THE ART OF
CONDUCTING

A GUIDE TO ESSENTIAL SKILLS
by
JOHN LUMLEY
and
NIGEL SPRINGTHORPE

RHINEGOLD PUBLISHING LIMITED
241 SHAFTESBURY AVENUE LONDON WC2H 8EH
TELEPHONE: 01-240 5740 FAX: 01-528 7991 TELEX 264675 GILDED G

First published in 1989 in Great Britain by
Rhinegold Publishing Ltd, 241 Shaftesbury Avenue,
London WC2H 8EH (tel: 01-240 5740)

British Library Cataloguing in Publication Data
Lumley, John
    The art of conducting: a guide to essential skills.
    1. Music. Conducting
    I. Title II. Springthorpe, Nigel
    781.6'35
    ISBN 0-94689-026-9

Printed in Great Britain by Perfectaprint, Byfleet, Surrey

Contents

Preface   *v*

1 The Conductor   1

2 Preparation   5

3 Technique   17

4 Interpretation   93

5 The Rehearsal   111

6 Organization and Programming   129

7 The Performance   141

Appendices

I The Orchestra   149

II Preparation of Manuscript Copy   183

Bibliography   185

MAY WE INTRODUCE OURSELVES?

Buying a copy of The Art of Conducting may be your first contact with Rhinegold Publishing Limited. If it is, then you'd probably like to know a little more about us.

We started life rather more than twelve years ago publishing a weekly news magazine called Classical Music - this is now a fortnightly publication and is well and truly established as the authoritative medium for the music, opera and dance industry.

Our first book was British Music Yearbook published by us in 1983. It gave us the experience of researching a major reference work and gave us the confidence to launch Who's Who in Arts Management and British Music Education Yearbook, both works requiring full time staff working around the year to ensure comprehensiveness and accuracy.

Keith Diggle's Guide to Arts Marketing followed and, like Who's Who in Arts Management, began to introduce us to a wider readership, that of the arts world rather than only music, opera and dance.

In 1985 we started to turn our attention to the wider world and introduced British Music Worldwide, a book unusual in that it set out to present the British music industry to the world at large with a view to stimulating greater use of British musicians, agents and resources. It did this by making the book 'A Gift from Musical Britain to the World of Music' - it was sent out free of charge to over 6000 top arts managers worldwide. We also brought out the first Rhinegold edition of the Directory of Artists in association with the British Association of Concert Agents.

At the beginning of 1986 we started to publish the recently acquired Music Teacher magazine, a long established monthly and later that year we launched The Musician's Handbook. In the same year we published John Pick's controversial Managing the Arts? The British Expereince.

1987 was a year of major growth. Our first edition of Arts Festivals in Britain & Ireland was published, and we started to publish the 40,000 circulation quarterly magazine Musician for the Musician's Union. There was also the First Edition of British Performing Arts Yearbook which recognised, for the first time, that theatre, music, opera, dance and mime all make up one performing arts industry needing one comprehensive source of information.

In 1988 we published The Art of Auditioning by Anthony Legge which is proving an invaluable reference book for singers, accompanists and coaches around the world. That same year also saw the introduction of our new quarterly magazine Arts Management together with Arts Management Appointments - a new weekly recruitment medium for the arts industry. We also introduced a postal book service which, for the first time, includes management books from other publishers both in the UK and abroad.

RHINEGOLD PUBLISHING Publishers to the Performing Arts - Britain and Worldwide
Rhinegold Publishing Limited, 241 Shaftesbury Avenue, London WC2H 8EH
Telephone 01-240 5749 Telex 264675 GILDED G Fax 01-528 7991 E-Mail 75:MUS023

CLASSICAL MUSIC * MUSIC TEACHER * MUSICIAN * BRITISH MUSIC YEARBOOK
BRITISH MUSIC EDUCATION YEARBOOK * THE MUSICIAN'S HANDBOOK
ARTS FESTIVALS IN BRITAIN & IRELAND * THE ART OF AUDITIONING
MANAGING THE ARTS? THE BRITISH EXPERIENCE * BRITISH MUSIC WORLDWIDE
DIRECTORY OF ARTISTS * BRITISH PERFORMING ARTS YEARBOOK
ARTS MANAGEMENT * ARTS MANAGEMENT APPOINTMENTS

Preface

This handbook of conducting is dedicated to all amateur musicians, students and teachers responsible for directing the performance of singers and instrumentalists, to help channel their enthusiasm and to ensure the promotion of live music for the enjoyment of performers and audience alike. The skills required to control such forces are developed chiefly by regular rehearsals with a group of musicians. However, personal study and practice is also necessary to enlarge upon natural ability and this text considers these various requirements in a systematic fashion.

The section on technique takes the reader through from basic requirements to more difficult areas, such as the management of pauses and more complex time signatures. The chapter on preliminary analysis of a work is linked with those on rehearsal and performance. Consideration is given to the various roles a conductor may have to take in an amateur musical organization, and how these roles can be distributed between the members of a small, enthusiastic committee. The appendix on instruments provides a concise account of the standard make-up of the modern symphony orchestra and wind band, together with an outline of a wide variety of percussion instruments. Archaic and historical instruments have been included here to give some idea of their limitations and of modern equivalents if 'period' performance is intended, and modern substitutes for these instruments, where appropriate, have been suggested.

The authors would like to thank Steve Store for providing the information on brass, military and wind bands, Celia Burrage for her painstaking preparation of the original typescript, and the book's editor, Andrew Stewart, of Rhinegold Publishing.

Copyright Aknowledgements

Extract from Britten's *War Requiem* © Copyright 1962 by Boosey & Hawkes Music Publishers Ltd. Reprinted by permission of Boosey & Hawkes Music Publishers Ltd.

Extract from *Shepherd's Calendar* (Michael Hurd) reproduced by permission of Novello and Company Limited.

Extract from Richard Strauss's *Till Eulenspiegel* © Copyright 1895 by Josef Albi Musikverlag. © Copyright assigned to C.F. Peters Musikverlag. Reproduced by permission of Peters Edition Limited, London.

Extract from Stravinsky's *Firebird* (1911) reprinted by permission of Schott & Co. Ltd., London.

Extract from Stravinsky's *L'histoire du soldat* reproduced by permission of the copyright owners, J & W Chester/Edition Wilhelm Hansen London Ltd.

Extract from Stravinsky's *Pulcinella* © Copyright 1924 by Edition Russe de Musique. Copyright assigned 1947 to Boosey & Hawkes Inc. for all countries. Revised version © Copyright 1949 by Boosey & Hawkes Inc. Reprinted by permission of Boosey & Hawkes Limited.

Certain scores have been referred to in the body of the text without attendant musical examples; for these, rehearsal figures and bar numbers are given. For **Chapter 4**, the reader will require scores of Beethoven's Fifth Symphony, Dvořák's Seventh Symphony, and Mendelssohn's Fourth Symphony, the 'Italian'.

For specific note names, the Helmholtz system of letter notation has been used, thus:

CHAPTER 1

The Conductor

Conducting may be defined as the art of directing the simultaneous performance of several players, or singers, by the use of gesture. Awareness of such a dictionary definition, however, does little to help an aspiring conductor when faced by an orchestra, choir, wind or brass band. Even less helpful is to be informed that conductors are born and not made, and that to conduct one requires a divine gift and an inborn magic. Who is to decide whether such descriptions are more applicable to an international maestro, who has impressed a group of critics, than to a local musician, who has inspired a small rural community? The aspirant must certainly be an enthusiast and have total commitment to the music he is conducting; by so doing he will enable others to enjoy and appreciate the art of music.

The responsibilities of the conductor vary to a great extent, according to the level and quality of music making. The capabilities of a youth orchestra and a professional orchestra are very different. A school teacher or the conductor of a youth orchestra acts to a great extent as a 'note-janitor'; he will train the orchestra over an extended period of time to play the correct notes in the correct manner. Much coaching is needed at this level to achieve the phrasing and articulation that professional musicians play without apparent effort, although such results can be achieved. The conductor of a professional orchestra can take the playing of the correct notes by his orchestra largely for granted. It is the conductor's job to inspire amateur performers to play or sing to their highest possible standards.

On a more practical level, a conductor should fulfill two basic requirements: to know the music in great detail and to have the technique to communicate this knowledge. These two qualities are expanded in later sections, the former under **Preparation** and **Interpretation** and the latter under **Technique**, **Rehearsal** and **Performance**, but each is worthy of some preliminary consideration.

A clear knowledge of a work is dependent on a total understanding of its musical language, in terms of melody, harmony, rhythm and form. Attainment of this knowledge depends on careful preparation and meticulous examination of the score. Interpretation of the work is based on musical scholarship, and represents a lifelong quest for new ideas and meanings, such study being paralleled by examination of the place of composers and their works in musical and cultural development and awareness of various stylistic practices. During preparation many other sources of information may be drawn upon. Of prime importance is to discuss the music with learned colleagues and, where possible, to hear live performances of the work. Recordings provide another excellent means of acquaintance, especially in the case of composer-directed performances, but be aware of some of the limitations of this method which are discussed in a later section (*see* p.13).

Successful communication between conductor and performers is largely dependent on technical ability. Experienced instrumentalists can play together with good ensemble without direction, but they do need someone to indicate entries precisely, to set tempos, and to control dynamics and balance. To achieve these aims a conductor should indicate time units with clearly visible gestures, beats being denoted by distinct patterns with no tendency towards indistinct or vague movements. In rehearsal the conductor should listen to the sound produced, recognizing any defects and putting them right efficiently, without wasting time and by using as few words as possible. The art of conducting is to be able to suggest details to the players and to encourage stylish playing by gesture alone. The conductor who can achieve this in concert can turn a performance into an exciting experience: gesture should convey one individual's conception of a musical work.

Remember that players do not hear the balance as a conductor does and, in turn, a conductor will hear a different balance from that experienced by an audience. The conductor should, however, ensure that through him and his performers the audience hears a balance and a clarity of line, which accurately reflects the composer's ideas. Effectively, the conductor is a referee, elected to decide upon details of interpretation. Whereas orchestral players themselves can provide some excellent interpretative ideas combined with very polished playing, admirably reflected by the occasionally seen conductorless chamber orchestra, the time allowed to rehearse for concerts is often pitifully short. A conductor thus has a necessary job to draw together a performance by rehearsing his own clearly thought out reading of the work. With little time for discussion and the exchange of ideas about the details of the performance, the conductor can guide, for example, the strings to a specific type of articulation, the intonation of wind chords and the clarity of ensemble in difficult rhythmic passages.

Alongside the basic requirements of beating time and developing an excellent ear, the conductor should acquire many other skills if he is to be successful. Proficiency at a keyboard instrument will help with score reading and becoming conversant with the various clefs and transpositions employed by orchestral instruments. In an ideal world, the conductor should be a virtuoso on all instruments, although in reality some practical experience with a string, woodwind and a brass instrument, and familiarity with all members of the percussion section of the orchestra is most valuable. Many will have come into conducting through directing choral groups and this aspect should be maintained and developed.

Performers often require information beyond that of gesture. Clear verbal instructions should always reflect your knowledge of a work, without ostentation, and should be relevant to the passage or problem to be discussed. As if these requirements were not enough, one could add that a knowledge of Italian, German and French aids interpretation, especially of vocal music. Amateur musicians often provide the total drive behind the musical life of a community, the focal point for which might be an enthusiastic and energetic conductor. In all musical aspects, it is essential that the extensive efforts required are equated with the great musical pleasures obtained. To a degree the conductor may also act as an entrepreneur. It is often he who gathers players together to form an orchestra, or singers for the performance of a choral work. When employed by a choral society, he will guide the committee to choose the right sort of repertoire to sing; it is often he who books the players when a scratch orchestra is used. In the early stage of his career, the conductor has to engineer his own opportunities, organizing orchestral concerts in order to gain the valuable and necessary experience to proceed. It is important therefore to impress the musicians being directed with your knowledge of the score; this will reflect the preparation undertaken and the way you interact with them and, most importantly, will affect the quality of the music making.

Tact is needed when delivering criticism, and this should always be constructive, avoiding sarcasm, and coupled with deserved praise. A cheerful dignified disposition, with control of emotion, may be difficult in situations which can frequently be taxing and sometimes provocative. Nevertheless, these should always be handled with patience; remember that you are dealing with living beings and not inanimate instruments. As director, the conductor may be called upon to give public addresses, and the role may need to be extended into that of judge and friend, as well as that of teacher. These various responsibilities will lead to the development of a natural self-confidence, on and off the rostrum, based upon knowledge and experience.

CHAPTER 2

Preparation

Learning the Score

Orchestras and choirs expect a conductor to know what is required of them. They will accept that an amateur or student conductor may be inexperienced and will generally make allowances for this, provided he has learned the score to the maximum of his capability and has the appropriate technique to ensure a workmanlike performance. The way a conductor prepares a score depends on both ability and experience, and it will probably change as time goes by: to begin with the process will be very slow.

Obtain a miniature or full score of the work to be conducted, preferably the copy that you will eventually use for performance. A close liaison with a reliable music shop as well as the local library is essential. Markings on a score may be the composer's own instructions or they may be editorial: the latter particularly applies to baroque and classical scores. Try to get an urtext score and parts, i.e. one which distinguishes editorial additions from the composer's original text. Conventions of layout of orchestral and choral music have varied greatly over the the course of many years. The first page of a full score (not necessarily in a miniature score) should list all the instruments required for a complete performance. Occasionally not all appear here, especially if an instrument is only employed in a later movement of the work. Check, therefore, the list of instruments printed on the introductory pages (if such is included) and the first page of following movements. Most modern orchestral music is printed with the woodwind, brass, percussion and strings placed successively from the top to the bottom of the page, the order of the instruments within each group being from the highest to the lowest pitch (ex. 2.1).

The modern convention usually places choral lines above the first violin part, but in earlier days the vocal lines were often between the viola and the cello parts. The use of the treble clef

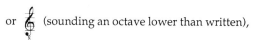 or (sounding an octave lower than written),

and of the bass clef for the tenor line is a comparatively recent convention. Nineteenth-century and older scores used a series of C clefs, which indicate middle C in a variety of positions on the stave. These clefs are now only employed by alto- and tenor-pitched instruments. The keyboard accompaniment (the figured bass of baroque scores) is inserted below the strings. A wider space is usually inserted between the staves of adjacent instrument groups to aid rapid identification. Similar instruments, such as two pairs of horns, three trombones and all the strings, may be bracketed together.

The printed arrangement, however, can vary considerably, particularly with older scores. Exs 2.2 and 2.3 display a common ordering of instrumental parts, mainly found in late nineteenth-century French music, which has been superseded by the

Ex. 2.1 Britten: *War Requiem* (opening page)

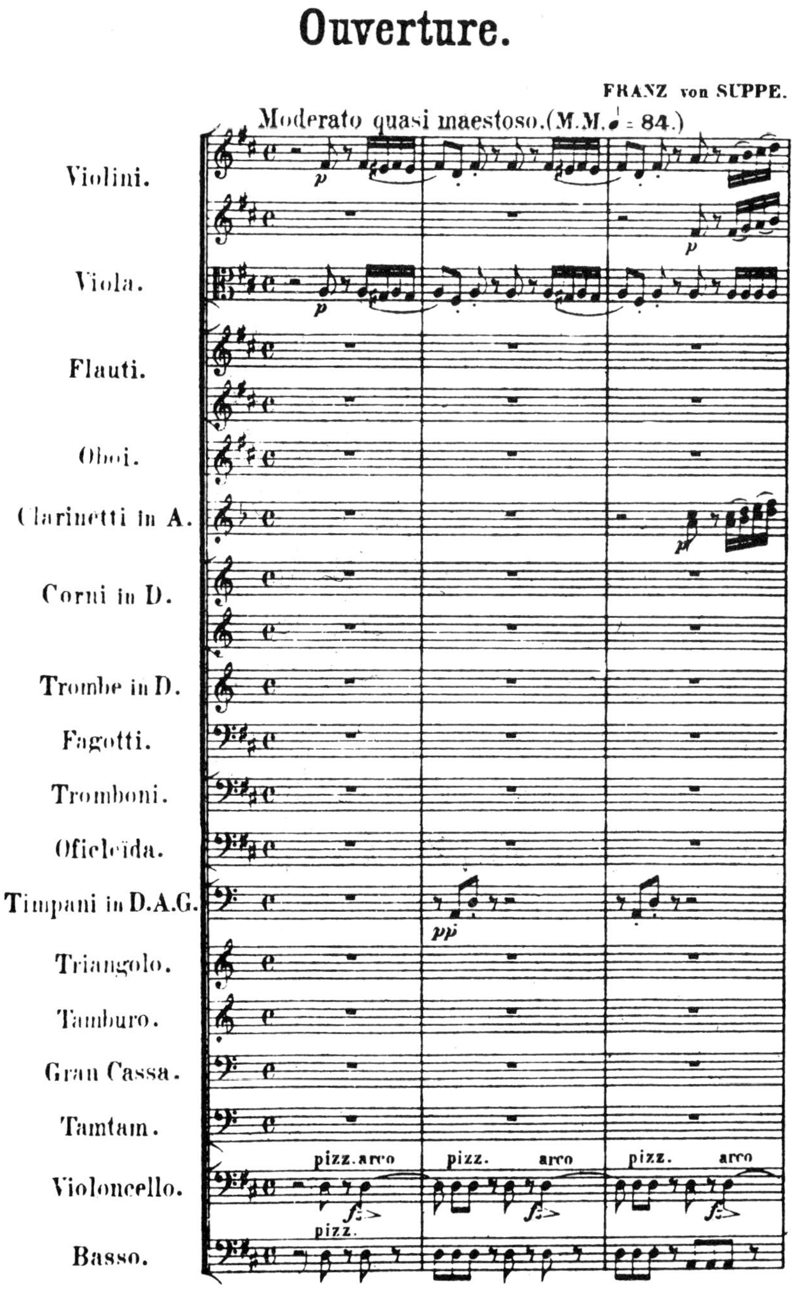

Ex. 2.2 Suppé: *Pique dame* Overture (opening page)

Ex. 2.3 Suppé: *Pique dame* Overture (final page)

Ex. 2.4 J.S. Bach: *Magnificat* (opening page)

layout by instrumental families as in Ex. 2.1. Notice that in the Suppé work the melody instruments are placed above the middle harmony parts and the bass parts. Most confusing is the arrangement of the string parts, found at both top and bottom of the score. In this case, the printer has only included details of instrumentation on the opening page of the score. Only when instruments are resting does the score give details of the instrumentation. This cheap method of engraving plates for a printed score is to be found in many works where a modern edition is unavailable.

Italian and French baroque composers generally placed woodwind, trumpet and timpani parts between the viola and cello staves, a convention that continued into the nineteenth century, while the German and English schools placed trumpets and timpani above the woodwind and strings (ex. 2.4).

Other arrangements found, especially in popular and theatre music, are much less satisfactory for the conductor. In some music for brass bands, for instance, instrumental parts may be grouped by range or family in a form of short score on three or four staves. Alternatively, a stave indicating the melody and the instrument playing it is placed over a piano arrangement of the whole work. In light opera and popular music the conductor often has to work from a vocal score with piano reduction on which he, or an editor, has marked orchestral entries. With this style of score the conductor is hamstrung to a large extent as he cannot easily find out what an instrument is doing at any particular moment. He therefore cannot help and give support in the same way as when reading from a full orchestral score. The players are left very much to themselves and much can go unnoticed.

Identify the position of each instrument in the score. When an instrument is silent for many bars, its stave may be omitted for a few pages and so it is important to know which instrument is playing on each stave of the page. This may be printed at the beginning of the page, but if not (see ex. 2.3), further information can be gained from the position on the stave, the clef, the range of the notes on each stave and, in the case of transposing instruments, from the key signature. Remember that all string instruments (apart from the double bass, which usually plays an octave lower than written), together with flute, oboe and bassoon, play at concert pitch, i.e. they are non-transposing.

An indication of the tempo (speed, rate, pace) will probably be included at the beginning of the work above the top stave. This may be in the form of a metronome mark or a verbal instruction. The latter is usually in Italian but it may be German or French, or more rarely in English: have a musical dictionary ready for reference. Metronome marks can be notoriously misleading with some composers and must be regarded with care. A discussion of the problems and pitfalls presented by metronome marks can be found in **Interpretation** on p.101. Setting a suitable tempo is crucial to obtain a satisfying performance. Initially, tempo should always be suggested by the music itself. There will nearly always be a passage or phrase which determines the tempo of long sections or movements. Use these to set the ideal tempo, broadening it if necessary in a hall or church with a reverberant acoustic.

Look for melody in the work; initially it will probably be in the first violin part or in the soprano line of a choral work. Once a melody is identified it will become easily recognizable as it moves through different parts. Sing or hum it out loud and determine the most appropriate tempo and rhythm for the line. A word or phrase which describes the mood and atmosphere of the melodic material should be noted, since such may also be useful to the performers. In choral music the text may help you in this respect, although beware of attaching undue weight to unimportant words. Follow the melody as it moves from instrument to instrument and between voices through the work or movement. Look for contrapuntal replies to the original melody and note the points of entry of the instruments. Phrasing is sometimes determined by breathing places for voices and wind instruments and appropriate bowing for the strings, but take care not to break up phrases artificially and so lose impetus and time. With some experience, however, it should be possible to look rapidly through the work as a whole before attending to details. At first, it is better to work through a line at a time or on a small section and so build up your knowledge of the music, rather like piecing together a mosaic. Although the ultimate aim is to see the work as a whole, there are many formal ways of achieving this: use whichever seems most natural.

Having read through all the individual parts and established vertical and horizontal relationships between the instruments, you are in a position to consider the shape of the whole work or movement. Look for changes of tempo and metre. Adjacent tempos may either be related to some small common unit or even purely l'istesso tempo (i.e. where the basic pulse does not change). If this is not the case, establish whether the composer intends a sudden change or a gradual transition through a rallentando or an accelerando, and over how many bars these changes are to take place. Consider how to beat the music, including the technical difficulties of the introduction, tempo changes, pauses and endings, and how such gestures will reflect the long-range melodic and harmonic implications of the music.

Identify the point of main climax in the work and points of lesser climax. Note the relative importance through the work of the various sections in terms of phrasing, dynamics and volume levels. Decide at what volume level crescendos and diminuendos should start, where they start, where they finish and the final dynamic level. The relative volume of the different instruments depends on whether they are playing the melody or an accompanying part: remember that held notes on the brass and woodwind can obscure melodic lines. Entries of solo instruments with important melodic material and entries of large bodies of sound are, like accents and pauses, relative to the overall structure and serve to give shape to a musical work.

Marking up Scores

The question of whether to mark up scores or not gives rise to heated controversy among conductors, as is exemplified by comparing the pristine scores and heavily annotated copies of different maestros. Simply using a virgin score should, ideally, give complete insight into the composer's wishes, but this is rarely the case. If you are uncertain of the standard ways of marking up a score, library copies are often already heavily marked and provide examples of the type of mark most commonly used. Mark library scores lightly and erase your additions before return: try not to be influenced by the bad habits of others.

The very process of adding marks to a score may serve to emphasize important facts, allowing quick recall during rehearsal or performance when there is little time to read the score. Clearly written additions make useful reminders, particularly when the conductor knows the score well enough so that he is conducting largely from memory. Excessive marking however will tend to obscure and reduce the value of the most useful additions. Important marks are the reference letters and/or bar numbers throughout the score. The latter can be placed every five or ten bars or at the beginning of each line or page, depending on the number of bars on the page. Similar markings must be made in the orchestral parts; such additions will save immeasurable time during rehearsal, particularly when performing unfamiliar works. Make sure the bar numbers in the score correspond with those in the parts. Errors do occur, for example, by counting an incomplete first bar, or including repeats (when often there are first and second time bars), codas and recitatives. Marks may vary in different editions, sectional letters or figures being particularly mobile (avoid playing from a mixed set of parts if at all possible). It is of great benefit to have your own score, so that you can mark up all the variations between editions and be prepared for subsequent perfomances: indeed, it should be regarded as a serious investment.

A useful inclusion at the start of a work or movement is the number of beats you intend to beat in each bar, changes being added as they occur. In complex bars, such as during rallentandos where the beat is subdivided or syncopated sections, mark the beats with vertical lines above the stave $\mathbf{|}$ $\mathbf{|}$ $\mathbf{|}$ $\mathbf{|}$ = 1-*and*-2-*and* etc.

The entry point of each instrument is usually obvious in a full score, but, if there is doubt or unexpected leads are encountered, a curved bracket may be placed in front of the passage together with the shorthand for the instrument in question. This is useful if an instrument has not played for some time, particularly if its stave has been omitted from any page. A further note of the number of bars rest the player has just counted (if it is a long break) can provide an understanding of the player's problem and possible source of error. Quite often a composer will ask for a change of instrument where a part is doubled or will request a change of tuning of timpani in between movements. Hand-tuned timpani require time to be re-tuned, and it is advisable to mark into the score a reminder that such changes are happening so that the next movement does not begin with half-tuned timpani, or with only half the string section muted.

When two or more systems (i.e. lines of music including all parts) are written on a single page, the editor may have placed a pair of short, oblique, parallel lines between them in each margin. If this is not so, their addition will remind you not to scan the page from the bottom up during rehearsal or performance and miss half a page.

At points of difficulty the well-known diagram of a pair of spectacles is useful, and when certain entries occur immediately after a page turn mark *v.s.* at the end of the page indicating *volti subito*, i.e. turn immediately. If a part of a page is to be omitted, place a double horizontal line at the beginning and the end of the cut and possibly clip blank paper over the section. Also clip together any consecutive pages which are to be omitted. Cuts, as a general rule, should be avoided unless you intend to do a 'standard' cut or a soloist specifically requests one.

In choral works mark in the page of the vocal score alongside the letters or figures of your full score. In some cases, such as in light opera, it is necessary to conduct a work from a vocal score, and in these instances it is important to mark this score with bar numbers and with each instrumental lead and to add any important missing phrases. Different coloured inks may facilitate the reading of such a score. It is particularly important to examine the orchestral parts to ensure that they correspond to your own. Ensure that these parts and the score are lettered and numbered since an incomplete score of this nature can present some of the most difficult problems of continuity during a rehearsal.

Listening and Hearing

There are several levels of listening. One may listen passively, enjoying the music itself and the musicianship of the performers. The conductor, on the other hand, must listen far more critically to the playing, so that he can lead the players and alter the phrasing, rhythmic vitality, balance and tempo where necessary.

Learn to recognize the sounds of instruments, instrument combinations and tone qualities. By listening to live or recorded performances of the work you will be able to gauge relative volumes and the balance of instruments in combination. It is possible to achieve uniform volume throughout an orchestral chord, while the participating instruments vary their volume to extremes: the tone colour of such a chord, however, varies with the relative volumes of the participating instruments. It is important to know the characteristics of different instruments, including their technical difficulties, extremes of range, areas of difference of tone quality and speaking times, together with the degree of volume change that is possible.

A conductor ultimately should be able to hear melodies and harmonies by visual study of the score. This, however, takes considerable training and there are several methods for acquiring and developing the skill. The first of these is the use of the voice. It does help to be or to have been involved in choir training and be used to singing lines at the correct pitch, pitching notes and intervals accurately in the chosen octave and recognizing the harmony of each chord. It is not necessary to have a beautiful voice but the conductor should be able to indicate vocally what he requires, to a choir or an orchestra. With the former the written words can be used for demonstration but, where phrasing and rhythm may be more relevant than melody, try to develop a language which conveys your intentions. Different rhythmical patterns, such as the dotting of the first quaver of a triplet, may be likened to the form of certain words, e.g. 'wonderful' in this case. The well-known use of 'um-pah' to indicate off-beat rhythms has its merits in a soft first and emphatic second syllable; a useful combination for emphasis on the second and fourth syllables is 'yi-pee-ya-dee'. Make up your own methods of learning and indicating different rhythmical patterns, possibly by choosing a short rhyme with appropriate emphasis. Regular use of the voice when studying scores will help provide vocal familiarity which can later aid communication with your performers. Many jazz musicians have developed the use of such nonsense syllables to great effect to show extraordinarily complex rhythms.

If you play an orchestral instrument this can be used to play through phrases in the music which may be tricky to sing or hear in the head because of extremes of range or speed. The piano, however, will probably provide you with the most useful aid in preparation. Help is certainly needed to hear the harmonic progressions and to recognize unusual notes, accidentals, phrasing and expression, and to practise reading the different clefs and transposing lines. If this proves impossible, it is advisable to find a skilled pianist who can play through the score for you. This can also be an aid to practising your conducting technique. See if your gestures produce the expected response.

The Use of Recordings

The use of recordings (both audio and visual) in a conductor's preparation is a constant cause of heated discussion and for the presentation of extreme views. Many an aspiring conductor has at sometime conducted a recording of a well-known work in the privacy of his own home and may even have stood, humbly, to receive an ovation at the end of the performance! Recordings are an established part of present-day life and form an essential part of a conductor's training, but it is important to consider carefully their specific points of value and their limitations. (*See also* pp. 96, 145).

In their favour, recordings do provide a useful means of acquaintance with a new work. Libraries are often remarkably well stocked and it is possible to borrow a copy of most works to see if you enjoy them and if they are suitable for future programmes. On hearing a work, study it along the lines already referred to: the melodies can be recognized together with the thematic and harmonic structure, the mood, and the emotional content. Tempos can be evaluated and the dynamics of phrasing and balance studied. Note how different approaches can dramatically alter the balance between different instruments.

Recordings can provide an authoritative performance, possibly by the composer himself. New technology allows us to hear such composers as Ravel and Prokofiev conducting their own works with surprising clarity. Where available, compare different interpretations. On following a recording through, it will be possible to recognize areas of difficulty which could give problems when facing an orchestra. Tape recorders allow listening at spare moments, be these at home or in a car, train or an aircraft, and repeated listening to sections of interest. This repetition enables you to pay attention to specific areas of orchestral balance or musical structure.

What then are the disadvantages of using recordings? The ultimate aim of all who study a work is to give a performance which reflects a personal insight into the music: an interpretation. Basing all your knowledge of a work on a single recording will give a very one-sided and unimaginative view of the music.

The vital preparatory beat and changes of tempo, so critical to the success of a performance, cannot be practised on recorded material; relating these to a recording may, in fact, give a false sense of security. A grave danger of repeated listening without a score is that syncopations or metrical complexities may be misinterpreted, the ear inadvertently misplacing the correct emphasis because details of the score have not been appreciated. Such habits and misconceptions can be very difficult to eradicate.

Remember that recordings usually represent a very artificial kind of performance; in such situations soloists and sections of the orchestra may be individually microphoned and the balancing altered electronically as the music progresses, indeed, often long after recording sessions are complete. Instruments can be doubled and sections reduced to obtain the required balance, or, in popular music, a solo line may be added later to a pre-recorded accompaniment. Whether such balance is reproducible, or desirable, in live performance must be carefully considered, as often such 'perfection' can be attributed to the technical skills of a recording engineer and the persistence of a good producer, besides the talents of musicians and conductor.

Within these limitations, however, it must always be remembered that a conductor has to start somewhere in preparing an interpretation. Whereas reliable learning by sight, with only the score as guide, should be the eventual aim, ensuring confident independence from all artificial aids, recorded music is now part of musical tradition and may justly form an important facet of the novice conductor's preparation of a new or unfamiliar work.

Seize every opportunity to attend live performances of works you intend to perform in order to observe how the conductor handles difficult areas and the fundamental matters of tempo, rhythm, and balance. A miniature or pocket score is desirable to follow the perfomance, but use it unobtrusively without causing any disturbance to other members of the audience.

In your preparation you will have found that score reading is more than a casual glance through the pages of a work and that it is not something which can be left to the first rehearsal. Look through the whole work repeatedly, and hear and decide what you require from each instrument and relate your assessment of the composer's intentions to the capabilities of the forces at your disposal. With this knowledge gained and with particular awareness of areas which are likely to give the conductor or the players any difficulty, you are now ready to approach an orchestra with the confidence of knowing what you require of them.

Preparation of Orchestral Parts

A scheme of bowing should be worked out between the conductor and leader prior to the first rehearsal. Having bowed the leader's copy and that of the principal of each section, all the copies of the string sections will have to be marked. If the basic bowing of all the works being performed has been worked out and written into all the copies prior to the first rehearsal, it saves considerable time, even if some minor alterations have to be made later.

Many other things need to be checked, notably the rehearsal figures or bar numbers. Do they conform in all the parts and do they conform with the conductor's score? Movements may even be numbered differently between scores and parts in scores containing recitatives. Special phrasing and articulation, modified dynamics, tempo fluctuations and such like, should be added at this stage if they are important in modifying the sound produced. Remember, the less rehearsal time available, the more valuable clear and accurate marking becomes.

When marking up orchestral parts — a chore whoever has to do it — the first job is to rub out all previous pencil markings. This is necessary as no two orchestras have identical views over phrasing and bowing, and some inexperienced players may have gone to extremes and bowed nearly every note! The conductor may be lucky and have a choir or orchestra librarian at his disposal who will do all the marking up necessary. More often than not, however, it is one of the conductor's responsibilities. Despite the request stated on most orchestral library and hire copies about returning them clean, parts are often in a bad state of repair on arrival. Make sure your markings are made with a soft pencil and are always removed prior to return.

Occasionally a conductor has to arrange and copy out orchestral and choral parts. Though he cannot expect to match the hand of an experienced copyist, he should produce an accurate, legible and unambiguous manuscript. Some notes on producing manuscript can be found in **appendix 2.**

CHAPTER 3

Technique

The conductor's baton technique is the means by which he communicates with the players and singers under his direction. It is not an end in itself and must become so automatic that he can concentrate on musical interpretation, rather than on matters of technique. The quality of technique, however, will be reflected in the music produced and therefore must be clear and descriptive, and incorporate an economy of movement. The aim should be to direct by gesture with minimal verbal communication.

Communication is achieved by arm and wrist movements and by changes in posture and facial expression, the most important element being the movement of the right arm, which indicates the tempo and dynamics of the music. These movements are often referred to as the conductor's beat; however, in this chapter, the term *beat* will be used more specifically to denote the rhythmical pulses required in each bar. These pulses are prouced by a sudden or gradual change in direction of the arm, which may be marked or barely perceptible. The point of change is known as the click of the beat; it indicates to the orchestra the precise moment at which to play. The terms *beat point* and *ictus* are also used by some authorities to denote the click of each beat. (The click can also be thought of as the moment of impact, as if you were to tap, or gently stroke, the top of an imaginary object.)

By convention, the position of each click and the direction by which it is approached indicate its place in the bar. A single beat encompasses the movement of the baton starting immediately after one click and ending on the point of impact of the next. The time taken between clicks indicates the tempo of the music; varying the emphasis of the clicks provides the performers with a means of recognizing the style of articulation and dynamic gradations of a work. Whereas in the following summary on technique the term click will be used purely to denote the beat point, a number of authorities use this term to denote the sharp, quick wrist motion which accelerates the movement of the baton just before reaching the beat point. Extra emphasis before the beat point can be used to gain a staccato effect or to ensure good ensemble, but it must only be used in special circumstances, never continuously, and not in smooth passages where the beat is already sufficiently clear.

The Baton

The right arm is invariably used for time beating, even by a left-handed person. With small groups of players or singers the hand alone is effective in controlling a performance, but larger groups usually require the use of a baton to magnify movements and allow all performers to see them clearly. The baton should be straight and white, and betweeen 12 and 20 inches long, depending on your height and the size of the forces to be directed. Experiment with various weights and lengths until you find a baton which is comfortable to use. Mace and maplewood are reliable, but fibreglass batons are much more durable, remain straighter for longer, and are more consistent in shape if obtained from the same dealer. Solid fibreglass batons, however, can be heavier than their wooden counterparts and a hollow, well-constructed model is recommended.

There is little need for a conductor to fashion his own baton these days, but he may want to modify the handle, which can be of cork or rubber. Opinions on its shape are almost as numerous as the number of conductors; certainly, your own opinion will vary over the years. Some general principles of baton construction are worthy of note: the weight of the stick should not be such as to produce fatigue within a few hours, or so light that it does not make a positive contribution. The point of balace should be approximately a quarter of the way along the shaft so that it is not held either too close to this position, making it inflexible, or too far away, making it difficult to control. A certain amount of flexibility is desirable, but very thin sticks are not easily seen and can be too 'whippy'.

When conducting with the hand, point the index finger towards the performers, raising it slightly; when using a baton, make this finger part of the grip. The baton can therefore be looked on as replacing the index finger and is usually held in line with the thumb. A secure grip requires three-point contact, best made with the pulp of the thumb, the side of the index finger just beyond the last skin crease, and the middle of the middle finger (fig. 3.1), although you should experiment to find the most satisfactory points of contact.

The handle of the baton lies within the hollow of the palm, the extent and the pressure of contact varying with the style of music to be performed. For very delicate movements, the middle finger contact may not be required, the baton being held between the pulps of the thumb and index finger. Even in these circumstances, however, the stick must always be under total control. As dynamics increase, so will the strength of the grip on the handle. Try to avoid a permanently clenched grip, and allow the fingers freedom to move. The varying shapes of the handle require different grips (figs 3.2a–c).

The most comfortable may be a ball-shaped handle which fits snugly in the hand, with little danger of loss of control even with over-enthusiastic arm movement. The grip must never be so tight that the handle appears to be clutched; the shape of the hand in the closed or open position should look elegant without affectation. This is not only for aesthetic, but also practical reasons: too much pressure or tension in the hand will cause unnecessary fatigue in the arm and shoulders. Relax the grip on the baton as soon as aches become apparent. The baton is an extension of the arm and its tip is the agent used to convey a conductor's intentions. As your skill increases, this focal point will more clearly describe your interpretation, reducing the need for verbal instructions. Sir Adrian Boult exemplified this when he described the actions of Nikisch: 'He spoke little at rehearsal because the point of his stick described the music with overpowering eloquence.'

In the rest position the tip of the baton is approximately in line with, and at the level of, the right shoulder. Viewed from above, an almost straight line can be drawn from its tip, along the baton and the length of the thumb, on through the wrist and elbow joints, deviating upwards towards the centre of the shoulder. Check this line on yourself, (it varies slightly with different individuals); the elbow should be held away from your side. The position must feel comfortable and relaxed. Wave your right arm around and practise bringing it back automatically to the rest position. Initially, your movements may be rather rigid, but with regular practice they will soon become smooth, flexible and descriptive of the music to be directed.

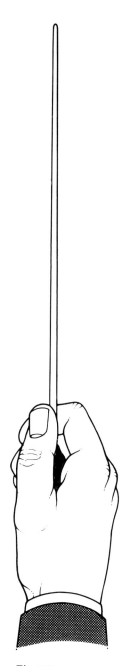

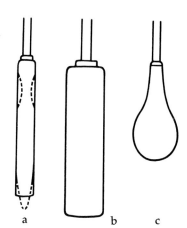

Fig. 3.1   Fig. 3.2

The Preparatory Beat

The conductor's most important task is to ensure that members of an ensemble begin together precisely and at the same tempo. Before a performer can produce a controlled instrumental or vocal sound, a definite physical movement has to be made. Different types of instruments take different times to 'speak': a bowed instrument produces a more immediate response than those activated by vibrations of the lip or of a reed. Each performer therefore requires preliminary information about the point of entry and the tempo of performance. This is communicated by means of a preparatory beat, which enables each musician to begin with perfect ensemble, without surprise or hesitation.

The preparatory beat should be in the tempo of the music it introduces, and comprises two distinct movements which travel in opposite directions, equivalent to one whole metrical pulse. At first, the preparatory beat will be discussed in relation to an entry on the first beat of the bar: the most common type of entry. Note that here the term *beat* indicates regular rhythmic pulse.

From the rest position the baton moves to its upper limit and then precedes vertically downwards to the next click, placed at approximately the point where the preparatory beat began. These distinct halves will be referred to as the *lift-off* and *attack* of the preparatory beat.

The lift-off must be vertical from the rest position. Additional movement before the lift-off is unnecessary; the action should be like withdrawing the fingers from a hot surface, but without violence. This movement is often referred to as the conductor's *upbeat*. If this usage is preferred, remember that it applies only to the vertical upwards movement which introduces the first beat of the bar; it does not equate to a full beat in duration or a complete preparatory gesture. ('Upbeat' is often used to signify the whole preparatory beat, but in this text is used only to denote the upward movement of a preparatory beat.) In effect, the duration of the preparatory beat, from the start of the lift-off to its upper limit, and from there to the click of the first beat of the bar, is exactly one whole pulse in value. Consequently, the lift-off movement conveys the tempo to the performers, the downward attack indicates the precise point of entry.

By convention, the click on the first beat of the bar is always approached by a vertical downward movement of the baton. The attack half of the preparatory beat, usually referred to as the *downbeat*, is always a downwards movement. Like the upbeat, it lasts only *half a beat* and is not a full beat in duration. The first beat in a bar is the only one approached by a long vertical downward movement, and thus, by such periodic downbeats, it is possible to count the number of bars performed. In this way, orchestral players can count rest bars without counting every individual beat.

The attack movement is equal in duration to the lift-off and ends on the click of the first beat. The length of the attack movement is usually of equal distance to that of the lift-off. The click of this first beat, therefore, is made at the rest position. The form of the two movements may be likened to the actions of breathing in and then out; it may even be helpful to link the preparatory beat with a measured breath.

The click of the attack is produced as if touching or striking an imaginary object at the rest position. The force of the click relates to the character of the entry and is controlled by the tension in the arm muscles and the tension of the grip on the baton. The lift-off (upbeat) thus cues the ensemble's timing and sets the tempo of the work, whilst the attack (downbeat) confirms the tempo, adds information on the dynamics and indicates the point of entry. The term *attack* can also be used as a general description of the nature of the entry; indeed, the two uses of the term are closely related. In this text, however, the word *attack* will always refer to the second half of a preparatory beat. The emphasis of an entry varies from a forceful bounce, through the usual firm but steady movement to a gentle gliding entry, different dynamics being indicated by the nature of the approach to the click.

It is possible to illustrate the path taken by the tip of the baton diagrammatically. Figs 3.3a–d show the lift-off as a dotted line and the vertically descending attack as a continuous line.

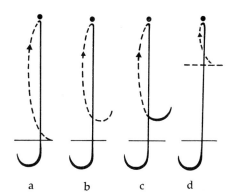

Figs 3.3a–d   a   b   c   d

The click is represented here as a thickening of the line and it has been directed to the left (the direction of this click is discussed later). The horizontal line indicates the rest position from which movements commence.

In fig. 3.3a the dotted lift-off is a little shorter than the attack, because the impact of the click usually takes it a little lower than the rest position. But note that the time taken for the lift-off and the attack are the same, and it is important that the start of the upward movement is a true lift-off, without the tendency to drop below the rest position. Any such depression (figs 3.3b,c) could produce a click and be misinterpreted by the orchestra. Short lift-offs (fig. 3.3d) are also ill advised, as the orchestra may be tempted to enter when the attack movement reaches the level of the starting point. In these and subsequent diagrams of preparatory beats, the black circle alongside the line indicates the half beat, i.e. where the lift-off becomes the attack.

The practice of beating an extra unit or units before the preparatory beat, in order to establish the tempo, should only be used if it helps the performers (as opposed to the conductor). It is generally unwise, since it may lead to confusion and some members of the orchestra may play before it is intended. If required, tell the orchestra that you are going to include it – "I'll give you three, four". Extra beats may be used to clarify distinct changes in tempo between one section of a movement and another.

Indicating the moment of entry is entirely the responsibility of the conductor and any vagueness here is immediately reflected in performance. The first few bars may not provide the key to finding the desired tempo. It may be more convenient to concentrate on a specific passage, further into the work, where the tempo is well established, e.g. semiquaver passages or a very strong rhythmic figure. The tempo of difficult solo passages should also be considered before you formulate your preparatory movements.

Beating Time

The number of beats to be indicated by the conductor in each bar does not necessarily correspond to the number indicated by the time signature of the music, but relates directly to comfort of movement and the clarity of the result. To avoid confusion, the first thing you must tell your players is the number of beats you intend to beat in each bar, e.g. "First movement of the symphony please, in four". In general, the size of your movements will increase with the level of the dynamics and as the pulse slows. However, they should also be relative to the size of your forces and to the style of the music. Small baton movements can be produced with fingers alone. Increase in the range of movements is achieved by successively including wrist, elbow and shoulder activity. The amount of forearm rotation used in these various movements is not great. For downward movements, the palm faces downwards and for movements to your left the palm is turned slightly to face in this direction. In upward movements and movements to the right, however, the palm usually faces downwards.

Extreme movements of the baton are rarely required and are usually undesirable, since they can take the tip out of sight of the orchestra. The usual area of movement of the tip of the baton should be enclosed by an imaginary square of approximately two and a half feet, the vertical sides of which pass downwards in line with the left side of your face and 18 inches to the right side of your body. The horizontals are just above your waist and just above your head (fig. 3.4).

The size of this area can be varied by altering the contribution from the four pivots (finger, wrist, elbow, and shoulder). Such movements must always be visible to your orchestra or choir. These right-arm movements must be steady and controlled, yet free flowing, conveying confident, accurate information. Do not forget, the elbow must never be locked in one position. Movements must be unmistakable, significant, and at all times at the service of the music. Never conduct with movements implying *fortissimo* and expect your orchestra to play *pianissimo*.

The tension in the arm and the grip on the baton, as you produce the click of each beat, causes the baton to rebound. Generally the more forceful the click, the more pronounced is the rebound, but the length of the rebound and its direction can be voluntarily controlled. You can test this for yourself by dropping your hand vertically to a click; as it rebounds, guide it at first to one side and then to the other, rotating your forearm slightly at the moment of impact to aid in its redirection.

By directing the rebound away from the position of the next click, it can be used as the first half of a preparatoy movement (i.e. lift-off) for the next click. This is an important concept; the use of the rebound as a lift-off when changing tempo will be considered later (*see* p.66). Usually, once the tempo has been established by the two halves of the preparatory beat, the orchestra is able to maintain the tempo by reference to the click of each full beat, without the need for half beat cues. The rebound is thus more passive than the lift-off for the preparatory beat, and is not always diametrically away from the position of the next click. After the start, therefore, the lift-off and attack of each beat tend to flow into one another as a continuous and curved motion.

Fig. 3.4

Figs 3.5a, b and c indicate the beat patterns for simple two-, three-, and four-beat time signatures. They represent baton movements, as seen from behind: the orchestra sees their mirror image. The square represents the area recommended for most of your baton movements. The horizontal line indicates the level of the rest position from which entries are commenced.

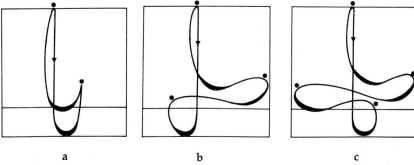

a   b   c

Fig. 3.5

The continuous beat pattern shown indicates the pathways taken once an entry has been established. To reduce the number of overlapping lines, the lift-off (upbeat) has been omitted: it may be added by superimposing fig. 3.3a over each pattern. For diagrammatic purposes, the downstroke in the different beat patterns has been moved a little to the left or right.

As already emphasized, the first click of any bar is always approached in a downwards direction. When there are two beats in a bar, the second click is placed near the rest position (fig. 3.5a).

In the case of three beats in a bar, the second click is placed to your right and the third near the rest position (fig. 3.5b). In fig. 3.5b, the second click is to the left, the third to the right and the fourth near the rest position. Note that the last click in each bar is placed near the rest position. This means that the rebound can be directed vertically upwards, enabling the first click of the next bar to be approached by a vertical downward movement of the baton, obvious to all performers who are counting bars.

The baton follows a longer pathway to certain clicks, these being the first click of each duple time bar, the second in triple time, and the third in quadruple. The longer movements serve to emphasize the natural metrical stress of these beats. The dots in the patterns have been placed between the clicks and represent the half beat, i.e. where the lift-off becomes the attack. This can be eaily demonstrated by beating in a slow tempo and counting out the half beats. Note that the relative lengths of the movement of each half beat varies, but their duration is always equal.

(Diagrams are helpful to indicate the patterns used for various tempos and also can be used to demonstrate pauses, time changes and endings. But remember that they are very limited in portraying certain other information which you need to consider in your movements. They are two-dimensional, and give no indication of baton movements towards or away from the body. In spite of the squares in figs 3.5a, b, c, they give little idea of the size of each beat. Accurate diagrammatic representation of overlaps could lead to confusion and, consequently, some artistic licence has been taken to prevent this. Diagrams lack information on the speed of the baton movement, either in absolute terms between clicks, or in relative terms through each beat. It is also difficult to indicate dynamic variations, and impossible to show whether variation is being produced by tension in the grip alone or by the inclusion of additional finger, wrist, elbow or shoulder movement.) The heavier markings used for the clicks in figs 3.5a–c serve to indicate some of the emphasis used to produce them. In practice, the curves may not be accentuated (e.g. fig. 3.6), but they can be looked on as relevant to music conducted at tempo moderato and at *mezzo forte* dynamic. Figs 3.7 and 3.8 are included specifically to show how the shape of the baton movements can change to suit music of different styles. Triple time has been chosen for this demonstration, since it requires a more open pattern. Remember that the time between clicks is constant, and, when definite lift-off and attack movements are present, each takes precisely half a beat: the overall pattern of the clicks is also constant.

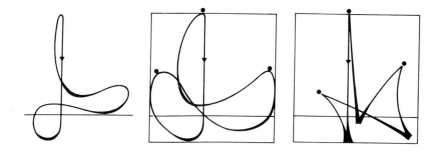

Fig. 3.6   Fig. 3.7   Fig. 3.8

Fig. 3.7 shows the pattern used to beat triple time in legato fashion. The baton tip traces a gentle flowing curve between the clicks. Even the clicks themselves flatten out and become less discernible and there should be no distinct indication of half beats. In ex. 3.1, the opening of Brahms's Second Symphony, the quiet and legato opening requires a small and smooth beat (fig. 3.7). Look to the cellos and basses to begin and, as soon as they have entered, address the horns and woodwind. With a slight broadening of the beat in bars 4 and 7 the players will follow the natural phrasing of the music.

Ex. 3.1

Slow beats can be difficult to retain in a smooth steady fashion. If there is ever uncertainty of the ensemble you must reintroduce distinct clicks. More reference points can be made by subdividing a beat (*see below*, p.34).

Fig. 3.8 represents the sharp, shorter, straighter pattern of movements used to indicate staccato-type emphases. Clicks are accentuated by a sharp rebound, using a firm grip on the baton, with less forearm rotation than required for legato passages. The approach to the click is faster than in legato, at its fastest immediately before the click. Because of this rapid approach to the click and the shorter distance travelled between clicks, the baton must move more slowly at places in each beat than in legato, and may almost stop momentarily. This is brought about by slowing both the end of the rebound and the start of the movement towards the next click, in other words a distinct lift-off and attack pattern is reintroduced.

Ex. 3.2

The opening of the third movement of Beethoven's Eighth Symphony (ex. 3.2) calls for a more vigorous movement from the conductor than that appropriate in bar 3 onwards. (No movement is required for the last beat of bar 2; continue with the smallest attack and follow with a very small legato beat pattern, which should become larger to show the written crescendo.)

Time Signatures

As already noted, the conductor's beat pattern does not necessarily consist of the same number of units as implied by the time signature, since all gestures have to be clear and comfortable at the chosen tempo. For any given tempo there may be a number of ways of beating a work, depending on the individual preference of the conductor and on his interpretation. The greater the number of conducted beats included in the bar, the greater the flexibility; however, each beat adds a point of emphasis, which may interfere with the flow of the music. A small number of beats provides a long smooth line but reduces flexibility. Try beating the second movement of Brahms's Second Symphony (ex. 3.3) at first in four and then in eight; note how the ebb and flow of the music is upset and too regimented when conducted in eight.

Ex. 3.3

Be aware that tempo markings may be editorial rather than the composer's own. Metronome markings provide a relation of numerical values to verbal directions. A tempo of 60 pulses per minute can be obtained from the tick of a watch, and the phrase *one-hip-po–po-ta-mus* can be used to remind you of this tempo and help with its subdivision. Tempos of around 72 to 120 pulses per minute can be indicated in a relaxed fashion using a beat for each pulse. As the tempo increases to over 152, or decreases to less than 44 pulses per minute, there is usually a need to combine or subdivide the beats. It is important to have a clear idea of the speed of different tempo markings. This you can achieve by remembering a few tunes, perhaps a waltz, a march and a hymn tune, to act as references when faced with a new or unfamiliar work (the march, *Colonel Bogey*, is a useful reminder of 120 pulses per minute). To verify a tempo against the second hand of a watch, count at the chosen tempo for fifteen seconds, beginning at nought. Multiply the number counted in fifteen seconds by four to give the number of beats per minute. By this method, twenty-two beats (in fifteen seconds) multiplied by four gives a crotchet pulse of M.M. = 88. These examples will serve as temporary expedients, until your understanding of the melodic and harmonic pace of a work automatically establishes its tempo requirements. With practice, it is possible to memorize accurately metronome speeds.

A beat pattern must be employed, at all tempos, with a clear vertical downward approach to the first click of each bar. The diagrams in the following sections serve to indicate the beat patterns and clicks; there has been no attempt to denote variation of baton speed or dynamics. The limitation of diagrams has already been emphasized, but they do help to clarify the aims of baton technique: design your own figures, adapting and modifying them to the music as you think fit. Musical examples can be supplemented by references to examples in *A Dictionary of Musical Themes*, edited by Harold Barlow and Sam Morgenstern. This will provide you with a variety of examples to help you to practise starts. The book is also recommended as a valuable guide to the themes of a wide range of the standard repertoire, but can only serve as a rough guide, since it fails to give indications of tempo or dynamic markings.

Two beats in a bar

Two beats in a bar is a common pattern, and is used in **C**, ¢ (alla breve), 2/4, 2/8 and, in fast tempos, for many other time signatures, particularly 4/4, 6/8 and 12/8. The pattern consists of a vertical downward approach to the first click, a short rebound being taken to the right. The second click is placed near the first with a vertical lift-off to the top of the pattern, preparatory to the next attack (fig. 3.9: ex. 3.4). Make sure that the first rebound is not taken too high as this could lead to misinterpretation, becoming the form of fig. 3.35, as in this pattern each down stroke is interpreted by the orchestra as the start of a bar (*see* p.41).

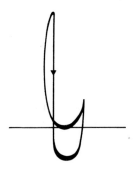

Fig. 3.9

A useful rule is to keep the rebound from the first beat, in this and subsequent patterns, to less than half the downstroke. Slight arm rotation enables the first click to be accompanied by simultaneous outward movement of the palm, adding definition; the second being accompanied by an inward turn. Practise this on the following passage from Grieg's *Peer Gynt* suite No. 1.

Ex. 3.4

Different features of phrasing, articulation or dynamic markings may suggest variations of any beat pattern. Fig. 3.10, for example, can be used to indicate the flow of a passage through the second beat, without the usual emphasis on the first beat.

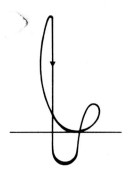

Fig. 3.10

If a note is held for both beats a second emphasis is not required, and the second click may be dropped and made the equivalent of an empty beat (fig. 3.11; *see also* p.55). Take care in all modifications of the beat pattern, however, that no unintentional changes in tempo are introduced.

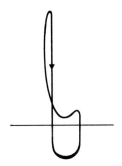

Fig. 3.11

In an accelerando, as the tempo increases, the second beat can be placed at a higher level until it coincides with the point of the half beat of the one-in-a-bar pattern at a predetermined place (figs 3.12a–f).

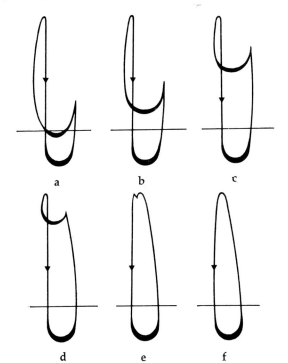

a   b   c

d   e   f

Fig. 3.12

Decide on the number of bars you intend to use for such a transition and inform the orchestra of the bar where it is finally to take place. Beating through the imaginary six-bar transition in the figure will demonstrate how, at the moment of taking up the new pattern, the beat resolves into a more relaxed pattern, with the loss of the second point of emphasis. In the bar before the change (fig. 3.12e) the second beat is in fact a half-beat punctuation of the new pattern (*see* p.37).

Four beats in a bar

Four beats in a bar represents the most common pattern you will encounter, and the main time signatures it encompasses are 2/4, 4/4 or **C** , 4/8 and 12/8. The chief emphasis of the pattern is on the first click, which is approached by a downstroke. The second stress is on the third beat, which is placed to the right of the pattern and approached through a long horizontal movement (fig. 3.13). The palm may be turned into each click in legato passages as with previous beat patterns.

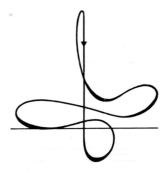

Fig. 3.13

To practise slow legato conduct the main theme of the second movement of Dvořák's Ninth Symphony, *From the New World*. Once you have mastered this, look at the opening brass chords, where a more forceful beat is required in bar 4.

The ability to produce a very smooth unexpressive beat as, for example, at the opening of Mendelssohn's overture, *The Hebrides*, is most important to set the atmosphere for the whole piece. Address the entire string section (thus preventing an over-enthusiastic contribution from the cellos) and cue the wind instruments with the eyes. Keep the beat small until bar 7, where enlargement will bring about the required expressive crescendo. Ensure that the instruments return to a true *piano*. Having practised the opening in four, try beating it in two: the opening can be conducted in either, and the ability to pass from four to two and back is needed later in the body of the score to maintain rhythmic control.

Ex. 3.5

A moderate staccato beat is required for 'The Hall of the Mountain King' from Grieg's *Peer Gynt* suite No. 1 (ex. 3.5). Make sure that the crescendo does not become too loud too soon.

Gradual change from a four- to a two-beat pattern in the course of an accelerando is shown in the following figures:

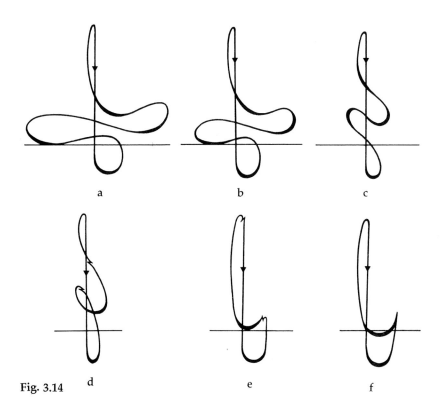

Fig. 3.14

Three beats in a bar

Time signatures requiring three beats in a bar include 3/2 (if not too slow), 3/4, 3/8 and 9/8. As for all the preceding patterns, the first click is approached by a vertical downwards movement, with a rebound to the left; the click of the second beat, carrying the secondary emphasis, is placed to the right; the third click occurs near the centre of the pattern and its rebound passes upwards to prepare for the first click of the next bar (fig. 3.15).

In slow tempos the forearm can be rotated so that the palm turns towards each click as it is produced, but in a fast tempo the palm should face downwards throughout the pattern. Not all music requires a click at each beat point. For very legato phrases, make the beat pattern look more like fig. 3.7 than 3.8.

Fig. 3.15

Ex. 3.6, from the opening of the second movement of Shostakovich's Fifth Symphony, requires a staccato beat (fig. 3.8), which also needs to be energetic and have bounce in the attack movement to achieve powerful and detached playing from the orchestra. Lift the forearm and bring it down forcefully; stop abruptly at the rest position and allow the hand to bounce at this point. The movement between the beats is slower than for the equivalent legato movement, which compensates for the greatly accelerated attack movement. In this example, a very strong beat is needed on the first beat in each bar.

Ex. 3.6

The waltz presents a specific variation of the triple pattern and requires graceful and flexible baton technique to indicate rhythmic subtlety. The main emphasis, although usually on the first beat of each bar, can be on any of the three beats and may shift during the work.

Many patterns have been developed to achieve this end. In slower waltzes the basic pattern can be retained with a definite downward approach to the first click, even when this is not the main emphasis. When the second beat is weak it can be indicated as a punctuation (fig. 3.16) or by a very small featureless movement to the right, the third beat passing vertically upward (fig. 3.17).

Fig. 3.16   Fig. 3.17

A slow one-in-a-bar waltz requires a special beat pattern where the second and third beats are combined. Each bar is conducted as if two in a bar with a quick first beat, and a longer but very light beat containing the second and third crotchets in the bar. Try this on the main theme from Johann Strauss's *The Blue Danube* waltz. The opening three notes are slower and require the normal three-beat pattern described above; the faster sections can be managed by a straightforward one-in-a-bar pattern.

Faster waltzes flow more satisfactorily if in one beat in a bar. Punctuate subdivisions, if required, and allow the baton to flow without the rigid vertical movement described for one in a bar (*see* p.41). This represents one instance where a vertical downstroke is not used (fig. 3.18). Sometimes one or both of the punctuations shown are dropped.

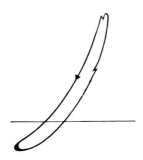

Fig.3.18

In accelerandos the pattern may be gradually closed down and changed to one in a bar. The number of bars over which this transition is to take place must be planned and practised before meeting the choir or orchestra (fig 3.19a–f). Note that one of the beats is dropped just before the transition.

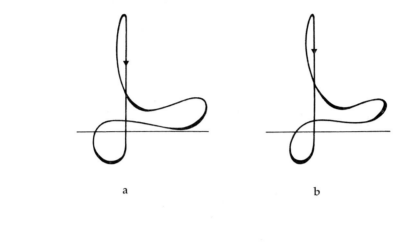

a   b

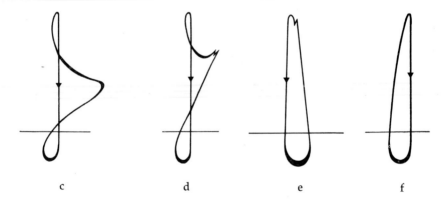

c   d   e   f

Fig. 3.19

Subdivision

With slow tempos, ritenutos and before pauses and breaks in the music, and where there are temporary rhythmic complexities, the individual beats of the basic patterns shown in figs 3.5a-c above may require division into two or more parts. They represent a physical counterpart of the verbal 'and' or 'and- a', i.e. one-and, two-and, or one-and-a, two-and-a, three-and-a, depending on whether the music is in simple or compound time. These subdivisions are indicated by additional clicks placed in the same area as that of the parent beat (overlapping it rather than as shown in figs 3.20 onwards), and thus they retain the overall pattern (fig. 3.20).

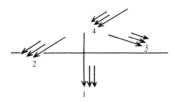

Fig. 3.20

The movements required for the subdivisions are smaller than those of the parent beat; contrast may be obtained by beating the main beat with the forearm and the subdivision with the wrist. Remember that although the length of the subdivision, in terms of distance, is shorter than the main beat, the amount of time taken for both (i.e. between clicks) is identical.

Subdivision is most common where there are three or four main beats in the bar and can take various forms. The most usual is where a definite click is required on each subdivision, as shown in figs 3.21–3.24. Duple subdivision is shown in Fig. 3.21, where the three parent beats have become six beats in the bar (e.g. for a slow 3/4 with paired quavers; but not when the six beats are derived from a compound duple time 6/8 as considered below). Fig. 3.22 shows the pattern for a triple subdivision employed in slow 9/8, where the three parent clicks in a bar have become nine.

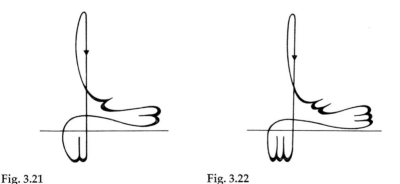

Fig. 3.21   **Fig. 3.22**

Duple subdivisions for slow tempos of four beats in a bar are also used to outline eight beats in a bar in 8/8 and 8/16 time signatures (fig. 3.23).

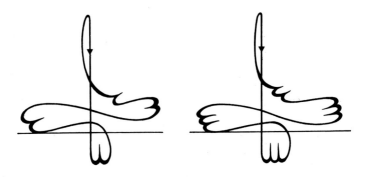

Fig. 3.23   **Fig. 3.24**

In compound quadruple time, 12/8 is beaten as either four dotted crotchet beats or in twelve, with the pattern in fig. 3.24. With large numbers of beats it is even more important to retain a clear basic quadruple beat pattern, with the subdivision smaller than the parent beat (exx. 3.7, 3.8).

Ex. 3.7

The overture to Rossini's *Il barbiere di Siviglia* (ex. 3.7) requires a subdivided 4/4 beat pattern: the opening needs care. An empty seventh beat is given with the baton (*see* p.36). A full lift-off on the eighth quaver will give enough information about the tempo for the orchestra to play the opening chord together. The semiquaver may be played as a demisemiquaver and similarly in bars 3 and 23. Keep the beat small in the *p* section by using wrist movements alone, without inflection.

Ex. 3.8

For the opening of Stravinsky's *Firebird* suite (ex. 3.8) a very legato twelve-in-a-bar pattern is required. Make the pattern very small but keep it very clear. In bar 5 the fifth quaver should be rather more firmly clicked to enable the trombones to play the off-beat chord together. A rather more staccato beat is required in bars 7 and 8, which can be executed with the wrist.

Two further forms of subdivision can be used to add emphasis or create time. In the first, the additional clicks act as punctuation marks: the baton makes a small, punch-like movement along the course of the beat pattern, as indicated by the zig-zag in the patterns of figs 3.25, 3.29, 3.31, and 3.36 (*see below*). The third punctuation in the triple subdivision in 9/8 or 12/8 requires a rebound to introduce the following main beat. The fourth form of subdivision is primarily used for complex triple rhythms, to avoid over-beating subdivisions and to maintain a degree of flexibility. This can be achieved by *marking time*, i.e. by beating a crotchet followed by the click of the third quaver (fig. 3.26). In effect the conductor should click one and three in each group, making the movement on the extra click very small and light.

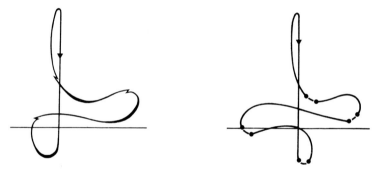

Fig. 3.25   Fig. 3.26

The subdivision of two in a bar over any length of music is very rare, since a duple subdivision of two is more likely to be conducted in four and a triple subdivision in six, following the patterns discussed below. Any subdivision of two in a bar is most likely to occur as a step between a straightforward two-beat pattern and either four or six in a rallentando or ritenuto passage.

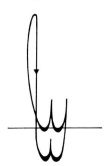

Fig.3.27

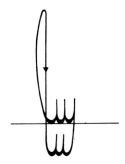

Fig. 3.28

Figs 3.27 and 3.28 show the patterns that are most commonly adopted in these cases. Punctuation-style subdivision may be appropriate in legato passages (fig. 3.29).

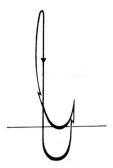

Fig. 3.29

Remember that when subdivisions are added, the baton moves faster than in the undivided pattern, since it has to travel further within each beat. If a preparatory beat, for example, is to indicate a duple subdivision, it will move twice as fast as if preparatory to the undivided beat. You must, therefore, always tell the orchestra if you intend to divide the beat. Practise the various combinations, at first counting out loud, then silently, whilst adding the appropriate emphasis to the voice and the beat, to ensure confidence in this techique before meeting the orchestra. Never overbeat subdivisions: they can disturb the rhythmic flow of the music. Where possible, try to adopt a more punctuated style rather than, for instance, giving an emphasis to each quaver in 9/8 or 12/8 by using a large movement for each stroke. Above all, let the music dictate the style of the beat.

Six beats in a bar

Six beats in a bar includes the time signatures of 6/4, 6/8 and 6/16. Varieties of the six-beat pattern and differences of interpretation are common. The emphasized beats are usually the first and fourth; these are approached, respectively, by a downstroke and a movement across to the right. The pattern can be viewed as a quadruple form with beats added to the weaker second and fourth, the additions made on the outside of the pattern (fig. 3.30).

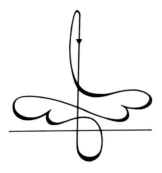

Fig. 3.30

In ex. 3.9, the opening of the second movement of Brahms's Fourth Symphony, a medium-sized and smooth beat is required until the diminuendo. The addition of the G sharp in the clarinet to the chord in bar 4 is one of the most important features of the opening of the movement, and a clear cue is therefore necessary. The *pianissimo* in bar 5 needs the smallest of beats; fingers only can sustain this, but the pizzicato requires an extra emphasis in the form of a click. Maintain the smooth movement between clicks to ensure no rushing in the string section.

Ex. 3.9

For the middle section of the second movement of the same work (bars 84-86, ex. 3.10), give a large staccato beat so that a broad, heavy and yet very detached effect is achieved in the orchestra. The first note in each triplet group should be stronger than each of the others.

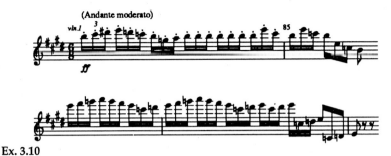

Ex. 3.10

Weak second and fifth beats may be indicated as punctuations (fig. 3.31), the third and sixth beats being preparatory to the emphasized first and fourth.

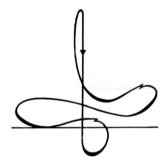

Fig. 3.31

This last pattern is useful for tempos which are not quite fast enough to be comfortable as two-beat bars. At faster tempos, the pattern shown in fig. 3.32 can be very effective and, once the tempo is established, it can also be converted into two beats in a bar or the punctuated pattern of fig. 3.33. Note that the approach to the fourth beat in patterns of figs 3.30 and 3.31 is to the right, whereas in figs 3.32 and 3.33 it is to the left.

Fig. 3.32   **Fig. 3.33**

One beat in a bar

Beat patterns of one in a bar are sometimes encountered in fast tempos (e.g. 2/4, 2/8, 3/4, 3/8, etc.). The one-in-a-bar waltz has already been considered in the section on three beats in a bar. One in a bar is not as easy to conduct as might be expected. The down click of the beat must be approached vertically, which gives the beat pattern a rigidity and limits the potential to indicate phrasing and expression. Attempts to introduce dynamic variations can result in a loss of stability of this single repetitive movement. The baton usually traces out a narrow loop to the left or right, the palm facing downwards throughout, with minimal arm rotation (figs 3.34a, b). In **fast** tempos, the up and downward movements overlap.

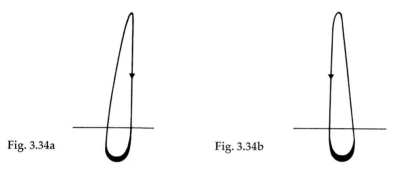

Fig. 3.34a   Fig. 3.34b

The quick one-in-a-bar-waltz pattern is a modification of the simple one in a bar. Where there is no need to highlight any aspect of the music in the beat pattern, the plain pattern used for the waltz requires a rather faster lift-off after the click than for the approach to the next click. In effect the baton slows at the top of its motion quite markedly (on the second crotchet in the bar) before descending again to the next click point. Some works allow the conductor to combine bars, which can add flexibility both to the music and to the conductor's movements. Grouping two bars into one is a useful technique and can be undertaken without disturbing those counting rest bars (fig. 3.35).

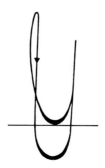

Fig. 3.35

The click of the first bar is placed slightly lower than that of the second, the forearm being slightly rotated so that the palm faces outwards. The rebound is carried higher than with two beats in a bar, but not as high as the rebound of the second click. The click of the second bar is also approached vertically, allowing players to count it as a whole bar. The palm is turned inwards to the point of impact and the rebound is to the left and to the highest point in the pattern.

The orchestra and choir need not be aware that you are beating a group of two bars as one. You will be able to feel the difference in the two pulses and use these to modify phrasing and dynamics. Larger groupings, such as four bars into a four-beat pattern, can be used to ensure clarity of phrasing. In the following example, from Walton's *Belshazzar's Feast* (ex. 3.11, rehearsal figure 65), the composer has indicated the grouping of four bars as one in the score; this is also found in the vocal and orchestral parts. Should you wish to introduce a similar (but unmarked) grouping in other works, you must tell the players exactly where it starts and stops.

Ex. 3.11

If subdivision is required in one in a bar it is usually as a punctuation near the top of the pattern (fig. 3.36). In slower tempos, however, it is more reliable to beat each bar in two or three.

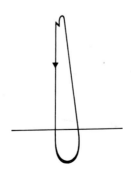

Fig. 3.36

Long sections of one in a bar can be tiring to beat; moreover, the natural phrase structure either may not be readily apparent on the printed page nor, as a consequence, felt by the performers. Shapeless phrases and the possibility of miscounted bars may become apparent as a result.

The first step a conductor should take is to analyse the phrase structure. A good example is that of the opening of the scherzo of Beethoven's Ninth Symphony. After the introductory eight bars, divided into two four-bar periods (note the silence is very much part of the music and must be counted out metronomically), the music proceeds in four-bar periods, with the addition of new instrumental lines with each period. Gradually, through the addition of more instruments and the marked crescendo, the music builds to the first climax at the *ff* bar 57. Beware: just prior to this climax Beethoven writes into the music two six-bar phrases (bars 45-50 and 51-56). The latter phrase, especially, can be viewed as a four- plus a two-bar unit. The conductor needs to point out the structure manually to the orchestra. The four-bar periods could be shown by a four-beat pattern; however, it is important to let the orchestra know of any such intention. In this case, it is best not to use such a scheme, as much of the insistent quality in the music may be lost. However, one should *feel* it in four without the orchestra ever being aware that you are not beating a simple one-in-a-bar pattern, either by keeping the general beat small but making the first of each four-bar period somewhat larger or, with the right-hand beat absolutely even, by marking each successive phrase with the left hand.

Five beats in a bar

Works or individual movements cast entirely in five beats in a bar are uncommon. The time signatures include 5/2, 5/4, 5/8, 10/8 and 5/16. Each bar can be looked on as a combination of a duple and a triple bar (e.g. 2/4 + 3/4 or 3/4 + 2/4) where the first beat of each is emphasized. The order of the combination varies, often within the same composition, though always includes the main accent on the first beat of each full bar, the secondary stress occurring on the third or fourth beats. Keep in mind the principle that the first click is approached vertically downward and the second emphasis is to the right. The two most usual patterns for five-beat compositions are given in figs 3.37 and 3.38 below (2+3; 3+2):

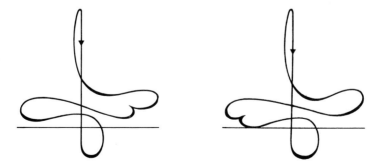

Fig. 3.37   Fig. 3.38

They can also be thought of as a standard quadruple pattern with the addition of an extra beat to the second or third pulse, respectively, of the same. The pattern in fig. 3.38 should be used for the example below (ex. 3.12) taken from Holst's *The Planets* suite ('Mars').

Ex. 3.12

Ex. 3.13

The 5/4 bars in ex. 3.13, from Mussorgsky's *Pictures at an Exhibition* ('Promenade'), orchestrated by Ravel, are best conducted as 3 + 2, and the 6/4 as in fig. 3.30. In quick tempos, when there is not time for the articulation of all five elements, the pattern is turned into two beats of unequal duration, indicating the two main accented notes and punctuating others along these lines if necessary.

When beating lop-sided two-in-a-bar patterns, keep in mind a duplet and a triplet figure. Shifts in emphasis between the 3 + 2 and 2 + 3 patterns often are present in the course of a five-beat section and, in the music of Stravinsky, for example, they can occur in alternate forms in consecutive bars. To practise duplets and triplets in isolation, study ex. 3.14 from Stravinsky's ballet, *The Rite of Spring*. All the bars in this short extract require just one beat: note, the 3/16 bars require a larger beat with a longer duration.

Ex. 3.14

When control of the baton with separate 2/16 and 3/16 bars has been mastered, practise beating lop-sided two-beat bars with a duplet followed by a triplet and vice versa. Ex. 3.15, also by Stravinsky (*The Soldier's Tale*, music to part 1, scene 1), contains both forms of 5/8. In this example beat crotchets in the 2/4 and 3/4 bars and one triplet beat for each of the 3/8 bars.

Ex. 3.15

Asymmetrical 5/16 bars can be split into a duple-figure quaver beat followed by a triple-figure dotted quaver beat. Study *The Rite of Spring* between rehearsal figures 188 and 192. Note that 2/8 bars can be beaten in two and the 1/8 bars in one. A very energetic beat is needed and the second beat of the 5/16 bars is, of necessity, a larger and more forceful motion. Make a clear difference between the first beat in the bar and the second, so that little confusion is made when two first-beat movements follow consecutively: i.e. when the music moves from 1/8 to 2/8.

The tempo of certain pieces is such that the most natural beat pattern falls half-way between the full five-in-a-bar and the lop-sided two-beat pattern. A punctuated pattern may be appropriate or, where the beat pattern is constant for a whole movement (e.g. ex. 3.16 from the second movement of Tchaikovsky's Sixth Symphony), a pattern more akin to 2/4 followed by 3/4 may be best used.

Ex. 3.16

The subdivision of five beats in a bar to produce 10/8 and 15/8 follows the principles laid out in the earlier section on subdivision.

Seven beats in a bar

A pattern of seven beats in a bar remains an unusual but necessary requirement. When it occurs (7/4, 7/8), examination of the score will indicate how it can be subdivided to give the correct emphasis: e.g. bars of 3+4 beats; 4+3; 3+2+2; 2+3+2; 2+2+3. Beat patterns are designed to match these requirements. In the first of the examples (3+4), a subdivided quadruple pattern (fig. 3.23) without the subdivided second beat, can be used. In the second example (4+3), dropping the subdivision of the fourth beat in the same pattern can be effective. In the third example (3+2+2), the pattern shown in fig. 3.39 is appropriate – modify this yourself to match the other two examples.

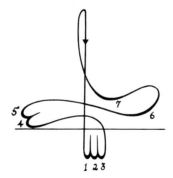

Fig. 3.39

Other complex patterns

We have dealt with time signatures involving one to seven equal beats in a bar, together with some, such as 5/8 and 7/8, which require groups of two and three beats. Complex patterns are most likely to occur beside others rather than solely by themselves, such as in the examples of 5/4 we have seen already. In theory, one could have any number of beats in the bar if the top figure in the time signature is odd: e.g. 7/4, 7/8, 11/4, 11/8, 13/8, 15/8, 17/8, etc.

In practice, odd-numbered time signatures above 11/8 are unusual; the composer is more likely to subdivide longer bars into smaller units, as may be seen in the 'Sacrificial dance' from *The Rite of Spring*. In ex. 3.17, from the vocal score of Michael Hurd's *A Shepherd's Calendar*, beat the 7/8 bar in three with a triplet beat first (i.e. 1-and-a, 2-and, 3-and) and the 11/8 bar in five with a triplet beat on one followed by the normal four-in-a-bar pattern (i.e. 1-and-a, 1-and, 2-and, 3-and, 4-and). Note that there are two downbeats (quavers one and four) at the beginning of the 11/8 bar and that all subsequent beats are duple.

Simple and less complex time signatures may be unusually subdivided: for example, in *The Rite of Spring*, Stravinsky employs dotted lines to indicate the beat pattern. On page 30 of the Boosey and Hawkes miniature score, beat in four at rehearsal figure 39 with three duplet beats and a triplet. The following bar, like those preceding, is in three.

Various signs can be used to mark such patterns in the score so that they can be seen at a glance. Those in most common use are △ indicating a triplet, and U and ⊓ indicating duplet beats, the first up and the second down.

Where the score or the composer does not indicate the subdivisions, it is up to the performer to decide. In the early works of Stravinsky, where the music is often extremely sectional, one can divide each section into its constituent parts. The process is to deduce in a bar of five equal notes whether the triplet follows the duplet or vice-versa and, in longer bars, in which order the duplets and triplets occur (cf. the sections on five and seven beats in a bar above).

Other time signatures encountered require a similar approach. Always indicate the beginning of the bar to the players or singers with a downstroke, and additional emphasis by a movement to the right, as demanded by the rhythmical form. A basic guide to follow is to beat in a modified two-, three- or four- beat pattern when there are respectively two, three or four subdivisions to be made within a bar.

Ex. 3.17

Entries on Beats Other Than the First

Works or sections beginning on beats other than the first of the bar are governed by the same principles as in the above. A full-length preparatory beat cues the orchestra to enter, with the click at its completion. The preparatory beat, as before, is divided into two halves of equal duration, the first moving away from the click, the second towards it. The terms lift-off and attack (*see* p. 20) are still appropriate. If, however, you are using the terms upbeat and downbeat, remember that they are neither full beats nor necessarily vertically up or down in the entries now under consideration. Figs 3.40, 3.41 and 3.42 indicate entries on the second, third and fourth beats of the bar. The vertical line represents the downward position of the first beat of these patterns and the horizontal line the rest position. The clicks are placed in the conventional positions for these beats in each bar, the bar then follows the remaining pattern as before.

Fig. 3.40   Fig. 3.41   Fig. 3.42

Entries within a beat

When the orchestra or choir has to start at a point within a beat, the preparatory beat follows the pattern as if introducing the next full beat. As the lift-off lasts exactly half the duration of the beat, by the time of its completion the musicians have the necessary information to time any entry between a half and a full beat, i.e. within the second half of the beat. They will receive additional cues from your posture, facial expression and, if necessary, from the left hand. You may, for example, breathe in or raise your head at the moment of lift-off and then give a nod at the point of entry (*see* ex. 3.18. Mozart: Serenade in Bb K 361, last movement).

It is better not to punctuate the entry by baton emphasis during the attack movement, as this can detract from the subsequent click of the full beat and disturb the rhythm of your movements.

Ex. 3.18

Start this piece as if there were a crotchet rest at the beginning; this is given as an empty beat prior to the preparatory beat. Use the left hand to hold the orchestra and prevent false entry. The players should enter at the end of the second lift-off; mirror these movements with the left hand.

Entries within the second half of a beat also depend to a great extent on stylistic practices. For instance, in ex. 3.7 above (p.36), the opening semiquaver often becomes shortened to a demisemiquaver. Double or overdotting, once applied narrowly to the performance of *grave* sections of French overtures, has become almost standard practice in the performance of much eighteenth-century music, despite the protestations of several musicologists that no firm evidence exists to confirm that such widespread rhythmic alteration was ever pracitsed. In more recent music, composers have often taken considerable care to notate the exact length of dotted rhythms, and the conductor should encourage performers to observe the exact relationship between the dotted and the following note once the performance style has been established.

For the opening of J. S. Bach's fourth orchestral *Suite* BWV 1069 (ex. 3.19, p.52), a single preparatory beat should suffice. However, to convey as much information about the tempo of the music, and precisely when the first full beat of the piece is to occur, the preparatory beat should start with a very positive movement. The beat should then be very smooth, with no inflection until the click itself. Whatever choice is made about the style and length of rhythmic interpretation to be employed, the approach to the preparatory beat must be confident. The left hand can be used to arrest the orchestra's attention; the right-hand beat should be small and clear.

In the overture to Mozart's opera, *The Magic Flute* (ex. 3.20, p.53), beat the adagio introduction in eight from bar 4. The first three bars, however, require special consideration: at a slow tempo, the conductor has the opportunity to beat the semiquaver at the end of bar 1. Beat four strict quavers for the opening chord. Stop the motion of both hands after the cut-off and hold quite still during the pause. Next, beat the seventh and eighth quavers as empty beats, and subdivide the eighth into two semiquavers beats. The length of the first semiquaver should be made clear to the players before the rehearsal commences. Make sure that the entry is separated from the subsequent chord, and allow time for the music to broaden at this point. In effect the opening may be perceived as shown in fig. 3.43.

Ex. 3.19

Ex. 3.20

Fig. 3.43

Entry on the half beat is initiated by a similar preparatory beat to that for an entry on the first beat of the bar. Additional entry cues come from head movement and the use of a clenched left hand at the entry point. In the case of slower tempos it is also possible to punctuate the entry by slight increase in grip tension on the baton at the moment of direction change, when the lift-off becomes the attack. Do not use this method if it interferes with the rhythmical flow of the preparatory beat. It often helps to think the beat before the preparatory beat (i.e. the third beat when the entry is within the fourth beat of a 4/4 bar), without necessarily beating this extra beat: the orchestra can usually sense its presence (exx. 3.21, 3.22).

In ex. 3.21, from the last movement of J. S. Bach's Concerto for two violins and strings (BWV 1043), there should be no need to give more than a lift-off to bring the orchestra in together. If this does not work, give both the second and third beats in the preparation. To attempt to start with just the lift-off – by far the most effective way – the conductor must feel the second and third beats very strongly (but without consciously moving). Continue the music boldly, and maintain a strong *forte*.

Ex. 3.21

Ex. 3.22

For the chilling fanfare that opens the first movement of Mahler's Fifth Symphony (ex. 3.22), make the initial lift-off a faster movement than the attack. This will give the trumpet player confidence to enter but will not encourage an initial dynamic greater than the marked *p*. Keep the beat small and direct it towards the solo player. To emphasize the crescendo, make the second beat of bar 6 larger than the previous beats.

Entries within the first half of the beat are more difficult to time, since, usually, the full preparatory beat will have completed less than half its execution by the time the correct point of entry is reached. With precise lift-off and additional cues, of the type mentioned, a skilled orchestra will be able to follow the conductor. If, however, there is any uncertainty in the attack, also show the preceding beat (i.e. the second beat in fig. 3.44) as an empty beat.

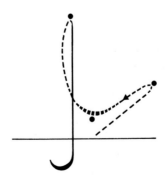

Fig. 3.44

The extra full beat provides the orchestra with a clearer sense of the tempo and the point of entry. It must be precise in its timing and clear in its form; but it must not contain any points of emphasis which could invite an early orchestral entry. The left hand is important here to hold the orchestra during preparation, so that players are not tempted to enter prematurely; the hand moves at the beginning of the beat of entry. In the third movement of Dvořák's Seventh Symphony (ex 3.23, p.56), give a whole bar's preparation to the opening and a staccato beat on the second beat of each bar to bring out the syncopation. Establish the tempo with the cello and bassoon melody firmly in mind; balance the upper strings so that their countermelody is not too prominent.

Empty beats

Beats which indicate time without directing performance, as referred to in the last section, are also used through long notes and rests and are known by a number of titles, such as empty, spineless, dead, walking-through, unobtrusive, and blind beats. The smooth continuous flow of the baton through an empty beat must keep the orchestra in a state of anticipation, as if hypnotized, awaiting the entry. The empty beat is placed in its appropriate position in the beat patterns of fig. 3.5a–c. If there are rests at the beginning of a work, these should also be beaten with empty beats followed by a distinct lift-off at the beat preceding the entry. Fig. 3.44 (*see* p.54) indicates an entry using an additional empty beat.

Cut-offs and Endings

Endings are indicated by a definite click of the baton. This click is often quite forceful and will produce a rebound, as if the baton point has struck against an imaginary object; however, the rebound must be controlled and come to a rapid stop, and should emphasize the end point. In the diagrams used to indicate end points, for the sake of clarity, the rebound has been omitted, the click here represented by a broadening of the line at the end of the pattern. The click for an ending is usually produced with the baton, but the left hand is often required, and in some instances, such as in staggered endings, the left hand may be used to effect the cut-off while the right hand continues the beat pattern. The ending is usually accompanied by a slight nod of the head, which provides extra information for the musicians and helps to show the precise cut-off point. The figures indicate endings produced with a baton; left hand movements can be mirror images of the same patterns. The cut-off movement works as if the point where the baton has come to rest on a held chord is crossed out (figs 3.45a, b), or, if it is still moving, as a crossing out of the click point of the next beat (fig. 3.45c). This crossing out is usually downwards and away from the body (i.e. to the right for the right hand), but it can be turned inwards, particularly if the ending is to be immediately followed by another entry. In the latter situation it is convenient to take the cut-off towards the click of the next entry. The baton will then be in a position to lift off from this point and move back towards the click point for the attack.

III SCHERZO

Ex. 3.23

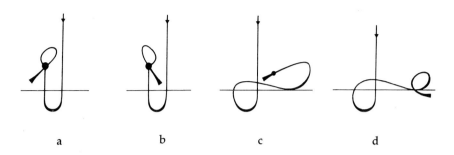

Fig. 3.45

To create an air of anticipation, the baton can be kept moving after a cut-off until it is ready to indicate the next entry. This can prevent both orchestra and audience from relaxing between consecutive movements, if so desired.

Most final notes consist of one or more full beats and, consequently, last until what would have been the click of the subsequent beat, as if the music were to continue. In figs 3.45a–c above, the cut-off is timed to what would have been the third click in the bar. The cut-off can be executed in two ways. In the first, the final note is introduced by a downbeat and the baton is then gently raised to just above the rest position during the second beat. The baton then makes a circular movement, and crosses out the held position, either down to the left (fig. 3.45a) or the right (fig. 3.45b). Alternatively, once the first beat in the bar has been clicked, the baton continues the usual pattern for the second beat as an empty beat, thus ensuring that there is no click or emphasis that could confuse the orchestra. The cut-off is then made by crossing out the position that would have been the third click (fig. 3.45c).

A movement or section may finish with a note tied to a half-beat note (e.g. to a quaver in music with a crotchet pulse). Here, instead of stopping at the click of this beat, the players continue for the extra half beat. There are two similar examples of this type of ending. The first is with a held chord as in ex. 3.24.

Ex. 3.24

Conduct the second and third beats of the first bar as empty beats. In the last bar, conduct the first beat with a short movement and without emphasis, and then make the cut-off movement on the half beat (fig. 3.45d). Use both hands to cut off the sound. The baton indicates the ending with a slight hook on the terminal click, crossing out this beat point on the half beat. The left hand mirrors the same motion, whilst closing the fingers into the palm of the hand.

The second example is often found in the music of Brahms, where a soft, feminine cadence is required. In the first movement of his Second Symphony, the wind chord (bar 522) is cut off by the pizzicato strings, the wind players stop the moment they hear the string chord. Give a very clear preparation for the first beat of the last chord. The click of the beat is more forceful here than in ex. 3.24 and the rebound becomes the cut-off for the wind players.

When the composer indicates a change of dynamic on the last note, this can be shown by gently raising, or lowering, the tip of the baton once the initial click of the note has been made (figs 3.46a, b). The movement can be mirrored, or replaced by, the left hand. The latter is necessary if the baton has to mark empty beats through the bar to the cut-off point.

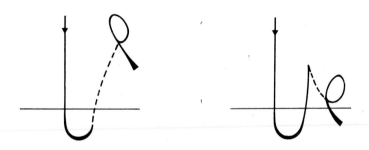

Fig. 3.46a   Fig. 3.46b

When the last note is of indefinite length, as implied by a pause, the baton is directed back from the initiating click to the rest position and held there. A gentle raising or lowering may be added to indicate volume change when necessary. The orchestra should be warned of the cut-off point in this situation, particularly if they are expected to make a final crescendo. It is given by beating an empty beat and crossing out its click point as shown in figs 3.47a and b (a – an opened-out form; b – overlapping as it actually occurs).

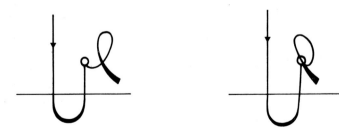

Fig. 3.47a   Fig. 3.47b

Some conductors make vigorous cut-offs vertically downwards. This variant is easily interpreted by the orchestra, provided there is a very definite end click to the movement. Remember to make your movements suit the music – large movements for loud music and small movements for soft. (*See also* p.71 for the discussion of examples of pauses on final notes.)

The last type of ending to consider is the abrupt one. This is often emphatic. In this situation the cut-off not only gives the dynamic and the end point but also indicates the length of the note required. Abrupt endings are more easily emphasized by downstrokes so that the rebound of the previous beat can be taken upwards to introduce them. A good example of an abrupt cut-off comes at the close of the 'Tuba mirum' from Verdi's *Requiem* (ex. 3.25). The ending is marked by a accent (>) and the word *tronca* (It. 'cut off'). Beat the usual four-in-a-bar pattern (in the bar before the cut-off). Move the arm and baton higher with each click. The two hands come together on the preparatory movement for the last chord and both are used for the cut-off. In the attack movement for the first beat of the next bar, instead of coming to a halt on the click, continue by moving the hands apart from each other at this point. The left hand is suddenly opened, the palm, in a held position, facing the violins.

Ex. 3.25

Ex. 3.26

Three forms of accent can be seen in ex. 3.26 from Elgar's *Enigma Variations*. The last, a dagger, requires a short staccato emphasis. Raise the left hand during the dotted minim and, with both hands, execute a forceful beat on the last crotchet. Stop all movement at the click point. There should be no need to make any form of cut-off motion. (Note the pause over the rest. A contrasting and more lyrical variation follows, and here Elgar ensures that the last chord of variation IV has time to clear.)

Changes in Tempo

Examples of changes of time signature and of tempo in the body of a movement or in a continuous section of a work are unusual in music of the classical period. Whereas in earlier scores these tempo changes tend to occur at the beginning of a new section, in music from the mid-nineteenth century they may take place from phrase to phrase or even from bar to bar.

Remember exactly where the changes of tempo take place, what a new tempo is to be and the relation of the new to the old. The time unit of the new and the old tempo may be the same (l'istesso tempo), or there may be a sudden or gradual change. Tempo changes may also represent only a temporary event in the course of a work and have no structural significance, e.g. a rallentando, ritenuto, accelerando or pause. Such events require careful attention, both in their preparation and technical management. Even if tempo changes are marked in the orchestral parts, the attention of the orchestra will have to be caught, since sudden changes are not possible without it. As you prepare for the change, the tension in your beat, and your stance, will alter and this will be sensed by the orchestra. Look at the players so that you can use visual as well as manual cues: your knowledge of the score in these areas must therefore be thorough. If an unmarked rubato is to be added, or there is any possibility of ambiguity, tell the orchestra precisely when, and how, the time change is to take place before rehearsal of the section or movement.

L'istesso tempo

Literally, 'the same speed', this indication implies that either a common pulse, or a common notational value, can be found between one section and the next. Three broad categories of l'istesso tempo can be recognized and are discussed below. Remember that the relationship between the old and new tempos may only be mathematical, as the mood of the new section may differ considerably. In such cases the style of the beat will need appropriate modification.

In the examples below, the indication of the common pulse or note value may follow one of two conventions (note that these two conventions are diametrically opposed!). Fig. 3.48a is taken from the third movement of Brahms's Second Symphony (bars 33–35): here the minim of the new tempo is in the same tempo as the crotchet of the old. The other and more modern convention states the same in reverse, and here the = sign is found over the bar line itself. Fig. 3.48a, therefore, could be rewritten as shown in fig. 3.48b, i.e. the crotchet of the old tempo is equal to the minim of the new tempo.

L'istesso tempo (where pulse and beat remain constant)

This particular category is the most straightforward example to conduct. It involves a change of time signature and, therefore, of the beat pattern. There is no change in the pulse of the music (exx. 3.27, Sibelius: Symphony No. 2 (second movement), 3.28).

Ex. 3.27

Ex. 3.28

Several examples of changes in tempo and metre occur in quite a short space of time in the third movement of Brahms's Second Symphony (ex. 3.28). Some of them are l'istesso tempo; others involve a change in the rate of the underlying pulse and are consequently more difficult to convey. The first change of time signature at the 'presto non assai' (bar 33) is an example of l'istesso tempo where crotchet = minim. The 2/4 requires one beat in a bar with only a moderate emphasis on the click to bring out the accent and maintain the *piano*. The pulse of the smooth three-in-a-bar pattern in the bars leading up to bar 32 is the same as the one-in-a-bar pattern of the 2/4, so the change in beat pattern is immediate and straightforward at the double bar. The return to 'tempo primo' at bar 107 is simply the reverse of bar 33: the one in a bar of the 'presto ma non assai' becomes the crotchet pulse of the 3/4 at bar 107. The next change of time signature at the beginning of the second section of the trio, presents a more difficult problem than in those described above. The strong pulse of the 'presto ma non assai' demands a staccato one-in-a-bar beat and the pulse is much faster than that of the previous sections, so the transition must be very clear. Make sure you pick up the first note of the second bar (bar 127) in case the orchestra is not quite together. Because of the change in tempo at bar 126, the beat for the first six bars of the new section may necessarily be a little larger than for the following bars, by which time the tempo will have been well established. A smaller, more precise beat is needed for the wind instruments at bar 132. They will not need any more encouragement than this. Ensure that the quavers from bar 135 onwards are well articulated and that there is no tendency to anticipate the beat.

The process of slowing down through bars 187-194 has been written into the music by the composer. The passage from the 3/8 to the 9/8 requires a change only in the beat pattern (from one in a bar to three). The change from the 9/8 to the 3/4 is also 'l'istesso tempo', but make sure you feel a duple rather than a triple beat. Pull the tempo back in the 3/4 passage and, with a broadening of the tempo in the hemiola rhythm of bars 192-193, reintroduce the slightly slower 'tempo primo' at bar 194. A light staccato beat is required until bar 192. At this point, adopt a smooth legato beat. Indicate the hairpins in the same bars by raising and lowering the hands.

L'istesso tempo (where pulse remains constant but metre changes)

Under these conditions the conductor does not have to alter the speed, merely the pattern of his beat. What is important, however, is the way that the beat reflects the metre. A duple metre should both look and feel different from a triple metre. In ex. 3.29, from the third movement of Brahms's Second Symphony a slightly more arched beat pattern, verging on punctuation, should sugest this difference.

Ex. 3.29

The greater part of the last movement of this work is in alla breve (two in a bar). Look at the climax of the movement where the opening music of the first movement returns. The minim beat of the 4/4 becomes the crotchet beat of the 'andante'. At the 3/4 make sure that the first quaver is short and cue the bassoons, horns and trombones on the second beat with a staccato beat. This will give a firm base for the off-beat triplets and to cue the trumpets and the woodwind.

L'istesso tempo (where pulse and metre change but where there is a common time unit)

Practise altering the pattern and speed of the beat with the rhythmic pattern in ex. 3.30, 'America', from Leonard Bernstein's *West Side Story*. The quaver pulse remains constant whilst the metre moves alternately through 6/8 and 3/4. Beat two (dotted crotchets) in the 6/8 and three (crotchets) in the 3/4.

Ex. 3.30

Such hemiola patterns are quite straightforward because of their regularity. If the common time-unit is very small, however, the change in the beat pattern can be quite profound, as shown in ex. 3.31.

The Overture to Mozart's *Don Giovanni* (ex. 3.31, pp.64-65) contains a form of l'istesso tempo, where the demisemiquavers of the violas continue through from the 'adagio' to become the quavers of the 'molto allegro' with little change. The conductor has to indicate a totally new tempo to the upper strings and cellos.

Sudden changes of tempo

Immediate time changes generally have a definite relationship one to another. Some composers not only relate changes within each movement, but also those that occur throughout a composition. Not all tempo changes, however, are such that the new is closely related to the old tempo. If the new tempo is faster than the old, there is a need to insert a full preparatory beat. The click of the last beat of the old tempo is made as an unemphasized baton movement, but the placement of this click ensures that the orchestra continues to play in the old tempo until the first beat of the next bar. The empty nature of the click means that the baton does not overshoot, and is ready to place an appropriately timed preparatory beat in the new tempo. The attack half of this preparatory beat ends at the first click of the new bar, arriving on it simultaneously with the orchestra, who, from the full preparatory beat, will be able to establish the new tempo and, from the character of the attack, will be able to introduce any required change in dynamic.

The conductor inserts the preparatory beat for the new tempo independent of the old. In effect, an estimation of the new beat/time interval is made using the old tempo as a reference point. By placing the preparatory beat across this interval, the conductor ensures that the click of the preparatory beat coincides with the start of the next bar. It is possible to drop the last beat of the previous bar and hold both hands steady until the preparatory beat of the new tempo. This catches the attention of the orchestra, and avoids confusion between the preparatory movement of the new tempo and the last beat of the old tempo.

Ex. 3.31

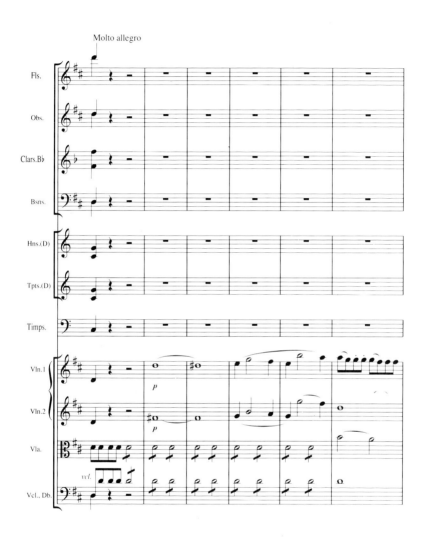

Ex. 3.31 (continued from p.64)

The quaver pulse of the 'adagio' opening of Beethoven's First Symphony should be noticeably slower than the main pulse of the following 'allegro con brio'. Beat eight and give an extra emphasis to the eighth quaver of the bar; a staccato lift-off will help gain a firm *forte* entry from the orchestra. Beethoven's own metronome marks here (♪ = M.M. 88 'adagio' and ♩ = M.M 112 'allegro') imply a considerable hastening of the minim pulse from that of the preceding quavers. The seventh beat of the slow introduction can be cut off with a slight movement of the left hand, before the right hand gives the preparatory lift-off on the last full quaver of bar 12. Use the left hand to maintain the *p* in the strings. It is advisable to ask the string section to lift the bow just before the demisemiquaver. Avoid beating the minim pulse of the 'allegro' too fast.

The left hand can be added to the lift-off movement, and, if emphasis is required, can be also included in the attack, thus indicating the half or the full length of the preparatory beat of the new tempo.

When the new tempo is slower than the old, often there is not time to insert a full preparatory beat within the last beat of the old tempo. Any attempt to overlap more than the last beat for preparation may interfere with the old tempo. As a rule, more than a beat's overlap should only be attempted when the old tempo is fast and well established. It is then unlikely to be altered by the lift-off of a preliminary beat crossing a number of beats in the old tempo.

Usually, in these circumstances, a half beat suffices to introduce the click of the first beat of the new tempo, which can be reinforced by movements of the left hand. Precise timing of the rebound from this first click within the new tempo increases its security. In effect, the start of the attack half of the preparatory beat is indicated as a punctuation mark at the top of the pattern. It is timed at the appropriate position within the last beat of the old tempo, estimating backwards, as just described, for the whole beat. The baton then descends to the click of the first beat in the new tempo.

In ex. 3.32 there is little time or opportunity to stop beating the 2/4 and to give a whole beat preparation for the entry at rehearsal figure 30. The orchestra will probably require some rehearsal on this change. Once they realize what the speed of the 3/8 is to be, the conductor need only enlarge his beat at figure 30 and even punctuate in the third quaver in this movement. Having maintained a very small staccato beat in the 2/4, a large energetic rebound at figure 30 into the larger beat will be enough for the orchestra to negotiate the change without loss of ensemble. There must be no slackening of the 2/4 tempo into the change.

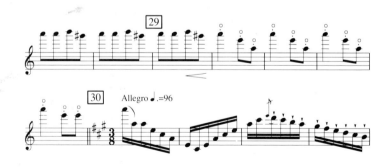

Ex. 3.32

Two changes to a faster tempo and back to a slower one can be seen in this short extract from Stravinsky's *Pulcinella* suite. Rehearsal figure 29 needs to be conducted as a very fast two in a bar. Economize on movement, as only four players are playing at this point. A small and clear staccato beat is needed, especially for the syncopated cello parts.

Beethoven's 'Pastoral' Symphony (fourth to fifth movements) provides a number of clear examples of the sudden tempo change. The transition from the minim beat of the storm music of the fourth movement to the dotted crotchet beat of the fifth is quite straightforward. To get a neat join, subdivide the second half of the last beat of the 4/4, so that the flute lingers a little on the last three quavers of the phrase. The slower two in a bar should come out of this with little trouble.

The change from the third to the fourth movement in this work is from a boisterous one-in-a-bar 3/4 to the minim beat of the following 'allegro'. It requires careful control of the baton. The beat of the new tempo is in fact marked slightly slower than the previous dotted minim beat. The cellos and double basses are marked *pp*, so the beat needs to be small and very clear. Cue the second violins, making the minim beat very obvious, so that they play on to the G with good ensemble.

Ex. 3.33

In ex. 3.33, taken from the third movement of Beethoven's 'Pastoral', push the tempo on quite energetically in the 'sempre più stretto'. Make the preparation for the 2/4 somewhat larger than the previous beats and conduct the two in a bar vigorously to bring out the accents and ensure good ensemble at the start of the new tempo.

Very often a new, slower tempo is not immediate, but preceeded by a rallentando or ritenuto, so that the new tempo comes out of the old without an appreciable break (*see below*).

Gradual changes of tempo

When the tempo is to be slackened over several beats or bars, decide on the number of beats the rallentando is going to encompass. Where it begins, start to lengthen the distance between clicks by placing them more towards the outside of the beat pattern, curving the enlarged path taken between them. This tends to open up the beat pattern. If the orchestra is aware of the moment you intend to make a rallentando, they will immediately respond to the change in beat pattern.

If the beat is already quite slow, it may be necessary to subdivide in order to manage the rallentando securely. Tell the orchestra the point where this subdivision is to commence and at which point the rallentando ends. The rallentando may have served to slow the passage down to a new slower tempo, so insert a full or half preparatory beat, as described in the previous sections, to establish the character and tempo of the following passage.

Ex. 3.34

This example from Elgar's *Pomp and Circumstance* march No. 1 requires subdivision of the 2/4 pattern in the third bar of rehearsal letter R and a 4/4 pattern in the fourth bar. Do not stop the movements between beats: make no pause on the last note of the allargando; the music must continue uninterrupted.

When the tempo is to be increased, give precise, light, short whip-like beats at the moment the acceleration commences. The lighter beats enable you to give sharp lift-offs from the clicks, and thus serve to lead the performers to the next click, which can be placed at a slightly earlier moment. In effect, during an acceleration, the lift-off from each beat is used as a preparatory beat for the next, shortening the durational value of each as you proceed.

As the tempo increases it may be necessary to halve the number of beats in the bar. This is accomplished by closing the pattern and marking weak beats as punctuation movements rather than clicks, as already described under the various beat patterns. Ensure that the score is marked with the precise number of beats and punctuation marks, and the bar of transition; also make sure the orchestra understands what is to happen. The acceleration may take you directly into the new tempo, but remember to introduce the character of the new tempo by a preparatory beat distinct from the last click of the old. If there is a change back to the original, or to a new tempo, introduce it with a clear preparation.

Rubato and tenuto

While often there may be variations in tempo and emphasis in music of the classical period, the concept is more apparent in music of the romantic period, where emphasized beats within a bar are slightly lengthened at the expense of weaker beats; however, the overall length of the bar is retained. The term tempo rubato is applied to the creation of such ebb and flow. Its literal meaning, 'robbed time', implies that the extra length of emphasized beats is stolen from the weaker.

To hurry the underlying pulse a little, the conductor needs to quicken the preparatory movements of each beat (i.e. the curved movements between clicks), so that the clicks themselves are placed slightly earlier, rather in the manner described above under gradual changes of tempo.

Drawing back is not as straightforward as accelerating the tempo. To slow music over a very short space of time, demanded by a ritenuto, a technique is required which is extremely useful also when accompanying a soloist. In these circumstances the conductor must be prepared to wait on certain beats. In a ritenuto, there is no gradual change: one beat may be in tempo and the next very much slower. To maintain good ensemble, it is best to wait on the beat but without stopping the baton. In figs 3.49a and b the heavy black lines indicate a very slow and controlled motion, as though the baton were being drawn through thick treacle. This slowing down, allied to a certain physical intensity, can be effected on any beat. The point where normal tempo resumes must be clear in the beat pattern. It is worth practising this technique, in particular, in front of a mirror before attempting it on an orchestra.

Fig. 3.49a   Fig. 3.49b

At the opening of Part II of Elgar's *The Dream of Gerontius* (ex. 3.35), the pace of the music ebbs and flows following the shape of the melody. Some of the points where the music is to be held back are indicated by Elgar's own painstaking marks of expression and phrasing. Gently subdivide the ritenuto beats (*see* p.34).

The Pause

A pause or hold mark ⌒ indicates a lengthening of the note or rest beyond its written value. (In America, a different terminology is adopted: the hold signified by the sign ⌒ is described as a fermata, since 'pause' is used to allude to a break in the music, such as is discussed below.)

The length of a pause note is unspecified and it is left to the solo performer or conductor to judge the amount of delay necessary at that point in the music. More often than not, whether marked or dictated by convention (as in operatic arias), the pause is a non-rhythmical addition to the metrical pattern of a bar, made for expressive purposes. Pauses can prove a technical hazard to the conductor, since their management (the stop and start and other related aspects) can be a minefield for the unsuspecting and poorly prepared.

The pause is one of the few occasions when the right hand may legitimately come to rest. The conductor has to indicate the length of a pause, the presence and length of any subsequent break and the point of re-entry.

Ex. 3.35

Avoid any change in volume during the pause unless this is specifically indicated by the composer. Where such a change is marked, it can be shown by slowly raising or lowering the left hand as described earlier. To stop the right hand at a pause is not enough to ensure that a sustained *forte* or *fortissimo* is maintained. Unless encouraged, most groups of players and singers will not sustain the loud dynamic right up to the cut-off point. The conductor must indicate the sustained intensity by the use of either or both of his hands until the cut-off motion is made. Beware of exaggerating the gestures necessary to maintain a loud dynamic. For *piano* chords, stop the baton hand and left hand on the pause to maintain the dynamic; the left hand will be required to keep players or singers subdued for softer chords.

1 Pauses at the conclusions of sections and movements

Many works have pauses on the last note and, in the main, need only the beginning and cut-off to be conducted. The manner and style of the initial beat and cut-off depends upon the dynamic and orchestration (*see also* pp.25, 58).

2 Pauses without a following break

Pauses which occur in the middle of a melodic phrase, such as those that can be found in an operatic aria, where a singer holds a high note to display technique, generally follow through without a break in the sound. The pause here is added to heighten the expressive nature of the music and also occurs regularly in instrumental works. In the following examples, the baton should come to rest on the beat point. To indicate the moment of re-entry, there follows a full preparatory beat with lift-off and attack halves. It is important to note that this preparatory beat is made whilst the pause is being sustained. The lift-off in this instance must be gentle so as not to pre-empt an entry, and is best complemented by the steady left hand holding the pause note. The direction of the attack half, which normally is in the opposite direction to the lift-off, must lead into the appropriate point in the beat pattern: i.e. after a pause on the first beat of a 4/4 bar, the lift-off and attack introduce the second beat of the pattern, and so on for subsequent beats. In figs 3.50a and b the ring represents the baton coming to rest on the click of the pause beat. In effect, where the pause is a whole beat in length, the beat-point click is gently repeated by the start of the lift-off. As with previous preparatory beat diagrams, the half-beat point (where the lift-off becomes the attack) is indicated by a dot.

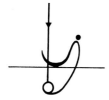

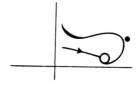

Fig. 3.50a   Fig. 3.50b

If the pause is held for one beat, as in fig. 3.51a, the effect is as if the third count is repeated, the preparatory beat starting at the same moment (fig. 3.51b).

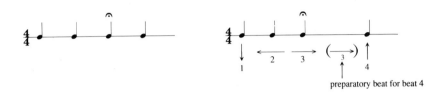

Fig. 3.51a   **Fig. 3.51b**

Where the pause note is longer than a beat, hold the baton still until the start of the preparation for the next note played (fig. 3.52).

Fig. 3.52

Ex. 3.36

At this point in the fourth movement of Mahler's First Symphony (ex. 3.36), the pause ocurs on a beat other than a main beat. The tempo is marked 'alla breve' up to this point. Beat one and hold on two (as if it were a 4/4 bar: the pulse has quickened since the previous bar). Prepare the next beat with a sharp lift-off as if it were the third beat of a 4/4 bar, but return to a minim beat so that the orchestra makes the accelerando, to arrive at the beginning of the next bar exactly with the baton.

3 Pauses followed by a break

a Where a break is marked in the score

Breaks after a pause may be indicated in a score with a rest or by one of the signs used to denote a break: these are discussed below. Examples may be found where both a rest and a break are combined, as in ex. 3.37, part of the 'Nocturne' from Mendelssohn's *A Midsummer Night's Dream*.

Ex. 3.37

The rests here have a definite duration, and breaks of a whole beat or more are conducted in a similar manner. The cut-off coincides with the start of the rest. Hold the right hand quite still through the pause and cut off with the left hand only. The preparatory beat commences at the moment of the cut-off and takes place during the rest. It gives adequate time for the players to breathe and reposition bows, providing information about the tempo and timing of the click of the following beat. Where the rest or rests following a pause last for a period of time longer than one beat, the baton continues from the preparatory beat in the appropriate beat pattern until the entry is reached.

If the rest that follows the pause is less than a beat in length, use both hands in the cut-off gesture and make the cut-off itself very solid. The rebound of the baton is usually the lift-off of the preparatory beat, players entering within the preparatory beat as described in the section on entries (see ex. 3.37 & fig. 3.53). Examples of this type of pause are rare.

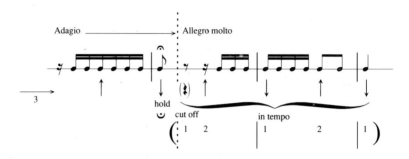

Fig. 3.53

The opening of the fourth movement of Beethoven's First Symphony should be beaten in four. The cut-off for this first pause serves as the lift-off for the preparatory beat for the fourth beat. The second pause needs care. Use just the left hand for the cut-off; it becomes part of the preparation as, in effect, it takes the place of the first beat in the bar. Both hands lift off together on the half bar, exactly in tempo (*see* fig. 3.53.)

b Where a break is suggested by the music but not marked

Very often a break has to be inserted after a pause to allow players to breathe or reposition bows ready for the next note, although the cut-off may or may not have been indicated by the composer. In the majority of cases the conductor will cut off the players in perfect ensemble as part of the preparatory beat for the next played note. The length of the break is therefore generally one beat.

There are occasions where players may judge for themselves when to cease playing, to breathe or to reposition bows, by the stage the conductor has reached in his preparatory movement. To make this clear to the players, ask them to insert a break or comma, and state how long or short it needs to be. Allusion can be made to further examples to illustrate this: at the beginning of the first movement of Borodin's Second Symphony it is important to heighten the tension created by the pause bars at the outset of the symphony by holding the semibreves as long as possible. The left hand should be employed to hold the pauses. The non-pause bars are beaten in two. The lift-off cuts off each of the pauses at the opening of the symphony. The third pause is treated in exactly the same way as the others, i.e. like an entry on the half beat (*see* p. 53).

At bar 176 in the second movement of Beethoven's Ninth Symphony, a very small empty beat is needed at the beginning of the pause bar to avoid any movement which might confuse the players. Use the left hand to cut off the sustaining instruments. To restart, either lift off the preparatory beat at the cut-off of the pause or wait momentarily, in effect adding a further pause over the break.

4 Pauses reached at different points in the bar

If a pause is given to one voice or instrument before the others, the left hand can be used to sustain this whilst the right hand continues to beat through the bar until all voices or instrumental parts have reached the pause note. Progress from the pause is as for the examples described in previous sections.

Ex. 3.38

The duet, *Ihr Schönen aus der Stadt*, from Haydn's *Die Jahreszeiten* (ex. 3.38) contains a chain of pauses that affect, at different times, both solo voices and orchestra. Figs 3.54 and 3.55 provide possible conducting solutions.

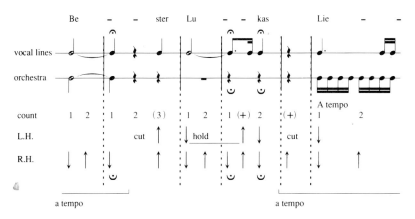

Fig. 3.54

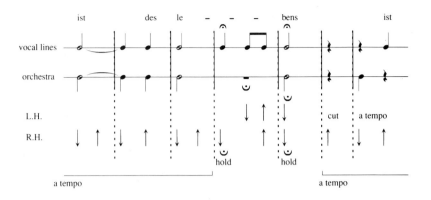

Fig. 3.55

Fig. 55 refers to bars 279-283, not shown in ex.38, where the movement into the second pause is shown by two beats of the left hand. The principle here is that the baton must be used to beat clearly the underlying pulse of the music, so that the orchestra may follow without error. The left hand has an important role, therefore, in communicating instructions other than the pulse and the number of beats.

Ex. 3.39

Here, Elgar's *Enigma* variation VIII (ex. 3.39), beaten in six throughout, requires the last beat before the pause bar to be divided with punctuation beats. Pause on the fourth beat, and take the clarinets and lower strings off with the left hand. Begin variation IX, 'Nimrod', with a slow and very smooth preparation. Keep the beat small to maintain the *pianissimo*. It is wise to cue the double basses with a glance and be prepared to balance the dynamics back to *pp*. Alternatively, do not indicate a measured cut-off to the clarinets and strings at the end of variation VIII. Tell the clarinets and strings to diminuendo 'a niente' and indicate this by gently lowering the left hand.

The dramatic quality of a sudden break in the music followed by an empty silence can be intense. Never underplay rests or breaks in the music. Most important is to achieve an absolute stillness from all the performers during the silence itself, as any small movement or rustle of music can ruin the effect.

Silences of this type may be indicated in several ways, either over a bar line or between notes in the bar itself, as in fig. 3.56. Some, such as the G.P., are measured breaks; the majority, however, are untimed.

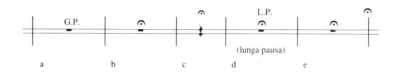

Fig. 3.56

A true musical caesura should be a moment of silence for the whole orchestra. The comma which occurs in all parts, or in complete sections at any particular moment, is not to be confused with the same sign which can occur occasionally in wind parts and vocal lines. The comma in the latter case designates a point at which the players must breathe, and so phrase the music: the rhythmic flow is unaltered.

The technique by which the conductor indicates these breaks is the same as for pauses, and depends on whether there is time to introduce both a cut-off and a whole preparatory beat. The hands must remain motionless during the silence between the cut-off and the preparation for the next beat.

5a G.P. (*General Pause*)

The G.P. is a measured silence marked by the number of beats contained in the printed rests, in all parts simultaneously. Most often the G.P. fills a whole bar and can even extend over several consecutive bars. The conductor can stop beating through the G.P., but must bring in the next written entries exactly in tempo.

There are, of course, exceptions that test the rule. In ex. 3.25 above, the *fortissimo*, which is abruptly cut off (*tronca*), needs time to clear; the more reverberant the acoustic, the more time will be necessary for this.

5b *Lunga Pausa*

A lunga pausa (literally, 'long pause') can be indicated in a variety of ways. The length of the pause is determined by the conductor. Most common is the instance of a bar's rest with both a pause mark ⌢ and the words lunga pausa (or L.P.) placed above each bar.

A measured G.P. may be extended indefinitely by the addition of a pause mark. The resulting break is considerably longer than a single rest with a pause. Occasionally all the available signs are used in combination.

5c *Pauses over a rest*

The management of a pause over a rest is similar to that over a whole-beat note (fig. 3.50a). In bar 4 of ex. 3.40, from the second movement of Dvořák's Ninth Symphony, beat the fourth crotchet beat to act as the cut-off for the orchestra. Hold the baton rock steady the moment it clicks on the fourth beat. Then, without any emphasis on the preparation, lift-off for the first beat in the next bar.

Ex. 3.40

5d *Pauses over a bar line or between breaks*

In theory, as the cut-off point is always the next beat, an extra beat has to be inserted to act both as a cut-off note before the break as well as to serve as the preparation for the next note. In fact, the break can be longer than a whole beat if the hands come to a stop at the cut-off point and remain still until the lift-off of the following preparatory beat. This can be seen clearly in ex. 3.41, part of *Enigma* variation XII, where the first beat of bar 3 acts as the cut-off of the opening introduction. A new preparatory beat has then to be made to reintroduce the third bar.

Ex. 3.41

Beat the first beat of bar 3 with a very small attack motion and cut-off. Hold still for a moment, then lift off for the first beat in bar 3 without any emphasis.

The fourth movement of Mahler's First Symphony has a number of pauses marked directly over the bar line. These *Luftpausen*, literally 'air-breaks', are used to create an effect of daylight between one phrase and the next, but are not intended to be substantial breaks. There is no need to make a specific cut-off motion before the first four pauses from four bars before rehearsal figure 13; simply freeze all movement on the half beat prior to the break. Immediately make a full beat preparation for the restart. The management of this pause is identical to that in ex. 3.40.

5e *Other short breaks between beats or over bar lines*

Several signs can denote a short break in the music. The comma can be found over the bar line or between notes (figs 3.57a, b). 'Tramlines' can occur in one of two forms, depending as much on the style of an individual publishing house as on the preferences of the composer (fig. 3.57c, d). All are treated in the same way generally, but are somewhat shorter than those breaks discussed in section **5d** above.

Ex. 3.42

Other unusual signs have been used to indicate breaks in a legato line or separate articulations. The published score of Shostakovich's Fifth Symphony (third movement, ex. 3.42) employs a sign very similar to a string-player's up-bow mark to signify a break in the third movement over the bar line immediately before rehearsal figure 90. (In a way, this is perhaps more than just a coincidence: after the preceding tremolando, the violin and viola players should be on an up-bow at the end of the bar.) The conductor may stop beating time with the baton during the last two beats of the bar and indicate a large crescendo. The cut-off and preparation should be made during the last quaver of the crescendo bar.

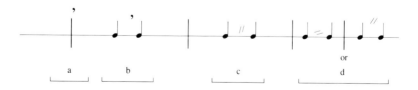

Fig. 3.57

6 Pauses associated with cadenzas

In a concerto of the classical period, there is usually a short rallentando, explicit or implicit, on to the sustained second inversion chord immediately preceding a cadenza. The chord is held for a suitable period of time according to the context of the piece (but not too long!), and cut off as described above (*see* p.57). The orchestral re-entry usually comes at the end of a trill. This is one of the cases where the soloist has to follow the conductor to the precise point of the desired tempo. The soloist can aid the conductor in the management of such a cadenza by inserting a turn at the end of the trill. Communication is therefore two way.

Not all cadenzas are found in concertos and neither must they necessarily end with a trill. Many end with a flourish, which leads back into the tempo primo without a break. In ex. 3.43, the conductor therefore has to subdivide the preceding run into rhythmic groups to gauge exactly the point of entry of the orchestra.

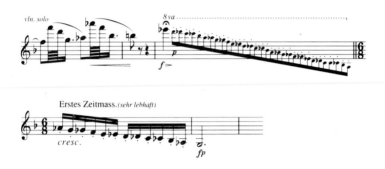

Ex. 3.43

Here, an unusual example of a fully-notated staccato glissando from Richard Strauss's *Till Eulenspiegel*, the conductor must take off the pause to enable the trombones, double bassoon and solo violin to finish cleanly before the violinist commences the measured demisemiquaver dash. Both the baton hand and the left hand then remain motionless, whilst the conductor follows the violinist down the run, mentally dividing five groups of six demisemiquavers. These should be played at the same speed as the semiquavers of the following 'Erstes Zeitmass'. Start beating in two again at the 6/8 bar.

In all the examples of cadenzas discussed so far, the orchestral parts have an indication of *lunga pausa* over one bar, whilst the solo instrument executes a cadenza. In the first movement of Stravinsky's Concerto for piano and wind (rehearsal figures 39–40), the rhythmic flow of the cadenza is so complex that to continue to beat all the way through may not in fact aid the orchestra. Instead, it is far better to stop beating at rehearsal figure 39, follow the soloists very closely and resume beating two bars before figure 40. Although some conductors would advocate a two-in-a-bar pattern here, the predominant pulse has been in quavers and dotted quavers, suggesting that to beat in four may give more security. In this case, however, make sure that the first few notes in the horns do not speak a fraction late.

Accents and Syncopations

When preparing a work, identify the rhythmical accentuations and phrasing requirements of each section. Articulation then can be indicated in the beat pattern by adding emphasis to the appropriate beats within any bar, and from variation in emphases between bars.

Accents

Emphasis on individual notes can be indicated in the score by various signs (*fz*, *sf*, *rf*, *fp*, *rfz*). *Fz* (*forzando/forzato*) and *sf* (*sforzando/sforzato*) are synonymous and sometimes are indicated by the signs ▼ or > above or below the note (even < has been used). These require a sharp and strong accent on one note. *Rf* and *rfz* (*reinforzando*, also *reinforzare*, *reinforzato* and *reinforzo*) is a repeated reinforcement of the note or expression on one or several notes. It is not necessarily an accent. *Fp* (*forte piano*) is simply a loud attack, the level of which should be gauged by the overall dynamic of the passage in which it occurs, on a note which is immediately reduced to a quiet level.

In Beethoven's music, the *fz* or *rf* are often implied by the repetition of a *forte* mark over several notes within a phrase. This can be seen vividly in the recapitulation of the first movement of the Ninth Symphony (bars 423–26), where a number of accents and dynamic emphases are used to heighten the movement's dramatic tension. Remember that all the markings described must always be considered in the context of the music.

Emphasis can be achieved by a precise and rapid lift-off from the preceding beat, thus allowing the baton to slow in the interval between it and the next. The movement is followed by a rapid, intense attack on the emphasized note which can be increased by using a slightly more outstretched movement of the arm. The concept of the rapid lift-off from a click point, as opposed to a downward emphasis, is very important here, since it is the preparatory beat which requires emphasis. We have already see the value of such a beat in the introduction of new tempos, in the management of accelerandos, and after pauses; it can also be used to re-establish faltering tempos. Independent of tempo changes, however, the preparatory beat is of great value to the conductor in accents and syncopation – a sharp lift-off is an effective invitation to the re-entry of individual or groups of instruments during a work. In general, the lift-off from a beat is the main indication of tempo and adds precision to the subsequent point of articulation, whereas the second half of the beat indicates the dynamic requirements of the entry. In a *fp*, therefore, the rebound from the attack half must be very small and may be heightened by use of the upheld left hand.

Syncopation

In cases of syncopation, where the emphasis is shifted off the main beats of the bar, half-beat and other emphasized subdivisions should only be indicated by the baton where the tempo is slow enough to make such additions without upsetting the syncopated rhythm or the clarity of the overall beat pattern. If the whole beats are clearly indicated by precise, straight lift-offs, an orchestra will play the off-beat rhythm without difficulty. A commonly found example of syncopation is where a crotchet beat is offset by a quaver, often used in accompaniment figures. It may even become a feature of the music at certain points:

Ex. 3.44

Ex. 3.44 (continued from p.82)

In this example from Sibelius's tone poem, *Finlandia,* give the beginning of the syncopation a good start by making the first beat of the first syncopated bar staccato and then use a very legato pattern.

Learn to sing syncopated sections with accuracy and beat through them while following the score. Once you fully appreciate the rhythmic importance of such passages, highlighting them in the beat pattern should be straightforward (figs 3.58a,b, exx. 3.45–46).

Ex. 3.45

The cross-rhythm in this extract from the fourth movement of Brahms's First Symphony (ex. 3.45) could be rewritten without the off-beat emphasis as in fig. 3.58a. The pulse, however, is one in a bar and falls into two-bar units (fig. 3.58b).

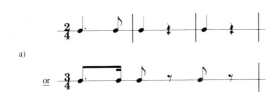

Fig. 3.58a

Fig. 3.58b

Ex. 3.46

Example 3.46, from the third movement of Schumann's Piano Concerto, requires a moderately small and slightly accented beat to bring out the syncopation. Make the beat that coincides with the crotchet rest more obvious than the other.

Ex. 3.47

For the opening of *Till Eulenspiegel* (ex. 3.47), practise conducting the horn solo without any accelerando until you are confident with the changes of emphasis. Note the change from 4/4 to 6/8 is l'istesso tempo. This solo should be well known to most horn players, but the conductor must indicate the main beats of the bar to ensure good ensemble in bars 11 and 13. The 'allmählich lebhafter' (gradually quicker) should move on quite noticeably.

When a syncopated rhythm is present over lengthy sections of a work, and common to the majority of players, it may be possible to insert appropriate emphasis within the beat pattern without detrimental effect. Subdivision by punctuation during the course of a beat provides a means to show such syncopations. Avoid unnecessary body movements here, as these can be disturbing to both the players and audience.

In baroque and earlier music, it is not uncommon for a duple metre to cross a triple within cadential progressions; this is the hemiola. Effectively, two bars in triple metre are articulated as if they were three bars in duple. This can be brought out by beating three beats across the last two bars of the phrase, but the rhythm must be made clear to the performers, as it involves a change of the normal beat pattern. Since the hemiola introduces a syncopation, it is expedient to continue beating the underlying pulse, rather than the superimposed one. This rhythmic device is often apparent in the music of Brahms (ex. 3.48).

Ex. 3.48

In this 6/8 example, the 'Sicilienne' from Brahms's *Variations on a Theme by Haydn*, it is best to continue beating the dotted-crotchet pulse whilst stressing the hemiola with the left hand. Keep a firm hold on the dotted crotchet beat; it is easy, but undesirable, to beat crotchets at this point: this should be avoided.

Another metrical variation sometimes encountered is that of conflicting rhythmical patterns in different instrumental groups (ex. 3.49, p.88). You may have to beat the smallest number of beats of the various forms, even if this is one in a bar, but you should also indicate the first beat of the bar to each instrumental group in order to outline their particular metrical emphasis. The indication of the appropriate downstrokes can be shown with the left hand.

In the ball scene from Act I of Mozart's *Don Giovanni* (ex. 3.49), three different orchestras play on stage, a different soloist singing with each. The pulse of Orchestra III coincides exactly with that of Orchestra I, in effect having a 9/8–3/4 or 3:1 relationship; the six 3/8 bars of each phrase in Orchestra III coincide with the two-bar structure of Orchestra I producing a hemiola relationship. Three 2/4 bar phrases of Orchestra II coincide with the two-bar phrase structure of Orchestra I. The conductor should therefore emphasize the first beat of every other bar of Orchestra I with a larger movement, where the bar line is common to each group.

Aleatoric Music

Conducting aleatoric works, or works with an element of indeterminacy, requires a different approach to that of more conventionally notated music. To a great extent, the concept of a constant pulse is inappropriate here. More likely, the conductor is required to act as a timekeeper, measuring out sections of fixed time duration (e.g. 2, 5 or 12 seconds) in which the players improvise around given parameters of varying exactitude.

From a technical point of view, the conductor is no longer required to conduct the beat patterns discussed above. A single downbeat should be used to mark out the beginning, subdivisions, and end of each section. In the aleatoric scores of Boulez, for example, the left hand is sometimes required to give signals indicating subdivisions of sections, the entries (and exits) of instrumental groups and soloists, and dynamic changes. In performance, the conductor may be required to indicate the order of sections, although this is often left to the performers. It may be necessary for the conductor and performers to agree on specific signs to indicate the choice of particular sections to be performed. If the composer leaves this choice of signal to the conductor, choose clear and distinct movements. These can include an upturned hand, such as the policeman's halt sign, which can also be turned to the left, to the right or downwards to indicate specific sections.

Most scores using graphic, pictorial or verbal notations are provided with a key to their explanation. Make sure that you understand the requirements of the symbols employed; each performer, however unfamiliar with the genre, should be encouraged to treat the techniques to be used as an extension of those required in more conventional music.

Berio's *Circles* contains many procedures and features typical of aleatoric scores. There is an absence of bar lines. Percussion (both tuned and untuned) make up the greater part of the instrumentation, and the work can be performed with only a few performers. The boxes scattered around the score contain series of notes and chords with which the players may improvise. The solo vocal line exploits extended

Ex. 3.49

techniques, often taking the form of an additional percussion instrument. Much use is made of glissandos on the tuned percussion (marimbaphone, xylophone and vibraphone) and harp.

Mastering the Beat

If at any time the players or singers do not enter or follow the beat, or if the ensemble is ragged or the balance poor, look on it as a deficiency in your technique and try to determine what is at fault. Never continue to beat faster or slower than the orchestra, but learn how to use preparatory beats to speed up an ensemble, and how to pull it back by lengthening your beat. In rehearsal, however, stop immediately and restart any section in which the orchestra takes a speed other than your own. An orchestra soon learns to ignore someone who is in obvious difficulty and who cannot rectify the situation or get their desired intentions across.

To obtain fluency and flexibility of right-arm movements requires considerable practice with the baton. Advice to undertake regular exercise is not necessarily heeded in any walk of life, but if you are conscious of limitations here, practise beating various time forms. Ensure that you can outline smooth clockwise and anticlockwise circles with your baton, increasing and decreasing their size by adding or subtracting wrist, elbow, and shoulder movements to basic finger control.

When studying the score try to concentrate on the clarity of right-arm tempo and dynamic movements and, upon reaching the end, beat through the work as a whole, with or without a recording. Recordings can be of great value in learning complicated rhythmic patterns before meeting the performers. Make sure that you conduct with the recording, rather than just following it. Remember that eventually your movements will have to lead the orchestra, directing rather than accompanying. Always listen to a variety of interpretations so that you become acquainted with the standard performance: never offer a mediocre copy of someone else's ideas.

Much can be done to improve basic conducting technique by standing in front of a long mirror and, if the facilities are available, by watching video recordings of yourself. Be critical of your conducting by continually checking to see if the baton, hands and face convey all the information you need to get across in the least fussy or stilted way. Listen carefully to the comments of teachers, friends and players on your technique and watch how other conductors cope with difficult areas. Particularly watch the use of their left hand and their gestures. Use these influences to develop a personal style, rather than merely copying that of others.

A conductor's beat naturally changes in style over the years, but whatever emphases, subdivisions or pauses are being indicated, the position of each click and the direction by which it is approached, must be retained: make them distinct and identifiable to the performers. Not only must the conductor aim to convey a sense of artistry to all his players, but also he must do so at all times with clarity and control.

The Left Hand

The left hand is not always in action, since little can be gained solely by duplicating the action of the baton. Continuous mirror-imaging is only required when forces are large, widespread or in the cramped confines of a theatre pit, where the orchestral players are separated on either side of you and cannot necessarily see the baton. Other indications that suggest combined use are areas of difficult ensemble and of definite emphasis, such as climaxes, and when great force of sound is required. The parallel movements of the two hands, as opposed to mirror-imaging, can create the latter effect, though such movements must be used sparingly.

At other times the left hand should be used independently and economically for specific functions, since it will then carry more impact when brought into use. At rest, the left arm can hang by the side of the body, but it may be more freely used when it is relaxing at waist level. The hand should not rest on the hip with the elbow bent, on a desk or stand, or be in your pocket. The left hand generally should undertake functions that the right is unable to achieve. It is of particular value in interpretation and expression, indicating dynamics, phrasing and articulation.

Well-established gestures which are recognized by performers include gradually raising the palm of the open hand to indicate a crescendo, and the reverse for diminuendo. For these, and most left-hand movements, the fingers are loosely held together. A clenched fist, with the back of the hand facing the orchestra, can imply force and tension over a phrase; these indications of expression may be directed at the whole orchestra or a specific section. Raising the index finger can indicate to a player that a note needs to be sharpened, the reverse being indicated by pointing downwards. One or more fingers can be raised to indicate the number of beats in a bar. Try to carry out these movements in front of the body and out of sight of the audience, with the minimum of display.

The left hand may be used for cueing instruments. It is not necessary to introduce every orchestral entry, especially if there are a number in quick succession: any such rapid movement on the part of the conductor could lead to confusion. Most players will enter automatically, but confirmation from the conductor can add confidence, especially if they have had a large number of bars' rest. Much of this can be undertaken with a specific glance or a nod of the head, but the left hand can be a far more reassuring invitation in difficult passages. Lift off in time with the baton from the preceding click, so that the movement prepares for entry on the next beat. If a loud dynamic is required on the entry, both hands can complete the attack half of the beat.

Another function undertaken by the left hand is to hold the duration of pauses, while the right hand continues to beat empty beats: this prevents misunderstanding and false entries. When performers need to hold a note, the palm of the left hand can be held upturned and, if necessary, to avoid false entries, the palm can be held out-turned and facing the players.

Sparing use of the left hand means that more notice is taken of it when it is employed, such as its use to change or stabilize tempos, or as a warning sign against premature entries or misplaced dynamics. Make sure that the left hand never interferes with the continuous pulse of the right: at no time should the hands cross. As with the right hand, any movement must be graceful and appropriate to the character of the music. The left hand can also be combined with the right for cut-offs at the end of a work, and is also used specifically in certain pauses, as already noted. Another of its functions is the apparently straightforward task of turning the pages of your score. This requires a little practice and must become automatic, so that it does not interfere with either the movements of the right hand or the conductor's concentration on the music.

Be sure that at all times movements are concerned purely with the interpretation of the score. Never be tempted to impress by flamboyant gestures but concentrate on directing the most polished performance possible.

Posture

The position of the conductor is dictated by the size and conditions of the hall or orchestral pit in which he is performing; this may even involve sitting. Ideally, however, stand at ease in an upright position with feet slightly apart, knees relaxed but not bent, weight carried on hips, elbows bent with hands at waist level, head and trunk bent slightly forward and looking down at the orchestra. Weight should be distributed evenly on both feet and not on the heels; avoid standing on tiptoe, as this can upset balance and be very tiring. Try to breathe regularly and in a relaxed fashion. This basic position must be linked with mental alertness, but not agitation.

The podium should be high enough so that every member of the orchestra can see the conductor from head to waist. Players should not have to resort to contortionist postures to be able to see the beat as well as the music on their stands. Care should be taken, in the case of a very high podium, that the first desks of the string sections are far enough back so that they do not have to move their heads to see the conductor.

The conductor should be able to see the eyes of all performers. The music stand should be just below waist level and should not restrict the movement of the baton. Arrange that there are no obstructions such as handrails, foliage, or other hindrances to the free flow of the baton.

At the outset, address the performers by standing upright with feet together and hands raised to the rest position, ready for the first preparatory beat. During the performance, however, try not to be fixed like a signpost in this position, but be free to move around.

Excessive gestures cancel each other out and can be disturbing to both orchestra and audience, and, if inappropriate, may even be comical. Poise rather than pose should be the maxim. Never look casual or sloppy, as this may be reflected in the manner of the performance. Certain extremes of movement, however, can be very effective in their result. Sudden crouching can help initiate a dramatic *pianissimo*. Such means, however, should be kept for a rehearsal, to stress specific points of dynamics: they can look absurd in a performance. The conductor should restrict movements to those that will convey the interpretation. 'Playing to the gallery' will be spotted by audience and performers alike. Avoid sitting down during rehearsal, as it may lead to a casual approach by the performers. Occasionally, rehearsals may be lengthy or piecemeal, as perhaps in rehearsing an opera. If a stool is used, it should be high enough, and the music stand appropriately placed, so that all concerned can still see the full extent of the conductor's movements.

With increasing experience, communication can be reduced to just a glance, facial expression, or, to a lesser extent, head and body movement. Simultaneous movement of the head, corresponding with the two halves of a preparatory beat, has already been alluded to. Shouting and stamping are undesirable. If such extremes appear necessary it is wiser to stop and issue a few brief and concise words, explaining what is required, and possibly singing the phrase or rhythm that is causing the problem.

In rehearsal, the performers' attention can be obtained by raising both arms just above shoulder level. When absolute attention has been obtained, the hands are withdrawn to the rest position, ready for the preparatory beat. In performance, raise your arms until both the orchestra and the audience have settled, and then withdraw to the rest position to introduce the work.

Before starting a work, look at the orchestra and not at the score. By this time you should have confidence in your knowledge of the work, and your movements should be well rehearsed and automatic even through difficult areas. With such training you will be able to concentrate on the most important task: listening to the ensemble, and ensuring that their performance corresponds to your interpretation of the music.

CHAPTER 4

Interpretation

This chapter has been divided into two sections. The first discusses general points of interpretation and how each is individually important, the second comprises an examination of the first movement of Beethoven's Fifth Symphony. The Beethoven work has been chosen because of its familiarity and because of its availability both in score and on record, and because of specific problems of interpretation. In the latter case there are decisions to be made by the conductor about a wide range of performance practicalities. Certain conventions employed by performers in Beethoven's time are no longer common practice; here, the concept of historically aware performance, for music of the past, must guide the conductor's choices of tempos, dynamics, articulation and phrasing, and balance.

The art of interpretation may also be divided into two distinct parts: the 'correct' reading of a composer's text, and the use of imagination and intuition in rehearsal and performance, to highlight a performer's understanding of the work. With amateur orchestras and choruses it cannot be assumed that the printed symbols of music notation will be interpreted accurately at first sight. Time and patience are the key to success at this level. Only when an ensemble can accurately reproduce their written parts should the conductor expect a response to his own personal interpretation. Music is an imaginative art; its notation provides a sophisticated but inherently incomplete code.

A performance of an orchestral or choral work expresses a conductor's concept of a composition; this view may differ considerably from other views of the same work. One of the conductor's functions is to ensure that the performers respect the written information on the page. This is quite distinct from an interpretation of a piece. Having achieved a correct reading of the score, the conductor then instils life into the music. How this is acheived will be discussed under a number of headings, including structure and balance, tempo, dynamics, melody, rhythm, accents and staccato, and ornamentation.

Tools for the Performer

The conductor is usually the only member of the performing body with a copy of every players' part: the score. What is reproduced in the score should be what is found in the players' copies, misprints and errors notwithstanding. In scores of music of the nineteenth and twentieth centuries, the printed text usually includes marks of expression and other performance-related information that the composer thought necessary for satisfactory performance of the work.

The development of more advanced printing techniques in the early nineteenth century offered composers the opportunity to be more specific about dynamics, expression, phrasing and tempo markings. This was linked to dramatic alterations in the standard of instrumental technique and the growth of the symphony orchestra. Romanticism in music led to a greater use of such dramatic contrasts. The published scores of Wagner and Mahler, for example, offer many marks of expression and tempo that would not have appeared in a baroque or classical score. These present a further problem, since literal marks of expression can have a variety of different interpretations according to context. (Composers' letters may offer further insight here, particularly correspondence with publishers.) The closer a work is to our own period, the greater the number of assumptions that can be made about performing practices; however, evaluations of each work to be performed should be informed by reference to any relevant books, articles, and anecdotal material that is available.

1 Scholarly versus practical editions

The editor's task varies considerably, according to the period of a work's composition. Ideally, a scholarly edition is produced by reference to all available sources, whether manuscript or printed editions, the best aiming to produce the most accurate reflection of the composer's original manuscript. Collected *Urtext* editions, i.e. those that attempt to reproduce the original text, seek to eradicate the errors and misinterpretations of previous editors or copyists. Most such editions are expensive, and often contain a substantial prefatory text on the work or works, together with a shorthand critical commentary on the sources used for the edition.

Many practical editions, i.e. those intended primarily for use in performance, reflect the most up-to-date research; however, the majority should be treated with a degree of caution, especially where a heavy editorial hand is apparent. Whenever possible, compare cheap editions, especially of choral music, with a good scholarly edition. Avoid excessively edited scores. For frequently performed repertoire, there are usually a number of good practical editions available. The editor's involvement with a renaissance or medieval source is vitally important to the finished result. Old notational and scribal practices must be fully and clearly translated into modern note values and metrical patterns. Decisions about performance practices may also have been made: for example, the question of *musica ficta* (additional accidentals) in medieval and renaissance works requires numerous decisions to be made about customs and conventions, based upon contemporary theoretical writings and the source of the work itself.

2 Sources

In most cases, a composer produces a work in manuscript form. If the work is entirely in the hand of the person in whose name it appears, this is called a holograph; if a composer makes handwritten additions or emendations to a copyist's work, this is called an autograph. Generally, an autograph copy is considered to be anything in the hand of its author. The earliest examples of composers' manuscripts date from the sixteenth century, although fifteenth-century examples have been postulated.

The transmission of the composer's work, before the invention of the printing press, would have been by hand-copied manuscript, the presentation and accuracy of which varied according to origin and destination. A work copied for use in a royal or ducal chapel usually differed in quality from the same work copied for use in a lesser institution, or as a 'working' copy. The first print-runs of music were small and expensive; very often they were modelled on contemporary manuscript styles. Alec Hyatt King's short guide, *Four Hundred Years of Music Printing*, provides an excellent introduction to the history of the collaboration between composer and printer.

3 Editorial practices

A cautionary note should be sounded here for the conductor interested in the performance of medieval and renaissance music: beware of the over-zealous editor. The transcription of music written before about 1600 is complicated by questions of the interpretation of extinct notational systems, implicit and explicit accidentals, textual underlay, and the extent to which scribal errors or omissions should be emended. Below is a short guide to a number of ways in which some of these problems have been tackled; individual styles are not discussed, only the basic concepts of editorial practices. The **bibliography** on p.185 provides a brief list of books and articles offering practical information on the following and related procedures.

(i) Barring and time signatures

To make an edition rather than a copy of a medieval or renaissance work requires more than simple transcription of the original source. Consideration must be given to the best way of presenting defunct notations in a form immediately recognizable today. Regular repeating bar lines were not used in most pre-baroque music (with the exception of keyboard and string intabulations). It is usual editorial practice to add bar lines to mark a work's metrical structure: either these may divide all parts into distinct bars (cutting through the staves) or, in the case of *Mensurstrich*, can be placed between the staves. The latter method allows individual voice parts to preserve an independence of rhythm, but makes the metrical structure less obvious to the eye. Conventional barring offers greater practical advantages, since performers are naturally familiar with it. Barring in the early baroque period sometimes has to be altered, to reflect more accurately the metrical structure of the music. The original scheme may be indicated by vertical lines above the stave.

Time signatures are added to coincide with the length of bar chosen by the editor of a medieval or renaissance work. This is not the place to discuss the question of editorial rhythmic reductions; however, when choosing an edition, legibility, clarity and simplicity should be the guide. Most editions today equate the modern crotchet with the semibreve of fourteenth- and fifteenth-century sources (4:1), with a 2:1 or 1:1 relationship used for sixteenth-century music. After 1600, note values should be interpreted as being the same as those of today.

(ii) Marks of expression and the metronome

Although found in some sixteenth-century sources, verbal expressions of tempo are rare until the next century. A good edition should preserve expression marks as found in the primary source. The basic Italian directions for tempo, and dynamics and phrasing were universally accepted and employed by the close of the seventeenth century. Marks in English, French and German were developed in the eighteenth and nineteenth centuries, but the dominance of the Italians in the major musical centres throughout Europe at this time led to the establishment of a 'standard' Italian usage.

The invention of the metronome in c. 1812 gave composers the opportunity to be specific about the precise measurement of tempo, although many composers resisted the idea of giving a 'rigid' or fixed tempo to their works in this way. A report in the *Allgemeine muzikalische Zeitung* in 1813 stated that both Beethoven and Salieri had shown interest in a new machine devised for the measurement of tempo. Johann Nepomuk Maelzel's metronome, patented in 1815, was used by Beethoven to make all of his extant metronome markings. Beethoven and Schumann frequently changed their minds about these markings as evidenced by autograph sketches and letters to publishers. Editorial additions to original tempo and metronome marks (if any) should be shown in square brackets to avoid confusion.

(iii) Dynamics

Performance instructions about gradations of sound, although occasionally found in medieval plainchant repertories, began to appear regularly in the seventeenth century, when the Italian *piano* and *forte* were used. In English consort music of the same period both 'loud' and 'soft' are to be found ('lowder by degrees' occurs in music by Matthew Locke). 'Hairpins' are not found before the beginning of the eighteenth century, although expressions such as Locke's and series of dynamic markings were used before this to acheive the same effect. Again, additional editiorial dynamics should be distinguished clearly from those of the original source. Often extra dynamic markings suggested by an editor are printed in a smaller typeface or a different fount, or are placed in parentheses

It is best to choose an edition which is not 'fussy', and which accurately reflects the composer's original text (or that of the scribe closest to the original source). In performance, decisions have to be made which may not be shown by any edition; indeed, practicalities of performance often cannot be prescribed by an editor or scholar. An *Urtext* edition of a baroque or classical work offers the conductor the basis for an individual interpretation, where knowledge of performing practice along with imagination are central to the recreation of a work in performance.

4 Recordings

Sound recordings, where available, can serve as a valuable aid when learning a score. Careful and repeated listening offers a good introduction to the shape and form of a musical work; however, the ability to apprehend the sound of a work from the printed or manuscript page should be cultivated at all times. Good aural perception is an essential requirement for any conductor; the ease with which we can now listen to recorded and live broadcasted music provides an excellent opportunity to become acquainted with new and unfamiliar repertoire. If misused, however, recorded interpretations can interfere with the natural process of learning a work, especially where the influence of the work of one conductor inspires slavish imitation. Modern recordings are often the product of concentrated recording sessions, where time is available to rectify mistakes, to record repeatedly a 'difficult' section, and to mediate artificially in matters of balance and overall shape long after the sessions have ended. It is best, therefore, to compare as many different recordings of a work as possible.

Since the Second World War, the number of specialists in period performance practice has expanded considerably. Many are accomplished performers of the classical symphonic repertoire who also take great interest in a specific and quite narrow field of music, presenting performances representative of the latest musicological research.

If possible, compare recordings of a Karajan or Furtwängler performance of Bach, or Beecham's version of *The Messiah*, for example, with those by Harnoncourt, Hogwood and Pinnock, for the vivid contrast provided between the expectations of style and taste in the interpretation of baroque music over the last fifty years. This is not the place to discuss the validity of the aesthetic of one style against that of another; however, today's musician must be aware of a wide range of stylistic practices spanning a considerable period of music's history. Aspects of rhythm, phrasing, articulation, expression, and tempo can be revealed when played on 'period' instruments that would be difficult, if not impossible, to reproduce using modern symphonic forces.

5 Advice

At first sight, the inclusion of this paragraph may seem out of place in a section headed tools for the performer; however, the foundations of knowledge must be built upon the ability to seek and use good advice. There is little more valuable than a discussion with a teacher or skilled musical colleague about aspects of performance, and about aspects of music in general. The ability to recognize just and constructive criticism, and to act upon it, is essential. Debate can be stimulated easily, especially if a certain strongly-held opinion is contentious: the views of others may help to clarify misconstrued or half-baked notions. An open mind should not be incompatible with firm opinions. Ultimately, a conductor's interpretation is determined by its individuality, with no room for self-doubt or reverent imitation.

Faithful interpretation requires a knowledge of the stylistic practices of the period and country in which the composer lived and also an understanding of the composer's music. A grounding in such practices, appropriate to the work's context and period, is essential in order for a performer to be faithful to the sense of the music.

Melody

Melody forms the heart of most music. A sequence of successive individual pitches may be considered as a melody (from Gk. *melos* 'song'). A melodic unit, or motif, can be formed from as little as two notes. Rhythmic organization is vital to the sense of a melody, whether it be conditioned by the rhythm of speech or prose, or by an artificial metrical system. Harmony has to be considered also as a fundamental element in determining melodic shape, especially in western music. The gradual erosion of the classical tonal system during the twentieth century, and the use of more angular or chromatic melodic lines, has further equalized the roles of rhythm, harmony and melody. Numerical series have been used to generate complex, but logical, melodic patterns which are much harder to recognize than those of tonal music, but which must be considered as melodies.

The ability to recognize melodic material, and to evaluate the importance of different strands of a contrapuntal composition, is essential to the success of an interpretation. Always distinguish and attempt to highlight melodic material from its accompaniment, especially at early rehearsals. Artificial balancing of parts may be necessary on occasions, especially in amateur orchestras or choirs and some youth orchestras, where not all parts may be adequately covered, or where one section is weaker than another.

In contrapuntal music, each strand should be readily apparent. Fugal subjects, where strict, are stated without accompaniment initially, and are subsequently interwoven with contrasting melodic lines in the form of countersubjects. These should also be pointed out to the choir or orchestra at the earliest stages of preparation.

Rhythm

With melody and harmony, rhythm forms the essence of western art music. Without precise rhythmic control true ensemble cannot be expected, nor will the music achieve a vibrancy or immediacy that can bring a performance to life. Indeed, a lack of rhythmic control can lead to sloppiness that can ruin an otherwise potentially good performance. Several aspects need to be carefully considered when approaching a score.

1. Duration of notes: notes should be given their full length. If a note is staccato then the question should be asked, does the degree of detachment have a measurable length?

A staccato crotchet may be equal in duration to a dotted quaver followed by a semiquaver rest or, depending on the context, tempo and style of the music, may be shortened still further to a quaver followed by a quaver rest. Alternatively, such a staccato might be played or sung as short as possible, according to whether the mark was used, for example, in an allegro or a lento passage. For a further discuusion of staccato *see* p.104.

Do not allow performers to hold notes for longer than the required length. Seated singers are particularly prone to this habit, which often happens at the end of a phrase or where a rest occurs, and can result in the next phrase starting late. This leads to a lack of ensemble, a choir that sings behind the beat and, ultimately, a sluggish and lack-lustre performance. Composers often fail to mark rests or other breaks to accommodate breathing time, requiring the conductor to prepare this in rehearsal.

2. Duration of rests: remember that a composer not only manipulates durations of sound but also of silence: the rests. Their precise duration is therefore as important as the sounding notes and no clipping of rests should be allowed, whether by hanging on to a previous note or by anticipating the next. Rests are often of structural importance in a work, carefully written out, perhaps over several bars (e.g. the General Pause, *see* p.77). As such they are an integral part of the rhythmic structure and pulse of the music.

3. Dotted rhythms: the greatest pitfall in the interpretation of dotted rhythms is that of rushed or inaccurate performance (clipping the longer note and anticipating the shorter); military and brass bands achieve an extra crispness in dotted rhythms by overdotting: shortening the note following the dot. A break is sometimes introduced

after the long note, combined with a generally crisp, staccato style of playing. The best of these bands play with bold, rhythmically light and exciting ensemble; however, this is often stylistically inappropriate and is used without discrimination by less able bands. Conversely, sluggish execution of the short note is often found in amateur choirs, where

♪. ♪ is incorrectly interpreted as ♩ ♪ (triplet 3)

4. Altered rhythms and rhythmic conventions in baroque and early-classical music: (the main arguments are introduced below. For detailed discussion of these topics reference should be made to the specialist books and articles listed in the **bibliography.**

Structure and Form

Many attempts have been made to define art in terms of form and structure. Definitions of form in art are various and ambiguous, but they attempt to outline its organizational function. Does form stimulate the sensory or emotional response felt when a work of art is apprehended for the first time? Or do surface details prevail upon the emotions? Whichever is the case, it would be impossible to comprehend a musical work without structural organization: its fundamental shape.

A single movement of a work has a structure which gives the music balance (a type of musical architecture); the same is true of the simplest melody. Numerous formal schemes have been evolved to provide contrast and tension, and to allow the simplest of melodic and rhythmic ideas to unify a whole movement or work (cf. the first movement of Beethoven's Fifth Symphony). Like speech, music can be shown to have a grammatical and syntactical structure: cadences provide an analogy with punctuation marks, and terms such as phrase, sentence and paragraph have been used in descriptive writings on musical language. Linguistic analogy, however, is of limited worth, since the development of thematic material and tonal relationships operates simultaneously over the course of most large-scale compositions. The form of spoken language is immediately understood: in music, formal articulations can be obscured by the complexity of melody, rhythm and harmony.

The consideration of different formal schemes, rather than the concept of form *per se*, is of greater practical value to the conductor, although there is much to be gained from a knowledge of the aesthetics of musical form. Dictionary definitions can be applied satisfactorily to a number of technical schemata used to provide the framework for many different types of composition. Prominent among these are the following:

Binary Form. Most commonly found in the movements of baroque suites and in other short pieces. It falls into two sections, both repeated, which share much thematic material; the first modulates to the dominant or relative major and the second modulates back to end in the tonic.

Ternary Form. Frequently used for short movements, such as the baroque *da capo* aria and the slow movements of classical symphonies and concertos. Two outer sections, similar in thematic use and key, enclose a central contrasting section. The Minuet and Trio has a ternary form on the larger scale, but also an adaptation of it for the individual sections: the latter, however, make use of repeat marks which alter the symmetry of the form.

Sonata Form. Used from the classical period to the present day for movements of symphonies, concertos and other large-scale works. This is considerably more flexible than the above forms, and indeed only exists in a loose set of principles for structuring a movement. It falls into three broad sections: the exposition, where thematic material is first stated, generally in two groups contrasted by key; the development, where this material is developed in a variety of keys; and the recapitulation, which balances the exposition in its statement of material, but in which both subject groups are played in the tonic. To this general outline may be added an introduction, transitions, codettas and a coda. In early classical works, the exposition and the combined development and recapitulation are both to be repeated.

Rondo Form. Found in a wide variety of contexts throughout the history of orchestral music. It applies to any movement or work in which one theme recurs in whole or in part throughout, separated by sections of contrasting material. In the fast movements of baroque concertos, the term 'ritornello' is used to distinguish a similar effect.

Variations. Found in movements from the sixteenth century to the present day. One or more themes are stated and then successively repeated in a variety of new guises. The Passacaglia or Chaconne is a type of variation form where a short theme (harmonic or melodic, e.g. the simple ground bass) is continuously repeated with various elaborations.

An important structural technique which is not used in such a consistent fashion is **Fugue**, where in a movement, or part of a movement, a theme is stated successively in different 'voices' and subsequently treated in a contrapuntal way.

From a thorough knowledge of such formal schemes, the conductor can pace the music and have an overview of a whole movement or complete work, balancing conflict and tension with periods of repose. As the composer had this in mind when creating the music, so also should the musician when he recreates the music in performance. Although the ideal of recreating music as it existed in the mind of the composer can never be realized by another individual, study of all aspects of music will aid the conductor. The process of understanding fully the structural features of music takes years of study. Methods of musical analysis, now an essential element of music education, offer many advantages to the student of conducting who wishes to investigate further the formal processes of music.

Tempo

As the conductor studies and gets to know a piece, he becomes more aware of the tempo necessary to give life to the music without making it seem unduly hurried or underplaying climaxes and cadential points. Factors such as auditorium acoustics, technically difficult phrases, style of articulation, and the alertness of performers will effect the eventual choice of a tempo.

Wagner considered that tempo was the essence of interpretation and stated that the whole duty of the conductor was to indicate the right tempo. Wagner's point is worth expanding. The degree of control invested in the modern conductor allows him far more influence over subtleties of tempo than to all but a few of his nineteenth-century predecessors. The concept of flexible tempo, as advocated by Wagner in his essay *Über das Dirigieren*, has influenced many conductors since. On the other hand Mendelssohn and Berlioz both favoured steady tempos, with the emphasis placed firmly on clarity of texture and crispness of articulation.

The tempo mark at the top of the movement gives the conductor a good idea of the tempo required. He should then look at the music itself to help gauge it more precisely. For instance, semiquaver passages or some other rhythmic passage may only work within a narrow range of speeds, either because of technical difficulties or because the rhythm feels imprecise if too slow or too fast. Choosing a satisfactory tempo is therefore one of the first things to decide upon. How is it done? Ideally, the score should provide enough guidance. Where the composer's original metronome or tempo indications are given, these should be related to the 'feel' of the sections they affect. Tempo marks can suggest as much about the style as about the actual speed of a work, especially as certain words were once associated with various genres of dance, characterized by metrical emphasis.

A movement marked allegro vivace must be taken fast enough for the vivacity and liveliness to be apparent, but not as fast as allegro assai or presto. Take for example the first movement of Mendelssohn's Fourth Symphony, 'The Italian', where the words 'Allegro vivace' are found. Choosing just the right speed here is essential; the qualifying adverb 'vivace' should offer a clue about the desired speed. The theme of the first subject needs to dance along and the repeated figure in the woodwind at the opening, which is a feature of the entire movement's thematic development, should bubble along with clarity and effortlessness. Flutes and horns can double tongue the opening quavers with ease, but the oboes and bassoons may find this more difficult. On the other hand, fast single tonguing is difficult on the clarinet; therefore, a compromise must be made to facilitate the woodwind articulation at this point.

'Should the piece be conducted in one or two beats in a bar?' It is possible to conduct the whole movement in one if the players are forewarned. Problems of ensemble and rhythmic flexibility would be created if this pattern was rigidly applied, however. Two beats in a bar affords more points of reference, essential for control of the fast quaver passages, or for the off-beat entries in the strings at bar 26 and the passage starting in bar 44. In each case, the players require a clear beat point to aim for. At bar 26 the second beat of the bar must be given to cue the string entry after two bars rest. To negotiate the syncopation at the beginning of the next bar the strings must play accurately on the second beat, without late entry or subsequent tardy execution. In this phrase, there are two strong beats to aim for: the second of bar 26 and the first of bar 28. The last three notes of the phrase must be phrased away with a diminuendo.

Unless an orchestra is rhythmically aware there will always be the danger of rushing or dragging at times: for example, in this movement, at bar 5 in the violins and in the passage at bars 20-24, the players may hurry the continuous quavers unless a firm grip is maintained on the underlying pulse (a two-beat pattern will encourage security and reassure less experienced players).

In the slow movement of Dvořák's Seventh Symphony, it may be necessary for the conductor to alter the number of beats shown to help articulate the phrasing and to clarify details of ensemble. In this case, not only does the music move from relaxed, lyrical sections to rhythmically intense and louder sections, but also the overall style lends itself to a fair degree of rubato. The basic speed of the movement is set by reference to the passages at bars 40-43 and bars 55-59. At these points there is a very obvious and strong underlying quaver pulse (quaver = M.M. 104-108), and the conductor must give eight strong beats in a subdivided four-beat pattern (*see* p.35). Once this pulse has been firmly grasped, turn to the opening of the movement. The beginning requires a four-beat pattern, slightly detached for the pizzicato chord in the strings. Amateur string players may be inclined to rush the quavers if they are not encouraged to listen to the clarinet's melody. There needs to be a slight ritenuto at the end of the first four-bar phrase.

Selecting a tempo thus requires a great deal of preparatory work on the style of music and the information provided by the composer in the form of tempo and metronome markings (where shown). It is helpful to get to know other people's ideas and to listen to live and recorded performances, and to talk to teachers and colleagues.

Metronome markings are peculiarly liable to typographical error, and thus it is perhaps judicious to check such details against other available sources, in particular the composer's autograph if possible. Many facsimile editions of works in the standard repertoire exist and can be found in most university and research libraries. (For a list of these, see the current *British Music Yearbook*). Metronome markings should not be taken as unfailing indications of absolute tempos: some composers are renowned for being inaccurate in the assessment of tempos for their own music. Wagner believed that metronome marks were of limited value and dipensed with them in his later works.

Once set, rarely is tempo totally inflexible. Apart from in ostinato figures, the tempo should fluctuate as the music runs its course. Benjamin Britten allegedly became most uncomfortable listening to a performance of music (especially his own) when the music did not move onwards from the opening tempo. Even so, the flow of phrases or music between sections should not be upset by inexactitude of pulse. Unless specifically marked, tempos should not change suddenly, the pulse being maintained constantly over shorter sections. Breaks in the body of the music should be timed exactly for best effect.

Choice of tempos is affected by the venue of the performance. Where there is a reverberant hall or church it may be necessary to broaden the tempo and play fast passages at a more relaxed speed than in a 'dry' acoustic, otherwise notes can become jumbled and forte passages will sound over resonant.

Dynamics

On the large scale, the relative dynamics of a piece are important shaping forces, and often coincide with and complement a work's structural organization. When such dynamic contrasts are carefully managed, they can help focus important events in the music. It is necessary, therefore, to exploit the fullest possible range of dynamics available from a performing group, one of the main faults of many amateur performances being the tendency to play at one loud, unrelenting dynamic. There is nothing more tedious than a monchrome performance executed at one level, without contrast; but it happens with alarming regularity! Considerable physical effort is required to make wide dynamic contrasts on most instruments. The conductor should encourage these efforts to be made during rehearsal until the desired effects have been achieved.

Not only must dynamics be considered as part of the overall balance of a work but also at the music's surface level. Sections which have a long and steady increase or decrease in volume can be made particularly exciting if the initial and final dynamics are sharply contrasted. In long crescendos avoid increasing the dynamic level too much too soon; it requires concentration to convey this to performers but, if accurately paced, is extremely effective when correctly carried out.

Occasionally extreme dynamic markings are requested. In the case of the climax of the first movement of Holst's *The Planets*, the crushing discord towards the end is marked *ffff*. Holst presumably requires the loudest possible sound at this point; indeed, a certain harshness of tone can be encouraged at this point. In *The Dream of Gerontius* Elgar prescribes that '"for one moment" must every instrument exert its fullest force' (rehearsal figure 120). Opposite extremes can be found. Tchaikovsky may hold the record for the quietest dynamic mark: *pppppp* at the end of the first movement of the Sixth Symphony. Although the loud sections of Verdi's *Requiem* are marked *ff*, with *tutta forza* used at climax points (e.g bar 382 of the 'Libera me'), the composer marks the orchestra down to *ppp* and the chorus and soprano soloist to *pppp* (*sotto voce*) in bar 367 of the same movement, to emphasize the contrast between the 'requiem aeternam' prayer and the following impassioned 'libera me', and to make the desired effect quite clear to the performers.

Solo dynamics (i.e. those required to project a solo line or lines over an accompaniment) are generally louder than their tutti equivalent. It is important to avoid straining or overpowering an orchestral soloist. Ensure that the accompaniment is quiet or subdued enough for the soloist to sound above it. Thus, a *pianissimo* from a solo clarinet, accompanied by a full string section, can be significantly louder than the quietest *pianissimo* obtainable on the instrument, to ensure that it does not sound distant in relation to the accompaniment.

Take time in rehearsal with an orchestra of players not used to playing together, for example, to balance chordal dynamics in the wind department, so that the players become aware of the relative balance necessary in the section.

Some composer-conductors (such as Mahler and Strauss), through their experience in rehearsing and performing various styles of music as well as their own, became particularly astute and careful when adding markings to their scores. Much of the orchestral balance can be reached by following such a score, if players are careful enough. Although many later composers have been influenced by this practice, blanket instructions are still common, e.g. *piano* for the full orchestra, rather than more careful and accurate dynamic markings appropriate to the individual instruments.

Variations of volume should be graded carefully to get the most out of the music. The gradations of these tints and shades from *pp* to *ff* are a severe test of a conductor's ability. Crescendos and diminuendos must extend between predetermined volume levels. Changes must occur gradually throughout the marking from the indicated position to reach the climax where intended. Guard against any tendency among an ensemble for undue acceleration through crescendos or slowing down through diminuendos, unless such effects are written. As far as possible follow the demands of the music itself.

Contrapuntal music requires careful preparation. The performers should be aware of the main subject and make important entries prominent. For the opening statements of a fugue, for instance in choral performances, the entries should be confident and projected. It is advisable to ask for the countersubject to be more quietly and lightly played or sung.

Accents

Accents of many different shapes and form can be used to modify a note in a variety of ways. Care should be taken to make each type distinct and appropriate to the style of the music, *sf, fz* or *sfz* (*sforzando, sforzato, forzando, forzato*) are the most explosive types of accent. The attack of the note is greatly heightened. Some separation of notes thus marked will facilitate clarity of ensemble.

Stravinsky's use of the *sf* mark is perhaps the most powerful of all, with the greatest degree of attack required. Listen to the opening of the *Symphony in Three Movements* for the music's granite-like qualities and to the extent that accents and short notes add to this. Here accented notes are shortened as a matter of course and staccatos are played extremely short.

Fp, forte piano, is similar to and is often confused with *sforzando*. The *fp* normally should not have the explosive start required for the *sfz* requires. Simply, the loud initial articulation should immediately give way to a piano (it is sometimes increased to *ffp* or *fpp*).

Tenuto (It., 'held'). This indication perhaps should not be grouped with accents at all. However, its treatment in loud passages can be similar to the *sf* but without the initial explosion at the beginning of the note. The note is held, but a measured break is inserted at the end of the note before the next is sounded, so that several crotchets would be sounded thus:

(These should be heavy and solid (rather like bricks) without diminuendo.)

Staccato

Staccato (It. 'detached') is usually indicated in modern scores by a dot over or under a note thus:

Fig. 4.1

It can be argued that this implies a reduction of the note's value by about one half. However, very short staccato (*staccatissimo*) is sometimes specified, where the note values may be shortened by up to three quarters of the original value. In Stravinsky's *Symphony of Psalms*, at rehearsal figure 9, the composer not only puts a staccato mark above each note but also marks the words 'leggiero et staccato' (lightly and detached). Note that for the horns he writes the superlatives 'staccatissimo' and 'leggierissimo'. A dagger sign is sometimes found to show a very short detached note with more than an element of force or accent (▼). In the 'Triumphal march of the Devil' from Stravinsky's *The Soldier's Tale* (rehearsal figure 7) he emphasizes the shortness of the staccato with the words 'tres court', and 'tres sec' (very short and very dry); the force and weight of the execution by 'au talon' (with the heel of the bow).

Ornamentation

The question of ornamentation in late renaissance, baroque and classical music has received considerable attention: books and articles offering valuable discussions of the subject can be found in the **bibliography**. Elaborate ornamentation has been used to add colour and interest to a melodic line, or to demonstrate a particular virtuoso's technical ability, either in fully-notated form or as shorthand signs. The interpretation of the latter often requires a degree of speculation, especially where the original signs are vague or ambiguous. Many theorists and composers gave rules for the performing conventions associated with ornaments, and some gave tables of the various signs and their correct manner of execution. Robert Donington's excellent article, 'Ornaments', in *The New Grove Dictionary of Music and Musicians* should be consulted for its compendious list of examples.

Jazz scores

Direction of larger jazz ensembles is ususally a specialist's job: the conductor of such groups is usually a performer who has taken on these duties. However, many of the skills required for rehearsing and conducting orchestral and choral forces also apply to the jazz ensemble. The conductor's job here is to give clear cues to the reed and brass sections, to highlight solo parts, to maintain crisp ensemble, and to gauge dynamics. A good jazz orchestra relies upon its rhythm section to maintain and constant pulse (keyboard, bass guitar or string bass, rhythm guitar and drum kit). The conductor sets the tempo at the outset and is responsible for any subsequent changes in speed.

The score of a work composed for such an ensemble is often quite rudimentary, reflecting the importance of the improvisatory element in jazz. In effect the chordal structure of the work is given in shorthand notation, with fixed instrumental melodies shown.

Interpretation of a Specific Work

The discussion of interpretive points is divided into two sections, roughly equivalent to the first reading of a score, and to a more detailed look at the music. The points made are not exhaustive: by its very nature the discussion is cursory. It contains a few ideas of what should concern the conductor for the satisfactory preparation of a score.

The first look through a score

Beethoven: Fifth Symphony (first movement)

First, establish the basic form of the piece. A check through confirms that in this movement Beethoven employs a version of sonata form, the structure of which is quite straightforward. Sir Adrian Boult, in *A Handbook on the Technique of Conducting*, recommends that before examining a score in detail, initially the conductor should read through the score several times very rapidly ('faster than it could be performed') until a strong impression is formed of the work's 'structure, balance of its tunes, its emotional sequence, its dynamic shape, (and) the pattern of its colours.'

The opening pauses in the Fifth Symphony immediately present problems for the conductor. One solution is discussed on p. 108. The one-in-a-bar tempo of the movement is set in bar 6; the pauses destroy any sense of pulse previous to this and serve to arrest the listener's attention. The music of bar 6 onwards remains at a *piano* dynamic, employing only the string section, until a repeat of the opening phrase (bars 18-24), when the strings take up the opening motif and pass it through the section. This time the music builds in tension and volume with the addition of wind chords, and the biting accents of the rising sequence bring the music to the first climax (bar 44). Note the single *f* at bar 44 becomes *ff* at bar 52.

A change in texture and character is apparent with the introduction of the second-subject theme at bar 63. After an assertive horn call (a brief transition), the second subject is stated, characterized by a smooth, *dolce* phrase. This is passed to the oboe and flute, and is lengthened by sequence, with the addition of more instruments to the melody and to the sustained chords: a climax is reached at bar 95 (note the bass line from bar 65).

There is the conventional repeat mark at the end of the exposition. It would have been usual to observe this in a symphony written in 1805, and it is important to the balance of the movement. Here the quavers in the strings should be played extremely heavily. Momentum must not be lost in the silent bars, either before the double bar line or at bar 57. Nor should there be any wavering of the pulse, or anticipation of the off-beat entries of the horn (bar 57) or in bars 119, 121, 125 and 126. Note that the greatest climax so far is at bar 102. This brings the exposition to a close. Save something for the final coda (bars 374-502). The opening of the development comes as something of a surprise in that it employs the opening motif, but with harmonic alteration.

The development of thematic material is begun in bar 129 with the extension and alteration of the first subject. Note the crescendos followed by the sudden return to *piano*. The music builds to bar 167; the reiteration of the chords continues to create tension until the explosive release at bar 180, based on the transition theme. Note the accents on the minims (these notes should become detatched). The off-beat entry of the bass line should be very solid; make sure the wind part (which is in contrary motion to the bass part) is quite clear. A new section follows that develops the minims themselves. A good balance between each section of the orchestra is necessary here, as is good intonation and balanced dynamics within each section, especially when the diminuendo takes effect. There should be no anticipation of the *subito forte* sections, and the return to the *pp* in bar 233 must be sudden and precise with no diminuendo on the chord of bars 231-2. Clear this chord a fraction early so that the following *pp* wind chord is crisp. A considerable crescendo is needed to bring the development section to end on the pause chords at bars 248-51.

The recapitulation is regular with the exception of an additional short oboe cadenza at bar 268, further prolonging the melodic tension. Do not conduct the oboist: simply cut off the orchestra after a crotchet (there will be a need for a slight ritenuto into the bar so that the crotchet here is a fraction longer than that of the basic pulse). Cue the first violins at the *a tempo*: this will act as a cut-off for the oboist's pause. The cadenza should be quite free rhythmically.

At the end of the closing section of the recapitulation (bars 362-372), inject much more energy into the music as you go into the coda. This section, in effect, is almost a second development both in length and in the way it re-uses a great deal of earlier thematic material and builds upon it. There is no great need for a marked ritenuto into bar 479, but it is worth subdividing if only to encourage the players to play a little more heavily (note the addition of the trumpets and timpani at this point). Ensure the following few bars are really quiet; it is easy to overblow in this section. The crotchets of the final bars should be clearly detatched.

The second reading

After the first reading the conductor should have an awareness of the shape and scale of the music's structure. The second and subsequent readings should concentrate on highlighting important surface details. Not only must the conductor become familiar with any technically difficult passages but also where cues should be given to important parts or players that have not been playing for a while. Every dynamic, slur, and phrase mark should be noted. Where the timpanist has to retune or change sticks between movements, time should be allowed for this.

The opening is difficult to conduct and requires careful preliminary planning. When facing the orchestra be sure of its attention; keep both hands raised and still in anticipation of the entry. A skilled orchestra should be able to time the first entry from the single preparatory beat shown in fig. 4.2. The black spot in the figure indicates the half-beat timing, although no emphasis is required at this point. With a single preparatory beat, the timing of the lift-off will require a clear and emphatic movement, shown by tensing the grip on the baton. If a single preparatory beat is favoured, some explanation may be necessary to the orchestra before playing. Correct the players if they make the opening motive sound like a triplet: i.e.

instead of

An alternative method is to add an empty beat (*see* p.55) before the preparatory beat, as shown in fig. 4.3. The orchestra must be informed of your intentions. There should be no emphasis at any time during the empty beat. The left hand can be used to hold the orchestra during the empty beat and then it can join with the baton hand to show the lift-off of the preparatory beat. With both approaches the attack movement of the preparatory beat should be powerful and end with a vigorouos bounce. The left hand then holds the minim pause while the baton hand prepares for the continuation into bar 3. The click at the beginning of bar 3 is also the cut-off point for the pause at the end of bar 2. Note that the minim is held over from bar 4 to 5, with a pause in bar 5. Beat an empty beat in bar 4, bring the pause off with the left hand, and begin simultaneously the preparatory beat for the second violins. In effect, an empty bar has been introduced. The cut-off in bar 5 and the entry at bar 6 can be treated in the same way as bars 2 and 3 (*see* fig. 4.4).

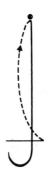

Fig. 4.2

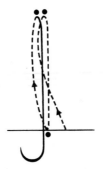

Fig. 4.3

Fig. 4.4

The tempo of the movement is such that it can be conducted in one in a bar (with the minim pulse equal to M.M. 108), so too should be the opening bars. Thus a strong attack of the preparatory beat at the opening will help the players to enter with good ensemble. However, listen carefully to the quavers to place the attack in the second bar with accuracy. The opening quavers need to be a little broader than those following in bar 6. The speed at which these opening quavers are played can be regulated by the size of the beat used in bars 1 and 3: the smaller the beat, and the greater the anticipation of the first beat in the next bar, the greater the accuracy of ensemble. With a larger beat, the orchestra will take more time here, and a slight ritenuto can be introduced if it so desired.

From bar 6 onwards ensure that the quavers are played spiccato and that the violins and violas are balanced with the bass instruments in tone and volume. Note the accents in the passages leading to the *forte* at bar 44. Balance the wind chords and check the intonation. The crotchet in the wind instruments at bar 51 is often played quite short. However, be sure to give full length to the chords in bars 56 and 57. A completely different style is required for the second subject. As the music from bar 63 is more lyrical, a legato beat is required. Keep it small to be in control of the shape of phrases and the *piano* dynamic. A firmer click is used to cue the cellos and basses in bar 65 and can be maintained to encourage rhythmic crispness. The short motif in bars 67 and 71, which is repeated by the clarinet and flute, needs shape.

The slurs not only indicate the shape of phrases here but also the bowing in the first violins. The bass part must be emphasized (bar 65), especially in the crescendo; it becomes increasingly dominant as the closing section is based upon the same theme. This also needs careful phrasing. Ensure that the crescendo commencing at bar 83 starts at a true *piano*. The sustained wind chords in this section should be carefully balanced, with no part too prominent. Do not allow the brass to overpower the rest of the orchestra at this point (the strength of the sound here should be provided by the first violins and cellos).

The quavers in bars 125-6 should not be allowed to lose momentum. The interruption in the harmonic flow should resolve itself as soon as possible into the return of the first subject at bar 129. Lighten the first quaver of the figure in bar 139 and at other similar places.

It is remarkable how Beethoven can build up a 10-minute movement on such apparently limited material. Nearly every bar has some recollection of the opening motif. The job of the conductor is to avoid turgid playing and to deal with the recurrent entries of the main theme in a musical manner. (This discussion may end here as the movement continues with similar material and should be approached in the same fashion.)

The art of interpretation is fundamental to perfoming; it is one of the most difficult yet most rewarding aspects of music making. The goal is to achieve an assured and convincing performance. In this respect, the learning process is never ending: the most experienced conductor often will revise his interpretation with each successive performance of a particular work. The student or inexperienced conductor should take every opportunity to experiment with his particular interpretation, and to see whether his understanding of a work can be conveyed to an orchestra or choir by gesture alone.

CHAPTER 5

The Rehearsal

Rehearsals are for the benefit of the performers, and not the conductor. Knowledge of the score, concepts on its interpretation and mastery of any technical problems must therefore be completed before meeting a choir or an orchestra. Every rehearsal should be planned in advance and have a clear preconceived goal. It is important for a young conductor to have attended other rehearsals to observe how conductors in different spheres of music structure their rehearsal time. This is particularly necessary if you are not an instrumentalist and have not performed under other conductors. When observing, try and station yourself as close to the podium as possible, hear what he says and watch his interaction with the orchestra. A conductor's function when managing rehearsals is to lead the orchestra, listen to their performance and correct anything which does not correspond to his concept of the music.

It is desirable to have a regular rehearsal site and if possible this should be where you intend to perform. Ideally the venue should have good heating, lighting and ventilation, refreshment areas and toilet facilities and a storage place for large instruments and music stands. The local church or church vestry is often lacking in many of these facilities, but an active group can generate enough financial support to upgrade available accommodation to satisfy rehearsal needs. At least the last rehearsal for any concert should be in the performance hall.

Orchestras

Seating

The seats, music stands and music should be laid out prior to the arrival of the orchestra. Seating plans vary somewhat between different orchestras and conductors. The shape and space on concert platforms also limits the orchestra to certain layouts. The most widely used layout for the modern symphony orchestra is shown in fig. 5.1a.

Certain variations on this format have been adopted by conductors. One of the most popular is the seating of the second violins on the right, opposite the first violins, with the cellos sitting in the position vacated by the second violins. The second violins suffer slightly by sitting on the right because their instruments face away from the audience. It is, however, an ideal position where the melodic interest is split evenly between the two violin sections, such as in the Elgar and Tchaikovsky symphonies. Exciting antiphonal effects, such as in Tchaikovsky's Sixth Symphony can be lost in the standard seating.

Note the proximity of the double basses to the cello section. Some would argue that it would be far more suitable for the double basses to be kept to the right of the conductor, i.e. on the side the bassoons and brass are generally to be found. A further variation in the arrangement in fig 5.1a, therefore, is to exchange the cello and viola

a

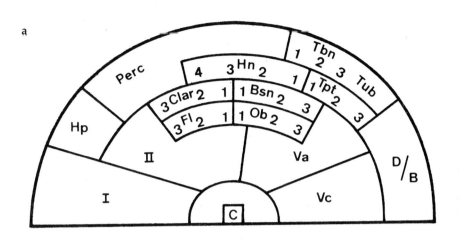

b

c

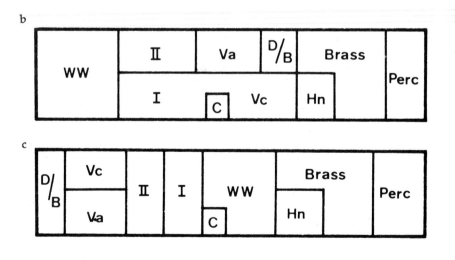

Fig. 5.1

positions and to place the double basses on the right behind the cellos. The arguments in favour of the seating plan of fig. 5.1a are twofold. First, it is convenient for the conductor and the audience to have the relative pitches of the string sections to be graded from the left to right, from treble to bass instruments. Second, the cellos can clearly project their sound into the auditorium from this position.

It is worthwhile experimenting with the various layouts and even adopting different layouts within the same concert, appropriate to the music being performed, as long as it does not result in too much disruption at the performance.

There is an accepted seating plan within the string sections of the orchestra. The conductor should find out where the principal and sub-principal seats are in an orchestra with which he is not familiar. The normal layout is to have the senior player of each desk on the outside for the first violins and cellos, with the senior player of the second violins and violas on the conductor's left-hand side. Be aware that in an unfamiliar orchestra, the violas may vary their position to conform with the cellos.

The leaders, and players on their side of each desk, usually play the top line in divisi sections and leave the turning of the pages to their partner. This allows continuous playing of music over a page turn with only minimal loss of volume. The seating should allow performers to sit as close to each other as comfort will allow, in order that they can hear the other instruments of the section and adjust tuning. Experienced players will adjust the position of their chairs and stands during the rehearsal, to get the best view of the conductor and maximum benefit from lighting and proximity to other players. While 'tidying up' the stage prior to the performance, whoever is in charge of stage management should not tamper with these alterations.

Try to ensure that the playing conditions are comfortable so that each performer at least starts happy and can concentrate on the music: extremes of temperature not only affect mood, ability and performance, but also the tuning of instruments. Lighting must be adequate and directed from above and behind the players so that it lights up their scores and the conductor's face. The conductor should face any bright light, such as a sun-filled window, rather then be silhouetted. The conductor's position has already been considered, but it is worth reiterating that he must be visible to all players from the waist upwards, in order that they can follow his beat by glancing from their music without losing sight of it behind their, or his, music stand. The conductor must also have freedom of movement so that he can turn to the leaders of each section, or to soloists, and can see the eyes of all the performers. Figs 5.1b and c show the standard dispositions of instruments within the pit orchestra.

The rehearsal

The timing of the rehearsal must be carefully planned so that no one is left idle for any length of time. Groups of instrumentalists not required in part of a rehearsal should be told at what time they will be needed. Where appropriate, sectional rehearsals and soloist rehearsals ought to be held separately. Avoid at all costs calling players to a rehearsal if you are not going to use them. Having provided a clear timetable, insist on punctuality; players must arrive long enough before the scheduled start to prepare and tune their instruments. A strict rehearsal schedule must be followed, a period of rehearsal being up to three hours, punctuated by a break of fifteen to twenty minutes with prompt return, no unnecessary time being wasted: good planning will enable this to be achieved.

A conductor's relationship with an orchestra will gradually evolve, and relates to his own character and enthusiasm, but he must always be aware that he is dealing with a group of individuals and should retain their interest in an assured and relaxed way, with good humour yet sensible discipline. There is no need to apologise for any inadequacy in technique: a well-informed orchestra probably knows more about your limitations than you do. If you have fully prepared the score the players will recognize this fact and respond accordingly. Nevertheless an inexperienced conductor may well feel self-conscious if working with a skilled orchestra: avoid over reaction, retaining the same discipline expected of less-able groups. Anecdotes are best avoided until you know your performers well, and should never be wasteful of time. Players not involved in a particular part of the rehearsal may leave the rehearsing area, but should do so with the approval of the conductor. If children are involved in the performance, treat them as you would the adult performers, and never hint by your speech or behaviour that their contribution is in any way less than that of the rest of the choir or orchestra

The leader of the orchestra is a key figure in the smooth running of the preparation and rehearsal. This player acts as the conductor's intermediary with the orchestra, and can help in discipline and advise on specific problems relating to string playing, for example, on bowing, as well as on more general matters. The communal spirit across sections, and in the orchestra as a whole, should be firmly encouraged, as teamwork reflects in both rehearsal and performance as well as at other times.

The leader or co-leader will probably also be involved in the initial tuning of the orchestra. It is usual to request silence and ask each section (strings, woodwind and brass) to tune separately. The oboe's A (= 440 Herz) is the usual point of reference, because it has the most consistent and easily controlled pitch, and is clearly audible. In its absence a tuning fork ought to be used. Where a keyboard instrument is included in the score, either solo or continuo, it must be used to provide the tuning note. Wind and brass bands normally tune to B flat. Sectional leaders as well as a conductor will often request re-tuning during the course of the rehearsal. Carefully listen for instruments going out of tune and compare your own perception of the pitch with that of the players: electronic tuning meters are available, and may prove a worthwhile investment.

Use the score for rehearsal. Although you may have committed much of a work to memory, the score is still needed for reference and for sorting out any queries from instrumentalists. The conductor, like the players, should always have a pencil and rubber to hand to make or change markings. The score, and the instrumental parts, should be provided with identification marks in the form of bar numbers, letters, and tempo and dynamic markings before the first rehearsal (*see* p.15). Know how the parts are marked and if there is any discrepancy between different copies. It is essential to be able to identify bars for discussion and places for restarting. On these occasions give the orchestra a specific bar or a specific letter (e.g. "third of letter A", "third bar of A, please"). Alternatively, count backwards or forwards from a letter with the orchestra, so that they are ready to restart on reaching the required bar. A lack of adequately marked parts is the responsibility of the conductor/librarian: it can be infuriating if it leads to time-wasting, and can cause considerable disruption to a rehearsal.

When you are ready to start and have drawn the attention of the orchestra, state which work you are rehearsing, where you are starting and what you intend to beat. It is at this stage that your efforts to obtain a clear baton technique will come into service. All gestures should be directed at the performers and not to an imaginary audience and must be in keeping with the mood of the music. Do not expect the orchestra to hold a written *piano*, if your actions imply *fortissimo*. Remember that the preparatory beat is based on memory of a phrase somewhere in the movement, where the rhythm is established and characteristic. This preparatory beat, should imply the tempo of the entry, with the attack half of the beat indicating the dynamic of the entry. Avoid a noisy deep breath with any sudden lift-off, audible grunts or singing along with the choir or orchestra.

At the first rehearsal with an unfamiliar group, listen with an open mind to the whole orchestra and to individual instruments for some time before offering any criticism. It is advisable to allow an orchestra to play through a lengthy section of a familiar work, to play themselves in, before giving any attention to detail. When rehearsing works for the first time, it is also helpful to play them through at the correct tempo. Experienced players will sort out many of the problems themselves. An orchestra made up of skilled musicians possesses a collective instinct to perform well: this must be encouraged, and on occasions it is wise to direct such an group with minimal intrusion.

Throughout this time, however, listen very carefully to the playing. The ability to detect various problems is one of the most important skills a conductor has to develop. Make a mental list of problems and be ready to tackle them once you decide to stop. Initially it may be difficult to remember all the faults detected and during early conducting days you may also be distracted by anxiety about technique. The problem is compounded by the fact that, to begin with, you will only be able to concentrate on one section of the orchestra at a time. The ability to detect qualities of tone and the niceties of specific instrumental groupings requires great experience, as does the quick switch from listening to one group to listening to the whole orchestra. If this a problem, stop and rehearse small sections at a time, but ensure that no player is kept unoccupied for any length of time.

The quality of playing within an orchestra is usually quite uniform and the novice conductore is not faced with as much difficulty as the previous sentences may imply. With an inexperienced orchestra the problems will be mainly of incorrect, shaky intonation, or missing notes and poor ensemble. With a skilled group you need not worry about these two factors, but will be able to concentrate on specific aspects of interpretation such as style, balance and phrasing. With such a group, a single wrong note is usually obvious both to the conductor and the performer, and the two may indicate recognition of the fact by catching each others eye, interruption being unnecessary. Deliberate playing of a wrong note to test a conductor's ability is a rarity and once recognized should generally be ignored. If it ever becomes a recurrent problem, it should be sorted out with the individual concerned after the rehearsal.

Correcting faults

Ideally a conductor should be able to control music by gesture alone. Much can be gained by this, but, on completion of the play-through of a lengthy section, or when an orchestra is having difficulty with a complicated passage, stop the players and start to correct the inadequacies verbally. Never stop an orchestra without saying why, and know what to stay before stopping. Insist on a rapid halt by all instruments and complete silence. State desired changes with as few words, and as quickly as possible. Speak slowly and clearly, stating which instruments and which bars are being addressed. It is annoying to have to repeat such information more than once.

Identify the place and ensure each player knows where it is; use simple musical language to indicate what you want and make use of your prepared vocalization to indicate any points of rhythm or phrasing. Restart as soon as possible, identifying the start point accurately (repeat this several times before starting), and give players time to find this place in their music. Stress the reasons for repeating a particular section; listen carefully to the repetition to ensure that your points have been understood.

When dealing with orchestras of lesser ability, attention should primarily be given to wrong or absent notes, and secondly to the accuracy of ensemble. Inexperienced performers are likely to have a tentative approach to technically difficult passages, with late entries and cut-offs as a result. This will need to be corrected by practising these areas and establishing within the group a confidence in the preparatory beat and its attack. If a single section is at fault, rehearse this and allow the others to rest. For general points, try not to direct individual criticism against a player, rather, give comments to a section or to the whole orchestra: the message will then probably reach the individual concerned. Criticism should at all times be constructive, without giving offence, and should aim to build up a mutual respect between yourself and the players.

The next factor deserving attention is the intonation of the orchestra. This is related to the initial tuning and the choice of fingerings used by the players, and is also influenced by the quality and inherent technical difficulties of each instrument. Players in amateur and youth orchestras will require more encouragement and training than experienced players and professionals. Always insist that your players give the necessary concentration and attention to detail. Above all, groups of players respond to inspiration from their conductor, and the collective enthusiasm of the players can often sustain higher degrees of excellence than their individual standards might suggest.

Specific problems of balance and dynamics will require positive attention, such as insisting on the maintenance of a *pianissimo* or a sustained *fortissimo*. Crescendos must increase steadily in volume throughout their length rather than produce a sudden increase at any one point, the reverse being true of decrescendos. Ensure that *fortes* are less forceful than *fortissimos*. Be clear in your mind where the peaks and troughs of the movement are and avoid making a climax out of every every forte passage.

One of the skills that you will need to develop is the ability to assess whether or not an orchestra is capable of playing in the way that you want; by so doing, one can avoid excessive repetition of sections and introducing an element of fussiness, which is likely to result in orchestral discontent. Do not repeat any section without telling the orchestra why, and what you would like changed. Remember that during a rehearsal, the extended use of certain instruments, such as the oboe and the horn, and the human voice, tire the individuals concerned and reduce control and enthusiasm.

If you have difficulty in obtaining a certain effect, ask the section concerned why. Such discussion will enable them to tell you if they realize correctly the effect you are requesting. Always be ready to take the score to the section for such a discussion, and ensure that there is no discrepancy of parts. If an individual point is not rapidly sorted out it is better to leave it for discussion with the player, or section concerned, after the rehearsal, or with an experienced colleague, rather than waste valuable time in rehearsal.

It is, therefore, the ability to listen acutely which you should cultivate during your rehearsals, and this must be achieved without getting behind, or losing control, or slowing the progression of the work. You should aim to obtain the maximum potential of the group you are working with, seeing how they respond to high pressure and insisting that their interpretation corresponds to your own views of the composer's wishes.

Even well-known works require thorough rehearsal, but little is to be gained by just playing them through, except in a warm-up. Certainly the application of a critical approach to the works of the great masters will provide you with some of your most exciting performances. Rehearsals must be so planned that each piece is equally well known by the time of a performance, but it is not necessary to play through each piece at every rehearsal. Allow rehearsal time for sorting out minor flaws, skipping through a work to these relevant areas and leaving nothing to chance. At the end of each rehearsal, leave time to polish sections and to review danger spots.

Times and schedules

Timing of rehearsals is critical. Never go over time at the end of a rehearsal or leave music unrehearsed. If you find yourself in the position of needing an extra 10 minutes to cover something vital, then stop rehearsing at the appointed time , have a quick word with the leader and invite the orchestra to leave if they need to. Amateur orchestras will generally give the extra time to a conductor who is going to use it constructively. Several members of the orchestra may leave at this juncture, but enough will stay to make the extra minutes worth while. Never go over time without prior explanation and the permission to do so from the orchestra; this will only lead to bad feeling and the great danger, if it is due to the conductor's mismanagement of the rehearsal, of not being invited back. Alternatively, if it is a scratch orchestra, players may refuse to play for you again. Where professional musicians have been employed, or you have been engaged to conduct a professional group, it must be stressed that to exceed the scheduled rehearsal time will incur overtime payments. If it becomes apparent that more rehearsal time is necessary, a request for overtime should be made after the half-time break. Players are quite entitled to refuse such a request, and it may be better to reorganize remaining rehearsal time to cover sections most in need of practice.

At the last rehearsal, the larger part of the programme should be covered to provide a unity of feeling throughout, without risk of over rehearsing or taking the edge off the performance. By this time you will be able to spend most of the rehearsal listening without the need to stop unduly. During the rehearsal leave the orchestra playing on its own and walk around the hall to assess the acoustics at various places, relating this to tempo and balance. The quality of tone tends to improve as you walk away from the orchestra, but the ensemble may deteriorate and it is important to be aware of what your audience hears. At both rehearsals and performances, try to invite a skilled and candid listener and perhaps also a less skilled person to comment on the quality of the playing and of the appeal of the music.

At the end of this final rehearsal, remind the orchestra and choir of the arrangements for the concert, the programme, the timing, the dress and any other factors (such as car-parking facilities or the lack of them!). The choir must note where they are sitting and to where they should return; spare seats should be left in the unlikely event of anyone having been excused this final rehearsal. Everyone must be able to see the beat and allowance should be made for the introduction of different footwear or hair-styles for the performance.

Handbags should not be brought into the hall, so security arrangements must be checked. Make sure that a strong-arm team is ready to check all arrangements concerning chairs, music stands, heavy instruments and the removal of any heavy furniture, such as a pulpit; see that they are supplied with a tool-kit, if necessary. A member of the orchestra (if amateur) should also be responsible for laying out scores and be armed with manuscript paper, paper clips and sellotape, and also clothes pegs for out-of-doors activities, where they will be needed to keep music on the stands. In instances where you have assembled an orchestra of professional and semi-professional players, you should try to persuade a friend or assistant to perform these vital tasks, or take responsibility for such yourself.

Choirs and Choruses

Most choral groups are made up of amateur singers and usually require a different style of training to that of professional vocal and orchestral forces. It is important, therefore, to be aware of the maximum potential of the performers. The reasons why people join and remain with a choir are many and varied: although they may often be related to the enthusiasm of a conductor, such factors as habit, associated social activities and the absence of counter-attractions, may be of some importance. Whatever the reason, aim to provide programmes which are enjoyable and to achieve a result of which the group is proud. At all times foster enthusiasm within the group, as this is their greatest attribute.

Initial assessment

Immediately after taking over a group the conductor may have little control over its composition. However, there is no place in a choral group for an 'atonal growler', for such noises obviously impair the quality of the sound. It would be advisable to spend a quiet moment with such an individual in order to establish whether there is any possibility of training him or her to pitch a note. If this proves impossible try to encourage the person to contribute to the life of the choir in some manner other than singing. Their contribution could be far more valuable socially and administratively by helping the choir with organization.

Although atonal growlers are unacceptable, your approach to singers who sing out of tune, or who are too prominent in quiet passages, or who have a tendency to swoop or wobble, presents much more difficult decisions. Decide whether such problems are correctable or acceptable and, if neither, what alternatives are available. Politically, it may be very difficult to ask a singer to leave; to do so may upset other members of the group. Generally, when joining a group, it is better to spend a few months settling in and assessing how much you can tactfully adjust the tonal quality, gradually modifying disagreeable sounds by working on corporate technique alone. It is surprising how a very good general choral sound can be achieved from a large choir which may contain a high proportion of only mediocre singers. Patient training of a whole choir can certainly improve the vocal quality of the average member.

Criticism

Criticism should be constructive, linked with encouragement and, as with other ensembles, not directed at specific individuals. When individual criticism is required it should be carried out in private and aimed at constructive correction of any problems. It can be far more valuable to correct individual problems with the whole choir as certain basic faults are often common to many singers in a group. Few singers have a problem totally unique to them. Once a regular group has been established and standards set, auditions can be considered for existing members on a regular basis as well as for potential newcomers to the choir. Insist on an attendance of at least three quarters of all practices before anyone is allowed to sing in a performance.

Regardless of your own ability on a keyboard instrument, a regular accompanist is a great asset to any choir. His presence will enable you to listen to the choir more easily and allow the choir to become accustomed to following a conductor's beat. The requirements of a skilled accompanist are legion; consequently, good ones are hard to find. They must not only be able to play accurately any music placed in front of them but also be able to add parts and to fill in, or bring out certain parts which are flagging, always keeping in time with your beat. Being able to score-read the vocal parts is a prerequisite. They have to be prepared to stop immediately with the conductor and also be willing to remain silent for much of the later practices when unaccompanied rehearsal forms the basis of training. The accompanist may also be your deputy should you ever be unavailable. In spite of this total involvement they may well not partake in any performance unless they play some other instrument or are acceptable as a choir member. To obtain such a skilled individual, it will normally be necessary to pay an appropriate professional rate for the job.

Warm-up exercises

Five minutes at the beginning of each practice can be usefully dedicated to vocal exercises. The purpose of these is to improve the control of breathing, volume and pitch and the quality of tone and enunciation. Arpeggios, ascending and descending scales, and held single notes form the basis of these exercises, but in addition, rehearsal of short difficult phrases and rhythms from works to be rehearsed can be usefully included. The exercises can be unaccompanied, although check that pitch is maintained with occasional reference to a keyboard or a tuning fork.

Start with a single note exercise on G or A (in the appropriate octave), taking a deep breath and sustaining it for 15-20 seconds or count seconds from one to twelve. Short sentences may be intoned, incorporating any known peculiarities of dialect. Crescendo and decrescendo can be added to these sequences. Sing a series of scales downwards, starting from D and on a decrescendo, noting various breaks in each voice and rehearse for security of this transition. Allow a few moments rest between each sequence and rehearse synchronous deep breathing before starting the next. The speed for such exercises should be generally slow and never more than moderato. Most exercises are carried out at *mp*. Always listen for individuals who have difficulty finding or maintaining the pitch of a note.

Vowel sounds are used for most of the exercises; most useful are those that can be sung with a wide-open mouth, ensuring that each note is a separate enunciation of the vowel. Concentrate on the production of good tone quality on each note in ascending and descending passages. Use 'ah' predominantly but occasionally vary this to 'oo' and 'ee', the latter still being produced with a slightly less open mouth. Add consonants that are produced with the lips, teeth and pallate (*P*'s, *D*'s and *L*'s) and ensure that they spring explosively into an open-mouth 'ah' on each note. Exercises are usually carried out seated, with both feet on the ground and hands loose by the side. Add a few minutes standing at ease on two feet and deep breathing exercises. When exercises begin a rehearsal, make sure that all members attend punctually and participate in this important aspect of training.

Technique

In a well-trained group, everyone should contribute to the final result. As choir members may have different levels of ability and training, they will learn at different rates, and it may be advisable to hold sectional rehearsals for weaker members. This constant repetition will enable them to be confident in their approach. For this type of rehearsal it is often better to act as your own accompanist, as you can rapidly return to difficult areas as required. Such additional training will enable you to keep all members of the group fairly active during a full rehearsal, reducing the time for fidgeting, talking and distraction. As with an orchestra, choir members should bring pencils and rubbers, and should also be prepared to purchase the music being performed or to obtain it from a local library.

Choir training is a highly individual matter and choirs vary so greatly that it is difficult to give specific advice to the conductor. However, some general remarks may be of value. At all levels of ability make sure that members of the group both know, and accurately pitch, the notes of the music to be performed. Encourage them to learn phrases by heart, but not at the expense of dynamic and phrase marks in the score. They will then be able to watch you and ensure competence of entry and phrase. You will find teaching an amateur choir to watch a conductor is one of the more difficult problems. Another desirable attribute for a chorus member is the ability to count rests accurately.

Words usually require careful attention to ensure that there is complete unity of approach. You will have to decide whether any effects of dialect, such as the long Yorkshire vowel or the altered vowel sound of the cockney, require modification. The textual underlay (i.e. the rhythmic setting of the words) may be upset in translation; any imbalance may require rewording. Ensure uniformity of the beginnings and endings of phrases. Attack on a vowel can be accentuated by a glottal stop, the moment immediately before phonation when the vocal folds separate, producing a definite 'edge' to the sound. This can also be used between the final consonant of one word and an adjacent word beginning with a vowel to articulate the two words and so avoid running the consonant into the vowel (e.g. *'ever and ever'*, not *'everandever'*). Sibilants at the end of a word may be more satisfactorily produced chorally as a voiced *z* sound, or their placement even may be left to a few reliable members of the choir. *Th* or *d* may be substituted for *d* or *t*, avoiding the dental or so-called 'wet' sound of these consonants in English. The prefix *ex-*, similarly, is better performed as *egg-* (e.g. 'excelsis' becomes *egg-shelseez*). Pronunciation of church Latin usually follows Italianate principles, although north-european pronunciation of sacred and secular Latin texts varies considerably.

Breathing-points in a vocal work are usually linked with musical phrasing, and the composer generally allows adequate time for choir members to inhale. Singers should be encouraged always to breathe in deeply, but be careful not to put sudden emphasis on the subsequent entry, i.e. controlled expiration requires training. Heads held up and sound projected upwards and to the back of any building should be routine and thus reduces the likelihood of shouting when performing in a large auditorium. Occasionally a passage cannot be sung with a single breath and in these cases breathing should be staggered (choral breathing), adjacent singers breathing at different times in the passage and in this way avoiding any loss of continuity of sound.

Ensure that high notes on non-emphasized beats are produced gently. When, for example, a soprano line has to leap an octave to an unemphasized second beat, the emphasis must be on the lower first beat, the voice accurately bouncing the octave without swoop or over-emphasis.

Once notes have been learnt, unaccompanied singing should be encouraged. The group should learn to respond to your actions. Such singing will allow easy transition to singing with an orchestra, and will also enable you to detect faults of intonation and extremes of volume and balance more easily.

Rehearsals can be the most enjoyable part of your association with a choir. You will generally talk to the group more than to an orchestra. As well as needing more direction, voices also need an occasional rest. Encourage the choir, without flattery and with positive criticism. Reserve favourite anecdotes for groups that you are sure will appreciate them. During rehearsal leave the group in no doubt as to the levels of achievement that you intend to reach. For choral as well as orchestral rehearsals set a distinct goal. Rehearsals should include as much variety as possible, mixing intensive study of difficult areas with singing through easier passages or sections which have already been mastered. Remember that easy sections will also require close attention at sometime during preparation, to ensure perfection and to provide a fresh approach. Vary the rehearsals as much as possible to sustain interest. When preparing works that will fill a whole programme, it is worth learning some short and contrasting pieces purely as an aside,where time permits. If the work to be prepared has long sections where the choir is singing with soloists - either accompanying them or waiting for important cues - try to engage some singers to sing these solos in rehearsal. Some of the choir members may themselves be competent enough for this. Below are two typical seating plans for large choir (fig. 5.2a) and chamber choir (fig. 5.2b).

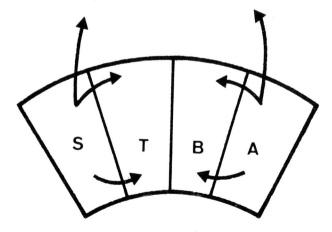

Fig. 5.2a

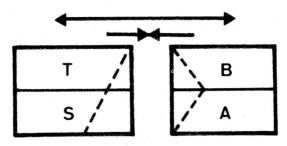

(Semichorus members may be placed conveniently within the space defined by broken lines without disturbing choral balance.)

Fig. 5.2b

Soloists

Ideally you should have at least one preliminary rehearsal with all the soloists under your direction in order to discuss tempos, phrasing and dynamics. Tempos should be agreed on, as should any changes in relation to the acoustics of the auditorium or to the nature of the forces available. Phrasing and dynamics should ensure an interpretation appropriate to the music being performed.

When orchestra and soloists come together, arrange for the latter to be as near to you as possible so that they can be seen and heard. A single instrumentalist or one or two vocal soloists is usually placed on the conductor's left, between him and the first desk of the first violins (figure 5.3a). A group of four singers in an oratorio usually stands both to the left and right of the conductor (figure 5.3b). The older British convention of placing a piano between the conductor and the orchestra, where the conductor's ears are swamped by piano tone, has been dropped. Now the usual placing of a piano is behind the conductor (figure 5.3c), where conductor and soloist can be in contact (the conductor should be able to see the soloist's left hand).

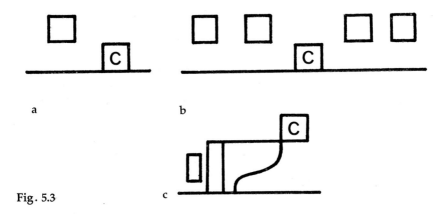

Fig. 5.3

Balance between soloists and an orchestra

Balance is primarily related to what an audience hears. If the orchestra can hear a soloist, they are not necessarily playing too soft; however, in certain halls, it is not always possible for the orchestra or choir to hear soloists even when the balance is satisfactory. In order to achieve excellence from your soloists you will need to listen intently. To a great extent your interpretation must be conditioned by the wishes of the soloists, but these should not conflict with your own impressions; indeed, careful preparation and collaboration should lead to a unity of purpose.

Singers have particular problems as soloists, since they have to produce and control words, as well as tone, and they may also be acting on a stage. Higher tones are more easily heard, but it is easier to produce good diction in middle and lower registers. The tessitura should be within the soloist's range otherwise the strain will be noted as well as difficulties of intonation. If a few bars are out of the range of a soloist, and an alternative is unavailable, it is wiser to rewrite these sections to ensure a relaxed performance. Try not to overtax any soloists during a rehearsal. Allow them to rest during any points of orchestral difficulty and remember that singers are not generally at their best in the morning. Singers will often sing half-voice in straightforward passages to preserve their voice.

Balance within solo vocal ensembles, where possible, should be defined prior to an orchestral rehearsal. However, more often than not, vocal soloists are professionals who come together only on the day of the performance. Nevertheless, they should know and understand the music well. With less-skilled soloists, at preliminary rehersals, you should sing or play the expected orchestral cues and train singers to count rest bars, reducing problems of entries and time changes at their first rehearsal with the orchestra.

Entries

Solo entries may not require a full preparatory beat as a cue when careful preliminary rehearsals have taken place. A nod or a look is often satisfactory: watch their breathing, or their mouths, to ensure that the click of your beat corresponds. It is useful to think, breath and mouth entries with a solo singer as this in itself conveys a great wealth of information. Similarly watch the breathing of wind soloists and the end of a bow of a stringed instrument for the completion of a phrase. Let soloists know when it is essential that they watch to ensure good ensemble and rehearse precise methods of beating their cues at such places. Your own interpretation should be already considered, so take care that these ideas, particularly in matters of tempo and phrasing, correspond to those of the soloists and are well rehearsed with the orchestra.

It is unnecessary and time wasting to play through a cadenza in a full rehearsal, but the orchestra must be acquainted with its ending. Ensure that key words and notes, which you have planned to coincide with your preparatory movements for re-entry, are satisfactory to bring in the orchestra at the appropriate moment. Allow some flexibility of this movement to compensate for any minor changes a soloists might make in performance.

Recitative

Recitative provides specific problems of accompaniment for the conductor. Again success is largely dependent on your knowledge of the work, particularly of the words and the rise and fall of the phrases. The latter provides a good indication of entries regardless of language. As usual, an accurate preparatory beat is desirable to introduce the chordal accompaniment, but the indication of every beat in the bar produces unwanted rigidity. Each bar must be shown with an empty downward movement for those players not involved in the recitative accompaniment and to help players in the accompanying group follow the soloist. Other beats may be given at appropriate points where there is a considerable amount of text or can be beaten one after another to clarify the placement of a rapid series of chords, no further gesture to be given until the preparatory movement for the next orchestral entry. Where there is only a short break between chords in the accompaniment, beat empty beats to correspond to the rests marked in the orchestral parts.

If a chordal accompaniment enters on the second beat of a bar, give an empty downward movement to indicate the first beat and use the lower end of the movement as the lift-off point of a preparatory beat for the next entry. When following a soloist, it is sometimes more satisfactory to indicate each chordal entry as a down beat, but in this case, tell the orchestra of your intentions. It may also be necessary to tell them the length of notes if it is not possible to give a clear cut-off in addition to the preparatory beat for a subsequent entry. You will have to allow for some flexibility of the preparatory beat, since sudden and unexpected entries or tempo changes may have to be followed. At all times ensure that a good balance between soloists and accompaniment is obtained. When a vocal soloist is accompanied by a keyboard instrument and cello alone, it is more satisfactory to leave them to perform without gestures from the conductor, provided the vocal line is well indicated in their scores.

The 'prima donna'

'Prima donnas' (both male and female) are more common among vocal than instrumental soloists. This is related to a number of contributory factors which add stress to vocalists in particular. The human voice is not as reliable and tires more easily than most of its instrumental counterparts. It is also more obviously affected by the emotional state of the individual and by minor throat or general ailments. Remember that a vocal soloist is under the scrutiny of the orchestra and choir, as well as the conductor, and insecurity of mood may reflect of lack of confidence under these circumstances. It may also represent a self-critical reaction. A vocal soloist has no instrument to blame for the results when these do not reflect their intentions.

Recognizing and understanding the factors contributing to a 'prima donna-like' attitude does not excuse such irrational behaviour or what may amount to frank provocation: most soloists in fact manage to cope remarkably well with the pressures associated with singing before an audience. You may have had some indication of weakness of character from a soloist during your individual rehearsal, but try to identify potential problem areas and work out how these can be circumvented. Tact is essential and there is no reason why a conductor should resort to an equally unacceptable attitude. Your aim should be to carry out constructive, smooth and effective rehearsals, avoiding excess strain on any individual and to provide encouragement and reassurance to all your forces.

However, a soloist is, by definition, a single individual and allowing the antics of one individual to waste rehearsal time is clearly unacceptable. Confrontation may be the only action, but this is better carried out in private when it should be possible to offer more constructive criticism. Your partnership with a soloist for a forthcoming performance may be irreversible but you can at least reflect in the knowledge that you need not ask any such soloist to work with you again.

Opera

Involvement of an amateur musical organization in an operatic production has much wider implications. The management team must be enlarged not only to represent the choir, orchestra and soloists but also to include a separate chorus master, producer, director, artistic director, dance mistress, stage manager, together with scenery painters, costume makers, props, make-up, house manager and box-office team. The position of the conductor in this group may thankfully be limited only to the musical aspects or he may be the director of the whole production. At all times, however, he must ensure high musical standards of the group, equating to their full potential.

Team approach

An early meeting with the stage director will enable the conductor to become acquainted with the former's concept of the work, his ideas on its realization and agreement over the edition, translation and necessary cuts. Proposed details of staging must be communicated as soon as possible. If there is a chorus master, the conductor should discuss the score in detail prior to the first rehearsal, sit in on an early rehearsal and be involved in the late pre- dress rehearsasls. Singers who do not routinely watch a conductor from a static position will have even more trouble when self-consciously moving around a stage. Teach them to react to gestures, using a baton for late rehearsals.

Emphasis must be given to the spoken and sung word to ensure that an audience can follow the story. Insist that the cast learns the words and music by heart at an early stage. Train them to speak the words through difficult rhythmical passages, watching enunciation and pitch. In conjunction with the stage director, work out where the chorus will be standing and how active they will be for each section and how this effects breathing and the projection of voices. When possible, the chorus should be facing the audience and in full view of the conductor when they are singing: this facilitates control of vocal forces. However, a rigid, static-block formation must be avoided; animation must be linked with visualization, and control of breathing and ensemble. This is the job of the producer/director.

Back-stage and off-stage choruses may have difficulty in hearing the orchestra or seeing the conductor. These sequences must be perfected in rehearsal and may need backstage video or amplification or an off-stage conductor. They will require particular attention to balance. Singing during active crowd scenes and dancing routines by the chorus must be fully rehearsed on stage, the direction shown to be appropriate and the tempo firmly established, to avoid rushing in performance.

Dance

In dance routines, and in particular ballet, the conductor must maintain a very precise tempo, with little room for change, since the performers have to complete difficult movements in perfect ensemble. These matters must be fully discussed with the director and choreographer. It may be helpful to record some excerpts at an agreed tempo with the orchestra or piano with which the dancers may rehearse.

Principals and minor roles

Meet with principal members of the cast early enough to ensure a thorough understanding of the score and agree on the edition and translation. Make sure that they bring scores to be marked with the agreed interpretation. The traditions of opera and its dramatic requirements allow for a much wider form of interpretation than in oratorios: the management of ornamentation, rubato, fermata and glissando need specific attention. The preliminary meeting with soloists, individually or in groups, enables the conductor to get to know them and their personality, temperament and musical ability, together with their strengths and weaknesses, prior to a rehearsal with the orchestra and chorus. This will allow smooth management of later rehearsals.

Rehearsing an opera orchestra

Just as the chorus and soloists require separate rehearsals, so does the orchestra. Whereas three to four rehearsals are usually sufficient to prepare for an 80-minute concert, much more time is required to sort out such details as multiple tempo changes for an operatic work of two hours or longer duration. Unfortunately, not even professional orchestras are afforded a great deal of rehearsal time. Amateur groups often have to make do with one orchestral play-through and a dress rehearsal with the full cast.

Make sure that the orchestral markings match those of the direction and the parts of the chorus and soloists. Initially concentrate on separate orchestral rehearsals until the vocal forces are conversant with both music and staging. The first combined rehearsal should be undertaken in a rehearsal room rather than on stage. The conductor is the link between vocal and orchestral forces and may be the only one of the group who can hear the combined effects or be in a position to sort out balance and manage the frequent tempo changes. He must be fully conversant with the opera's plot, the score and the libretto and be ready to bring in all musical entries on cue and with appropriate emphasis.

On-stage activities must take priority, but tempos must be agreed during rehearsals, and areas where there may be variation in different productions should be clearly identified. Rehearse all possible encores and ensure that all forces know how they will be cued, and where they begin. The production must incorporate some flexibility to relate to the atmosphere and temperament of each audience and individual performance, creating on each occasion a unique and memorable event. The soloists' main priority is their dramatic role and their eyes cannot be fixed on the conductor, therefore it is important that his position and the lighting ensure that he can be easily seen from the stage so that cues at difficult and critical times, and where there is any unsteadiness of ensemble, can be given. Be ready to meet the eyes of the soloists at these times; usually, a glance will direct all, although be prepared to give a clear movement of the baton if necessary.

Tutti rehearsals

Rehearsals should be carefully planned so that no one is left waiting around unnecessarily. A rehearsal schedule should be prepared and every effort made to stick to it: late arrivals should be suitably chastized. The order of rehearsal is not critical in the early stages and dialogue can be rehearsed separately from vocal sections. A piano is a more appropriate accompaniment for initial stage rehearsals, the orchestra only being introduced once staging has been established. Difficult orchestral parts, with or without chorus and soloists, can be rehearsed during scenery changes.

Principals and chorus should not have to sing to full volume throughout rehearsals or during repetitions. Amateurs, in particular, may lose their voices after a long rehearsal near to the date of performance, and the amount of singing by inexperienced soloists should be carefully monitored, gradually increased, but should never be overtaxing. When not required, the chorus should be out of sight, backstage, with adequate intervening doors to control any off-stage noise. Call and video systems will ease immediate recall when needed. For later rehearsals the emphasis must be towards continuity, with singers and orchestra performing to performance volume, so that balance and diction can be checked.

The dress rehearsal should comprise an uninterrupted performance of the whole opera. During this, full notes should be kept by the conductor and director of all problem areas. Difficult orchestral corners can usually be sorted out during scenery changes. A further vocal rehearsal must be scheduled for discussion of problem areas before the first performance. This is often conveniently undertaken in a rehearsal room, working through the opera with soloists, chorus and a pianist.

Rehearsals with orchestras, choirs and soloists can be marvellously constructive and exhilarating, developing intense communal spirit. Such enjoyment leads to the confident expectation of a worthy performance.

CHAPTER 6

Organization and Programming

Much of the decision-making and direction for an orchestral and/or choral group may come from the motivation and enthusiasm of the conductor. However, the more adventurous the endeavours of the group, the greater the need for a team approach, to take over the administration of the unit and allow the conductor to concentrate on musical matters.

The team must consist of enthusiasts, each with a specific task to which they are suited, with appropriate mental or physical ability. They should know what the task involves and be happy with it, being fully committed to the necessary workload in terms of time, time of day, telephone availability and transportation requirements. They should be reliable, persistent and dependable. If any prove unsuited to the task, and this cannot be remedied after frank discussion, an appropriate replacement should be found. Each member of the team, however, should be mentally attuned to sorting out any job when it is absolutely necessary.

Important offices include those of secretary and treasurer, other useful positions being those of concert manager and public relations officer. Further positions should only be created for individuals who are enthusiastically and constructively able to promote the activities of the group. If the conductor is not the prime leader of the group, an independent chairman with some experience of committee activity should be appointed. At all times the spirit of the total musical forces should be taken into account, developing a friendly personal atmosphere and ensuring that everyone feels fully involved in committee selection.

Secretary

An efficient secretary can take on much of the administrative responsibilities of a musical group, such as building a directory of addresses and telephone numbers, contacting all members concerning rehearsals and concert dates, places, times and dress, also sending out scores to performers so that they come to rehearsals fully prepared. Secretarial services might also include keeping attendance records and organizing concerts, but additional help may be taken on for these and other services, such as music librarian, social secretary (looking after refreshments, parties and group functions) membership secretary and publicity manager (organizing advertising, tickets and programmes).

Treasurer and finance

The treasurer preferably should have some accounting experience with a knowledge of banking, insurance and taxation. This person should be available during the day time to get to the bank and to be reached by other members of the group when necessary. A treasurer should plan budgets, open a bank account, carry a float, pay bills, and maintain a balanced account, which is submitted to appointed auditors.

Expenses include: stationery, postage, telephone bills and the printing of brochures, posters, leaflets, other advertising, programmes and tickets. Standing orders may be authorized for the National Federation of Music Societies, the

Performing Right Society, and for a music and dancing licence and public liability insurance.

Rehearsal costs may involve the rent of a hall, heating, lighting, repairs, refreshments, purchase or hire of music, music stands, and the upkeep and tuning of keyboard instruments. Concert expenses may involve hire of a hall, staging and (for orchestras) additional instruments, such as a keyboard, archaic or uncommon instruments and (for choirs) a whole orchestra. Artists, whose hospitality costs must be considered, may include guest conductors and vocal and instrumental soloists, as well as resident professional musicians, such as a conductor and accompanist. The payment of travel and other expenses within an amateur orchestra can be fraught with problems and such practices must at all times be seen to be fair.

Income for various expenditures may come from subscriptions by the members themselves, or from the sale of tickets and programmes. Advertisements within the programme may bring in additional revenue, as may donations, collection boxes, trusts, covenants, guarantors and benefactors. Grants may be obtained from arts councils, via the regional and other arts organizations, local authorities and educational concerns for specific concerts. Sponsors must be sought continually, events being named after them and due prominence given to them in the programme. Funds may be raised by the sale of refreshments at concerts and appropriate fund-raising events, such as raffles, garden parties, sales, discos and sponsored musical activities.

All members of the group should be made aware of the need for some degree of sponsorship for musical events, regardless of their amateur or professional status, and a network of potential subscribers built up in all public and private sectors. Information may be obtained from the Charity Aids Foundation, 48 Pembury Road, Tunbridge Wells, Kent, TN9 271 and the Association for Business Sponsorship of the Arts, 2 Chester St, London SW1X 7BB tel: 01-235 9781.

Librarian

The librarian has a vital role in any substantial musical organization. Few amateur groups have the necessary resources to purchase sets of vocal or orchestral material. The librarian must liaise with the conductor at an early stage to decide which edition of a work is desirable and whether it is readily available. He should be responsible for issuing music before the first rehearsal begins and for collecting it either after a concert or at the next rehearsal. Other responsibilities include the provision of folders for loose sheet music, logging details of performances, press clippings and printed programme information for archive purposes, and recording sources of hire material for future reference.

Programme Planning

The reason for a concert

The primary reason for promoting a concert is to provide a group with a target date on which to complete the preparation of one or more works and perform them in front of an appropriate and, it is to be hoped, a large audience. The guises in which this aim is achieved, however, are numerous, and the objectives of each form of promotion influence the type of music and the size and style of the concert venue.

The promotion may be by the group itself, or an associated music society, in which case the members will be responsible for ensuring an audience and covering costs while receiving the benefits of any profits. The concert may also be promoted by a local authority, be part of a festival, or be in aid of a specific charity or small private function. In some of these instances an audience will be provided by those promoting the concert and they may attract sponsorship to cover costs. In general however, the group will be heavily involved in funding, stage managing and promoting their own activities.

Programme content

The choice of programme may be the personal task of the conductor or carried out in conjunction with the committee. The conductor should certainly ask the opinion of colleagues in order to broaden his repertoire and to find new and interesting works of an appropriate standard. The orchestra or choir may have a general plan for the performances over one or more years, or there may be an annual commitment to a certain festival.

Aim to keep everyone happy and particularly consider the taste of the usual audience. Audiences most enjoy familiar music, but mix a little education with entertainment. Do not undertake a full programme of modern, early or unusual music unless presenting it to a specific audience which knows what to expect. If soloists are involved, include music of their choice or match them to the chosen programme. The NFMS produces a catalogue listing choral works by composer and indicating the forces required, the length of the performance and the availability of music for purchase or hire. The Federation's equivalent publication for orchestral works follows a similar pattern and both are essential requirements for all conductors. Of equal help can be the hire library lists of large music publishing houses, such as Novello or Boosey and Hawkes, in helping to programme concerts: they list works held in the catalogue of published works with orchestral forces, soloists and durations shown.

If the orchestra or choir is to tour, they may be asked to submit a programme or a copy of their repertoire to the local organizing committee. Discussion of the programme is certainly advisable to ensure that there is no repetition between it and other local performances. Works may be chosen from the canon of a single composer, or include a variety of music with a suitable balance of keys and tempos. Try to avoid changes in the size of orchestral or choral forces within each half of the programme to lessen any disturbance caused by the necessary re-arrangements.

The standard style of orchestral programming, inclusive of an overture, a concerto and a symphony, is a useful start but there are many other options; perhaps incorporating a number of shorter items, a new work and arrangements. The major work in the programme, usually a symphony in an orchestral concert, is by convention performed in the second half. Newly commissioned works require particular attention in placement within a programme and, if possible, a close liaison with the composer so that the conductor is fully aware of the details of the composition. Musical arrangements may offend the purist, but they do allow inclusion of much interesting operatic material in the concert hall. Gilbert and Sullivan or Viennese evenings, concert performances of operas, and even instant play-throughs of well-known operas and oratorios, can be most enjoyable if performed in an appropriate environment.

Each programme should be less than two-and-a-half hours in length. A useful plan is about 80 minutes of music divided into two halves by a 20-minute interval. Each work within the plan should, as far as possible, suit the chosen concert venue. Large-scale works need a suitably large auditorium for them to sound effective. Such a work can overpower the audience in a small hall with balance and contrast a victim as a consequence. Take particular care with the choice of the final work; it should be such as to send the audience home fulfilled. Although good programming can show off the skills of the orchestra and its soloists, the calibre of each may be related to the money available. Ensure that there is adequate rehearsal time, including a rehearsal in the concert hall.

The choice of an opera should be made in close liaison with other experts involved, particularly the director and producer, and this should continue throughout the preparation. The track record of a company will indicate both their ability and their traditions. It is possible that a conductor may also be the musical director. Be sure however, that specific requirements for such a position are precisely documented in any contract and the time given to any extra duties does not interfere with the musical standards and disciplines.

Programming and grant applications

The regional arts associations give clear guidelines as to the criteria by which allocations of grants are distributed. Choirs should use a professional orchestra at least for one concert a year, rather than an *ad hoc* collection of local amateurs and semi-professionals. This is important in building up standards of performance as well as keeping professional musicians in employment. Try to include the music of living composers. If at least one programme a year contained a major piece by a living composer, composers would be kept busy and audiences would become more conversant with recent compositional styles.

Publicity brochures

Once the plan for the year's activities is complete, it should be written down and distributed to all members of the organization so that they can reserve dates in their diaries. Concert dates can also be distributed to local events diaries and brought to the attention of likely audiences. A photocopied sheet will provide preliminary notice to performers, but this should be supplemented by an attractive brochure which can be used to publicize events widely and attract new members and sponsors.

The brochure should be of the best quality that can be afforded and efforts made to cover costs with advertisements. It should be tastefully and colourfully laid out and printed on good quality paper and the size be such as to fit standard envelopes, to allow ease of distribution. The cover should be headed with the title of the group and its logo, and the contents should outline the details and aims of the group, its charitable status and number (where appropriate), and the names of its officers. There should be information on how individuals may join the choir or orchestra, the format of auditions and rehearsal times, and who to contact, with addresses, and telephone numbers. All details should be carefully checked each year before sending it to the printers and any photographs updated. A professional designer, though often expensive, may save many hours work and, ultimately, provide a return on the investment.

The brochure should include the concert dates and places, the programmes and the names of artists, together with appropriate pictures and addresses and telephone numbers where tickets and information can be obtained. Discuss and agree on the format of all printed material, giving clear instructions on content, heading size and layout, and allow plenty of time for copy dates and photographic reproduction. All proofs must be carefully checked. A good working relationship with the printer will be amply rewarded when difficulties, such as unavoidably late copy material, are treated sympathetically. Complimentary tickets will further their interest in the group and its activities.

Concert Organization

The organization of group activities needs early planning and involvement of reliable members of the team to carry out the various jobs discussed below. A check-list is worth keeping to hand, with space for each item to be initialled when undertaken.

Concert check-list

(Design and print a list tailored to the needs of the society. Leave space for the name of the person or persons responsible for particular tasks, together with a target date for each task to be completed.)

1. *Plan programme.*

2. *Find a sponsor.*

3. *Book hall* (note caretaker's name, address and telephone number).

4. *Hire: soloists, orchestra, organist, keyboard instruments* (also fix fees).

5. *Fix rehearsal dates and venue(s) and inform choir, orchestra and soloists.*

6. *Music: collect and distribute vocal scores; collect, mark and distribute orchestral scores.* (Remember copyright law; number all hired vocal scores and parts. Collect and return hired parts after the concert.)

7. *Publicity: prepare and distribute posters and handbills.* (Newspaper articles and adverts, other media, 'What's On', travel agents etc.)

8. *Tickets: fix price; liase with typesetter and printer. Distribute to sellers and send complimentaries.*

9. *Programme: design, collate notes on works and artists, photographs, advertisements; print and collect.* (The NFMS has a database of well-informed programme notes, available for a small fee.)

10. *Stage/concert manager(s): stage, chairs, stands, delivery and return of heavy instruments and other furniture.* (Also, lighting, backstage facilities, security, soloists' reception, transport, accommodation and bouquets.)

11. *Front-of-house: box office, cloak room, bar, guest reception.* (Also, hall seating layout, furniture removal and return, decor, flowers, stewarding, programme selling.)

12. *After performance: letters of thanks, return of photographs, collection and distribution of press clippings, if any.*

Early planning and communication

The first decision to be made is whether a concert is to take place and, if so, its provisional date. The venue will be linked with the programme and artists, together with sponsorship and the expected audience. Liaison is necessary with local authorities and other societies to ensure that there is no clash of dates. Once the programme has been decided, specific jobs are allocated to the team, and a two- or three-month schedule laid out with feasible target dates for each task. Regular committee meetings help to co-ordinate the programme, maintain enthusiasm and momentum, monitor progress and ensure that target dates are met.

Once concert and rehearsal dates are finalized, the secretary should notify all members of the orchestra, choir, visiting soloists and conductor, together with extra or deputy instrumentalists. Additional forces, such as a school choir may be involved in specific concerts and adequate rehearsal time must be planned. Information should include the time, place, programme, the time and length of each rehearsal and when each instrumentalist will be required. With unfamiliar venues, additional directions and maps should be forwarded together with notes on parking and facilities for eating and changing. Concert information must include details of dress.

Soloists should be informed of the proposed form and length of hospitality and where they will be staying, by whom and where they will be met, who will look after their transport arrangements to and from the rehearsal and concert, and where they can have private rehearsal. They should each receive two complimentary tickets and be told where more can be purchased.

The hire and transport of keyboard and heavy instruments and their reception, positioning and tuning must be arranged in plenty of time to ensure punctuality and reliability of delivery.

The venue

The committee should inspect every conceivable concert venue in the area, listing good and bad points and the type of programmes that may be suitable. Once a site is proposed for a performance it is essential that at least one member of the group looks over it in detail and fills in a checklist of the various points considered below. This applies to every site which has not been used previously by the group.

A site at first may be looked over unofficially during other activities, but when making the final decision as to whether it is appropriate for a concert, an official visit is advisable. The approach is made to the individual or committee in charge and telephone contact made with the keyholder and guide. Specific dates and times for a concert may be proposed, in which case availability can be checked and a provisional booking made. When the proposed concert site is some distance away or abroad, checking concert house facilities is more difficult but an informed delegate, such as a local concert administrator, is essential. It is helpful in these circumstances to send a questionnaire so that all requirements can be adequately catered for.

Concert venues vary considerably, from purpose-built concert halls to theatres, cinemas, civic and public buildings (such as council rooms, libraries, universities and schools), churches, and stately and private homes. Size and cost are of prime importance when deciding a programme.

Before setting off, check the name and telephone number of all contacts and, on arrival, recheck dates and availability, the time that rehearsals may begin, when and where instruments and music stands may be delivered, who will meet them, where they can be contacted and who looks after the keys and security. There may be a specific time laid down for departure and possibly a penalty clause for overrunning. Enquire of any other constraints and, if possible, time the visit to correspond with rehearsal or concert times, to check what other adjacent activitities and concert clashes are to happen in the area.

Note first impressions of the cleanliness and decor of the hall. Decide whether flowers or foliage will be required to improve its image. Is the size of the hall appropriate to the size of the musical forces and the likely audience? Will galleries be needed and what form of seating is available: is it fixed? If mobile, will it be in place and who takes responsibility for moving it, laying it out and deciding on the position and size of the aisles. Will additional seats have to be borrowed or hired? Consider the positioning of the orchestra, choir and conductor.

If there is a stage, is it big enough for all the forces to be seated comfortably? Can they be seen by the audience and if not, can anything be done about it? Will additional staging be required to raise the choir or part of the orchestra? Is this available locally or on hire, who will move it and what will be the likely cost? Is there a conductor's rostrum or stand and is it high enough to ensure that he can be seen by all forces? Musical groups that perform regularly in one particular venue may find it easier to invest in their own furniture, such as staging and a rostrum. If a keyboard instrument is required, is the local piano or organ appropriate in quality, state of repair and pitch, and who maintains and tunes it? If a one has to be hired, the quality and size must be suitable to the requirements of the player and of the orchestral balance. Enquire when it can be delivered, what are the security arrangements, is there room for it on the stage and is the stage strong enough to support it: who will move it, and can it be moved between items? A constant temperature is desirable. The cost of the keyboard and other hired instruments, such as timpani, has to be carefully considered, and whether additional sponsorship and funding will be required as a result.

Placement of timpani may have to be modified because of lack of space or excessive reverberation, or to create antiphonal effects. Never place the trombones behind the bells of the French horn section: the effect on a trombonist's embouchure can be disastrous. Clicking a thumb and finger together or clapping will give some indication of the reverberance of a hall. A solid, domed wall is preferable to a curtain as backing for a choir, while low ceilings (especially artificially lowered ones) and arches, screens, carpeting and upholstery can reduce brightness of sound. In such buildings as churches, where high ceilings and domes may give rise to excessive reverberation, a compromise placement of the forces may have to be accepted. It is best to keep in front of the choir-screen. Much sound can be lost from the choir, unless they are right up against the back wall. In a large church or cathedral, it may be possible to perform with the audience with their backs to the altar and performers in front of the west window. Church authorities need to be consulted before attempting such an arrangement. Concert halls are usually designed with sound quality in mind, and additional sound boards or ceiling baffles may have already been constructed. Unfortunately, many conference halls have acoustics carefully designed to suit their particular non-musical purpose. It may be that musical programmes can be chosen to show off the sound qualities of a building, highlighting antiphonal, spatial and off-stage effects.

Extraneous noise must be identified and reduced to a minimum. Noises may include creaking floors and staging, noisy heating and ventilation, fluorescent lighting, chiming clocks, adjacent church services, kitchens and bars, and the noise of outside vehicles, railways and aircraft. Many of these noises can be lessened or avoided during the concert. Communicating doors and windows may need to be closed, noisy appliances turned off and the time of the concert chosen to avoid high noise periods. Make enquiries well in advance of the concert about any conditions that might be different at the scheduled time of performance from those encountered in rehearsals.

Lighting during the rehearsal and concert must be adequate for the musicians easily to see their copies and the conductor. The need for additional spotlights must be recognized and arranged. Audience lighting may be reduced during performance and the person responsible must be properly instructed. The temperature and humidity during rehearsal and concert must be considered together with the possible need for additional heating or ventilation and their early employment on the chosen day. Backstage facilities may be negligible in a church and an adjacent building may be required for storage, changing and toilets. In a theatre, although the decor is often uninspiring, cleanliness is essential and may require improvement. Adequate-sized male and female changing rooms are desirable, with chairs, coat hangers, mirrors, shelving and tables, together with toilet paper, soap and towels.

Check if there are any additional rooms where conductor and soloists can prepare and warm up and a green room where members of the group can meet the public or press. Arrange for the rooms to be marked, if this is not already the case, and note access routes to the stage and any intervening doors. Consider the need for stewards to control the noise and maintain security and whether rooms can be locked. If security is potentially a problem, an individual should be designated to look after valuables during rehearsals and concerts. Storage rooms with reliable security are also desirable for instruments between rehearsals and concerts. In a theatre, it may be possible to arrange for the box office to be used for advanced ticket sales. In the front of house, an attractive entrance is desirable. In the foyer, a reception area where tickets can be sold and an additional room for meeting important guests is required. Consider how to prevent noises of crockery and glasses from reaching the auditorium. Cloakroom and ticket facilities must be checked. Local arrangements for manning cloakrooms and stewarding ticket sales, refreshment areas and bars must be noted together with the costs.

Regular concert halls will have music and dancing licences and may be affiliated to the PRS, in which case the appropriate documents pertaining to the programme will have to be filled in. This may be covered by the group's membership of the NFMS or an occasional licence may be required. The third-party liability and fire insurance of the building should be checked together with the fire exits. Parking facilities for distinguished visitors, performers and audience should be established, public transport to the area noted and local maps obtained. If eating facilities are not available within the hall, local restaurants should be checked for quality and size in relation to the musical forces for possible meals before or after the concert.

Once the desirability and feasibility of a venue has been established, the booking should be confirmed in writing and a deposit paid. A careful note should be kept of all the jobs which will need to be done before and during the rehearsal and concert, and this reported back to the committee so that appropriate plans can be made.

Publicity and public relations

Good publicity is of the most critical importance to the success of a concert: choirs and orchestras need support. The choice of public relations officer on the committee is, likewise, one of the most important considerations. If possible, it should be someone who has some experience in advertising and public relations, able to prepare attractive advertising copy and sustain pressure on the committee, and to introduce frequent new ideas of promotion. Every method of publicity should be exploited and the group should aim to create a reputation for musical quality. Good relationships with the local authority, education authorities, local university, schools, parochial church councils, concert hall managers, and librarians are paramount; mayors and dignitaries at home, and ambassadors and consuls abroad, should be encouraged to attend all important concerts. This in turn, will attract publicity, reviewers and sponsorship.

The timing of publicity for an event depends on its size. For larger festivals and important artists, where it is essential to fill venues to cover costs, waves of publicity start three to four months before an event. However, care should be taken to avoid overlaping the publicity for adjacent concerts. Usually, publicity should last four to six weeks, with emphasis over the last two weeks.

Printed literature should be elegant, appropriate, creative and imaginative, with the stamp of quality. It should be headed with the logo and title of the group together with any associated promoters. The programme, place, time, artists, with names of leader and conductor are included and also ticket costs, where they can be purchased and details of parking and other facilities. Allow plenty of time for printing and proofing.

A4-size posters are most serviceable for widespread distribution and display in all shops where permission is obtained, the concert venue, church halls, local university, schools, waiting rooms and hospitals. Larger posters can only be placed on special poster sites and should be reserved for unique events. One of the most useful sites is the local library and here the librarian is a good ally. The publicity team should be armed with adhesiveo tape and drawing pins at all times.

Leaflets have the same target audience as posters but are also distributed with all information sheets and circulars to members. Word of mouth is the strongest mode of persuasion across a community and is infectious. Total involvement of the group is necessary and all members should be instructed on how to promote this enthusiasm. Unique events may warrant the production of car or luggage stickers, labelled pencils, and T-shirts embellished with the group's logo.

Other promotions include newspaper articles and printed adverts. More control is available over the latter which must be carefully worded in view of the likely cost. There is less control over articles and diary inserts but it is important to provide informative copy material, information on artists and photographs to the relevant reporters in plenty of time. Information should be offered for inclusion in 'What's

On' magazines, tourist information and parish magazines. Local radio and TV channels should be informed of all concerts, with emphasis placed on unique events.

Printed programmes and tickets

Printed programmes are important promotional material and must contain comprehensive information, including the history and aims of the group. The design must be attractive and encompass the group logo. Quality printing is desirable. Aim to cover some of the cost with the addition of one or more advertisements. In the programme, list the movements so that there is no intervening applause and note the place and time of the interval. Request no smoking or recording in the auditorium. State in the programme if refreshments and bar facilities are available during the interval.

Notes on the music should be authoritative, written by a knowledgeable musician and aimed at the likely audience. If a choral or operatic libretto is to be reproduced, avoid placing awkward page turns in the printed programme that correspond to quiet passages in the music. Detail the reason for the concert and thank any sponsors. Include notes on the artists, the leader and the conductor if possible, together with photographs. If travelling abroad, consider what language is appropriate for the programme.

Tickets, like all printing, should be tastefully designed. Ensure that the place and time, the name of the group, the title of the concert and any charitable involvement are included. The cost of the ticket is related to the forces involved, the specific artists, the facilities and the importance of the event, also whether it is a charitable concert and whether refreshments or an ellaborate meal are included.

When pricing the ticket, don't assume that the concert will be a sell-out. Consider the season as a whole with season tickets, group bookings, reduction for advanced bookings and specific rates for senior citizens, students, the unemployed, and children. Complimentary tickets should be distributed to artists, officials, sponsors, the promoters and anyone who is particularly helpful to the group, such as the local librarian and members of the press. For overseas trips arrange complimentary tickets for all travelling supporters. The timing of ticket sales should match the advertising and should take place at the concert venue, advertised sites, through the choir, orchestra, regular supporters, friends, shops and offices.

The day of the concert

The notes made by the individual who visited the concert venue will prompt many of the preparations required. A concert manager should be appointed to direct the day's activities in a firm but diplomatic fashion. The manager links with the concert hall management and looks after distinguished patrons, the artists and musicians. A concert manager requires a team of helpers which should include ticket and programme sellers, and front-of-house and backstage stewards.

Petty cash should be available for payment of tips, bouquets for female soloists and the costs of such items as transport. The team should be armed with paper, adhesive tape, drawing pins, paper clips and felt-tipped pens. A paid or voluntary 'heavy squad' may be required to set chairs, staging, heavy instruments, music stands and deal with the removal of any furniture, such as altars, pulpits, lecterns, and even doors. An equivalent group must be available for rearranging furniture at the end of the concert.

Preparation of the hall

Heating, lighting and ventilation should be switched on in time to prepare conditions for the rehearsal. The person in charge of lighting should know the order of the programme and ring five and two minute bells before the start of each half of the programme.

The cleaning of the hall should be attended to, flowers and foliage set out, seats arranged and numbered, and reserved places marked. Additional platforms should be laid down in plenty of time together with the conductor's rostrum. Music stands, music and a programme should be in place. Backstage changing rooms should be marked, and chairs, coat hangers and tables in place with toilet paper, soap and towels installed.

The hospitality extended to guest artists and their transport to the rehearsal and concert must be assured, as should their return to their host or hotel for relaxation prior to the concert. Call all forces to the rehearsal and the concert in adequate time. The deputy leader must have the orchestra tuned prior to the starting time. The stage or concert manager should start applause from behind the scenes as the leader walks on, likewise for the conductor and soloists.

In the front of house, ticket and programme sellers and box office officials should be ready with their wares and have a cash float. Stewards should be acquainted with seating arrangements and know to whom to refer any problems. Doors should be opened at the specified time, usually 30 minutes to an hour before the concert. Arrange for the stage manager, or designated individual, to be on hand to greet honoured guests and arrange a line-up of officials when appropriate. Press and hospitality rooms should also be prepared on formal occasions.

Refreshments and bar facilities must be prepared for the interval to ensure rapid service within the allotted time and light refreshments ready for the musical forces. The timing and entry routine should be repeated to schedule after the interval. The stage manager should organize curtain calls and the presentation of any bouquets.

The post-concert committee meeting and evaluation

Undertake a careful appraisal of the quality of the musical and organisational activities after each concert. Each member of the team should report and the group learn from its mistakes and constructively improve its activities. Artists must be thanked, and fees distributed, returning publicity photographs and sending copies of any reviews. All bills must be paid and accounts audited, and profits forwarded to any associated charity. Letters of thanks should be sent to all sponsors. Teamwork of this nature will ensure efficient running of the group and allow expansion of its horizons based on a firm organisational foundation.

CHAPTER 7

The Performance

It is essential to have a specific performance in mind when preparing a substantial work, as this will provide a suitable stimulus for the conductor, orchestra and chorus for the necessary intensive study. The approach to a performance differs from that of a rehearsal, since the conductor is no longer listening to correct errors but is aiming to direct a complete artistic performance.

If a conductor's technique has been of good quality during rehearsals, it should be equal to all the demands of a performance. However, ensure that all the rehearsed gestures are made: these will be recognized by the orchestra and will instil confidence. On the other hand a conductor experiences the music in a way that is not possible in rehearsal. An experienced conductor has enough confidence in his technique to let the music speak through his gestures, with minimal awareness of the technical process. This in turn is communicated to the performers and offers them a degree of extra guidance and inspiration that lifts their performance.

By the time of the concert the programme should be well known to conductor and performers, and the conductor will need only minimal reference to the score. Although conducting without a score can help to increase the contact with, and control of, the players, this must only be undertaken if a conductor is totally confident of his memory of the score. Remember to take on the baton if there is no music stand on which you can leave it. If a score is used, make sure it is placed on the stand prior to the start of the concert. Its value is as an aide-mémoire for cueing and to help sort out any mishaps; also, if in an opera pit, reflected light from its pages helps the orchestra to see the conductor's face and arms.

On any rare and, with luck, unscheduled occasions when you have to conduct in a hall in which you have not rehearsed, listen intently to the sound of each instrumental group and to the balance obtained. You should be able to hear all soloists clearly, but remember that some of the orchestra may not, so retain a clear beat to ensure good ensemble.

The atmosphere of a performance communicates itself not only to the conductor but also to the orchestra, who will become receptive and sensitive to the music whatever their mood prior to the event. Even a tired orchestra, which may have arrived late or may be disgruntled because of delayed transport or other mishaps, reacts to the stimulus of a concert and their total absorption in the work can lead to a good performance.

Concert dress

An orchestral group must be uniformly dressed. If all the players agree on a set uniform they will appear more efficient and professional and also be less distracting to an audience. Apart from evening concerts, where changes of fashion have had little effect, there has been a general relaxation of the once quite strict rules of formal dress.

Evening concerts

For most evening performances, professional orchestras and choirs continue to wear white tie and tail-coats for the men and long black dresses for the ladies. Amateur orchestras, when in smaller venues, or purposefully to create a more informal atmosphere, usually wear black tie and dinner jackets, with either long or short black for the ladies. A recent innovation for summer concerts is the white or cream dinner jacket, and, as black for the ladies can look drab, coloured dresses have also been encouraged for these concerts.

The conductor should generally wear the same as the performers. The only exception acceptable at a major concert allows for the white tuxedo when the orchestra is in black dinner jackets.

Morning or afternoon concerts

For daytime concerts, it is no longer expected for the orchestra to wear morning tailcoats and grey waistcoats. A dark suit is now the standard dress together with short black dresses for the ladies (much to the chagrin of the lady cellists who have been known to wear black trousers), although the latter is often relaxed to allow coloured dresses. Evening wear is worn during the day for groups normally performing in a distinct uniform, such as choirs and choral groups.

Amateur concerts

In the field of amateur music the rules of dress and etiquette are often broken. The amateur orchestra most commonly dresses in black tie and dinner jacket. A youth orchestra may wear a school uniform or white shirt, black trousers and an orchestra tie. According to etiquette the conductor should wear black tie and dinner jacket as well, but may wear white tie and tails. Youth orchestras can respond to this well, since it gives them a feeling that it is a special occasion. This is less true of the adult orchestra and one suspects that vanity on the part of the conductor is often a main consideration. Nevertheless, at formal choral concerts, soloists should be encouraged to wear white tie and tails. The conductor must, on these occasions, comply with the soloist to give a united appearance, even if the orchestra is in dinner jackets.

Concert Protocol and Stage Etiquette

At the start of the concert

The conductor should arrive appropriately dressed at the concert hall between 20 and 30 minutes before the performance, ensuring that no one is anxiously awaiting him. Give words of reassurance to inexperienced performers and a smile of confidence to all. Arrange for a quiet room to be available where you can have a few moments to sit down, relax and think through the programme in peace and quiet.

The chorus (if there is one) should file in, in seating order, ten minutes before the start of the concert. Every member of the choir should remain standing until all members have reached their seats, at which point the whole choir, as one, sits quietly. The orchestra makes its way to the platform five minutes before the scheduled start time. Once there, it prepares itself for the performance by checking seating, stands and the positioning of instrument stands for any extra instruments, such as double bassoons and bass clarinets. At this point check that all the performers are on the platform and seated, and so avoid making the discovery that some key player is absent the moment the concert is about to start.

The co-leader directs the tune-up, sometimes section by section, and must insist on silence from the orchestra as the oboe gives the tuning note. The oboist takes the A from the keyboard player, if one is used, or from a tuning fork or electronic tuning device. If a piano concerto is programmed, the co-leader plays the tuning note on the piano. It is best if the strings tune first, followed by the woodwind and brass. Whilst the tuning process takes place, the co-leader remains standing, and sits down only when each section is satisfactorily tuned. Subsequent tunings in the concert will be overseen by the leader.

In a concert there is an inevitable hush once the orchestra has tuned; this heralds the arrival of the leader, soloists, and conductor. Do not let thoughtless or nervous players continue to play at this point.

The leader should enter and, after a bow to receive the applause, sit down. Finally, the soloists and conductor walk on to the platform. At this point, the chorus (if in the first piece) should stand, unless there is a specific reason for it to remain seated, e.g. in works where the chorus does not enter for a considerable time or where it takes a secondary, accompanying role. A conductor should not come on later than the soloists, but should follow them closely. Never insist that the orchestra stand with the arrival of the conductor; if they do, it is a great sign of respect. Try to appear full of confidence, full of authority, dignified but friendly. Once the soloists are in place, lead a bow, either from the side of the podium or if there is too little room, from the podium itself. It is not usual to shake the hand of the leader before a concert in Britain, but this is often customary elsewhere in Europe. Raising the orchestra to its feet to receive applause is an option at this point. When there is sufficient quiet in the auditorium, and only then, the conductor should raise his baton hand. If there is still noise, turn the baton sharply down until there is absolute quiet, then, with a second quick gesture which alerts the players, give the preparatory beat.

Between pieces in a programme

If the conductor does not need to leave the platform after an item, e.g. to bring on a soloist, all that is required is a bow. First turn to stand facing the audience and then make a formal bow and a second and longer one if the applause is enthusiastic. If it is continuous, shake hands with the leader and invite the orchestra to stand. If the conductor leaves the platform, the orchestra should sit when the leader does. The leader should not leave the podium until the end of the half, or the end of the concert. After the interval, the leader again makes his way to the platform after his colleagues.

At the end of the concert

At the end of a loud work, cut off the orchestra (and/or chorus) with a clear and precise gesture. A fast and loud work should be ended dramatically, with some bravura in the cut-off. If a final movement is to end very softly, hold out the diminuendo and do not release the attention of the audience until a moment of complete silence has occurred at the end. The hands may be dropped to the side.

This is the signal to start the applause. If it does not come immediately, wait for it, clasp your hands in front of you and bow your head.

Receive the ovation as already described. Turn to the choir (if there is one) and invite them to stand, then the leader, and invite the orchestra also to stand. After a moment leave the stage but return immediately. Do not allow the applause to diminish. After a few moments, invite the orchestra to stand again. Orchestral soloists require special congratulation, and before asking the orchestra to stand a second time, point out each player or group of players and invite them to stand followed by all the forces once again. If a choral work is to finish the programme, arrange for the chorus master to come on to the platform at this point, if he has taken responsibility for the training of the choir. This is a courtesy that the chorus will appreciate greatly.

The conductor should promptly return to the platform for the first time, but he may take more time on subsequent returns if the applause allows. However, he should not let the applause die for lack of interest. This is not showmanship: it is false modesty not to acknowledge the applause, for courtesy demands the performers to indicate some kind of thank you to the audience for their support and approbation.

Stage etiquette with soloists

a) The concerto soloist

At the end of a concerto, the soloist occupies the limelight, not the conductor; therefore, the conductor must step back and even join with the audience in applauding. The soloist may then turn to the conductor to shake hands and then the leader, so that the conductor and orchestra are included in the applause. The conductor must not impose himself or offer a hand until the soloist wishes to acknowledge the conductor. The leader should stand when acknowledging the soloist's handshake and then immediately sit unless the sign is given by the conductor for the whole orchestra to stand (the soloist should not do this, though he can request it of the conductor). The conductor follows the soloist on and off the stage.

b) Vocal soloists

The conductor also follows the soloists both on and off the stage at the end of an oratorio work or concerto for more than one soloist. Turn to the audience and, after standing motionless for a moment, lead the soloists in a bow and then turn to each to shake hands before moving to the leader to shake hands and invite the orchestra and choir to stand.

Opera

When conducting performances of an opera the conductor's primary concern is for the singers on stage. His presence must be unobtrusive and yet he must be awake to all eventualities. The lighting must be such that both the beat and the conductor's face can be seen from the stage for cues and other encouraging signs. During any spoken dialogue there must be absolute silence from the orchestra pit with no whispering or fidgeting. A balanced full orchestral tone can be encouraged when there is no vocal line, but at all other times it must be such that the singers are clearly audible.

The orchestra must be trained to respond rapidly to the beat so that tempos can be quickly changed, to take up any slack if a singer unexpectedly changes tempo or adds extra rubato on the night. Flexibility of the beat is essential in such a situation. The technical skills of the conductor can be severely tested if the orchestra and soloist(s) fail to synchronize. You may be the only person who can recognize the relative position of the two forces. Conduct precisely until you have decided how the situation can be remedied. This will usually be by telling the orchestra to lose or gain the relevant number of bars or by telling them when the soloist arrives at the next rehearsal figure or tempo change. It may even be necessary to stop quickly to establish such a point of reunion. Do not look viciously at the performers after any such mistakes, but take a positive approach, with the emphasis on continuity. This will ease any areas of tension, and will reduce the likelihood of these problems being communicated to the audience. Between acts offer encouragement to the singers, which helps to keep their confidence and concentration for the remainder of the performance. If necessary, arrange extra rehearsal time to sort out all difficulties before any subsequent performance.

Theatre etiquette

In a theatre pit, the leader arrives with his colleagues and oversees the tuning process himself. The stage manager will then bring down the house lights. It is a moment full of anticipation and again it is unfortunate if it is broken by thoughtless members of the orchestra who continue to practise their favourite concerto. The conductor enters once the lights are down and can start the overture immediately.

After the house lights have dimmed and at the end of the interval (or the last interval if there is more than one), a spotlight should be directed at the pit. Take a special bow at this point on behalf of the orchestra, which is probably invisible to many of the audience. This is their only chance to receive their due acknowledgement.

At the end of the performance, no-one should leave the pit until the last curtain call has been taken and the house lights been brought up (even if professionals often do). The conductor may be required to make his way to the stage for the last call, after all the cast have taken theirs. It is not so uncommon that a gesture from the stage to direct applause to the orchestra has been made to an empty pit.

Recording

The widespread availability of sound-recording equipment means that one can easily obtain a recording of an event, be it a rehearsal or performance. Recording should be used to facilitate understanding and to improve a musical group. The quality of a recording relates directly to the quality of the apparatus and the care with which it is set up. The types of recordings are best considered under three headings.

The first type of recording is one to provide a rough idea of the progress of rehearsals and performances. It may be obtained using a cassette recorder or from equipment built into the hall. Such a recording can be very informative and can provide immediate information on tempos, rhythm, intonation and ensemble.

Balance is more difficult to assess and depends on the position of microphones, but you should be able to pick out obvious defects.

The second form of recording is a permanent one, made by a professional or an enthusiastic amateur at a performance. This will usually entail at least two microphones to give a stereo recording. More microphones can enhance the fidelity of the recording and make it possible, if a mixing desk is available, to balance and highlight soloists and parts of the orchestra. The players must be happy with the prospect of only one take if a concert is to be recorded so that the final package will be with warts and all. It may be possible to do it in private with the possibility of several takes of sections that are unsuccessful, thus producing a more polished edited version. In the case of an opera it may have been taken from more than one performance. The final version may be produced as a disc or a cassette and include all or a representative part of the work undertaken. The target audience for such a recording is usually made up of the performers themselves and their friends, representing a production of fifty to a hundred copies, for which payment may be required in advance. Always ask permission of performers before making a recording, and be prepared to explain what it is for. This is not simply a question of good manners: when dealing with professional musicians, it is a legal requirement. You should not record professional musicians without their prior consent, and if, in addition, the recording is to be sold commercially, special contracts and fees must be negoiated. They will not usually object to a recording being made if it is for the conductor's personal use, or for restricted distribution to choir members only, providing they are asked in advance. Make sure that setting up and balancing of recording apparatus is completed in rehearsal and that there is no risk of having some enthusiastic recording engineer crawling around the auditorium or stage during a performance.

The third type of recording is one intended for sale. This represents an entirely different, and very expensive, enterprise. Such ventures are pointless unless the necessary finance is available to ensure high-quality music and reproduction, and an outlet for the recording is available. Recordings of this type may be made in a recording studio or a building regularly used for the purpose. Any other building must be carefully assessed by the recording engineers to decide whether the acoustics are suitable, or whether additonal carpeting or screening is required. If an organ or keyboard instrument is to be used, ensure that any existing instrument is tuned to concert pitch.

The date, time of day and availability of the hall must be established and at equivalent times the building must be checked for extraneous noises such as generators, clocks, air-conditioning, bells, birds, cars and aircraft.

All furniture and heavy instruments must be in place prior to a recording and each session must follow a set timetable. Close liaison is required between the conductor, producer and engineers during recording. Such recordings should only be undertaken when the project is financially viable and when the standards likely to be achieved will be a credit to the musicianship of the forces involved and to the music to be recorded Strict rules govern the use of recording time when professionals are involved, and these should be checked with Equity and the Musicians' Union when the project is first proposed to establish details of cost and restrictions.

Assessment

Much of the comment in this work has been directed at self-assessment; emphasis has also been given to the need to encourage skilled and unskilled observers willing to give frank criticism of all aspects of your conducting. Listen carefully to comments from observers and members of the orchestras or choirs you conduct. If you work regularly with a single orchestra you will gradually get to know them, and frank discussion may provide important insight into your abilities. Never be offended by such friendly criticism and always look to eradicate faults. Never enter into a battle of words with a critic: there is always the possibility that they are right. Exercise self-restraint, turn your attention to future performances, and make use of the experience gained. In time you may be asked to judge others, whether they be conductors, choirs, orchestras or soloists. This can provide further insight into musical interpretation, particularly with respect to the control of dynamics and balance, and, with vocalists, the clarity of diction. Take particular note of comments on balance: in rehearsal, you or some reliable member of your team should take the opportunity to listen from various places in the hall.

A Performance of any kind should represent total mental and physical commitment to each work and enable you to present a memorable account to an audience, some of whom may be hearing a composition for the first time. After the performance, first go to the choir and orchestra changing rooms to say a few words of thanks to all members of the group. After this you can accept visitors and meet any enquiries. It is hoped that the organization within the group is such that the conductor is not then required to take down music stands, sort music or stack chairs. Leave the post-mortem of the evening's activities to the next day when you can spend some time going over the scores and listening to any tape recording made of the concert. Thoughtful examination and discussion with others helps to identify strengths and weaknesses both of the performance and of the group, and should point the way to future developments.

Postscript

It might be argued that music, to all but a few, can only exist in performance, and that on the page or in the mind it can never be fully experienced as a complete expression of a composer's intentions. Successful interpretation is dependent upon an intuitive act, influenced by knowledge and experience of performing conventions and understanding of the differences between musical notation and its realization in performance. The conductor of the symphonic, operatic and choral repertoire has the power to shape and dictate an interpretation of a composition; good technique is essential for an individual's vision of a work to be transmitted to a group of musicians.

Awareness of the latest research in performing practices associated with a particular period, place or composer is important, especially where the style of the music to be performed is unfamiliar, or where heavy-handed editorial decisions may have obscured the original composition. Ultimately, however, conducting is a practical art and must reflect a balance between intellect and intuition. In each performance, the conductor must have a sincerity of purpose and the conviction that the work to be performed, and the manner of its performance, is worthwhile.

The Orchestra

The basic complement of the modern orchestra was established towards the end of the eighteenth century. This is the orchestra required for performances of Haydn's 'London' symphonies and Beethoven's early symphonies. Since then it has grown in size with the addition of extra woodwind, brass and percussion instruments, and by a gradual expansion of the numbers of each string section. The standard size of the string section of a present-day symphony orchestra is eight desks of first violins, seven desks of second violins, six desks of violas, five desks of cellos and four desks of double basses, with two players to each desk.

Several important steps were taken in the development of the symphony orchestra at the beginning of the nineteenth century. In his Fifth Symphony (1805), Beethoven introduced the piccolo, double bassoon and trombones for the first time together in the same work (though each already had been heard separately providing special effects in oratorios and operas by Mozart and Haydn, for example). Berlioz introduced both harp and cor anglais in his *Symphonie fantastique* and included, in addition to trumpets, the cornet (*cornet à pistons*). Wagner prescribed even larger orchestras for the performance of his operas and helped to invent new instruments to add new sonorities, the most significant of which is the Wagner tuba. Mahler and Richard Strauss require something in the order of quadruple woodwind, eight horns and six to eight brass players as a standard orchestral complement, and both call for extra off-stage choirs of brass instruments (twelve horns and four trombones in Strauss's *Alpine Symphony*), as well as choral groups and solo voices. However, the ultimate in large forces for a single work surely is the minimum requirements for a performance of Schoenberg's *Gurrelieder* (1909-1913): 8 flutes, 5 oboes, 7 clarinets, 5 bassoons, 6 horns, 4 Wagner tubas, 6 trumpets, bass trumpet, 6 trombones, contrabass trombone, tuba, a large percussion section (7 players) including chains and iron plate or anvil, 4 harps, celesta, strings, large SATB choir (including 12-part male chorus), 5 solo voices and a *Sprechsgesang* part.

The String Family

The entire string section of the orchestra (violins, viola, cellos and double basses (i.e. the bowed instruments) may be referred to collectively in foreign scores as *gli archi* It; *Streichinstrumente* Ger; *les cordes* Fr. The German term, *Saiteninstrumente,* is used to describe other instruments with strings (such as guitar and harp).

Violin, viola, cello

Today's orchestral string section is an amalgamation of two distinct families: the violin and the viol. Those instruments which belong to the violin family (violins, violas, and cellos) have the same general design. The body is fashioned from several woods, often with a maple back and a spruce top, finished with many coats of varnish. Harder woods (for example, ebony) are required for the finger board, tail piece, end pin, chin rest, pegboards and pegs. The sound post (a wooden bar standing inside between the back and top of the instrument) is placed below and to the right of the bridge. Its purpose is to pass the vibrations, produced by the bow on the strings, from the bridge into the body of the instrument where these can resonate. This adds both volume and tone to the sound. The sound post also acts as a brace, without which the tension of the strings on the bridge would crack and splinter the wood.

The bow stick is just over two feet long and is generally round or octagonal in cross-section. Better quality bows are of pernambuco wood. The horse-hair (bleached in all except the double bass bow) is fastened to the head at one end and to a movable nut (the *frog*) at the other. The hair of the bow is tightened to playing tension by turning a screw cap which draws back the nut. The bow itself should always keep the slightly concave shape even when tightened. To avoid permanent warping of the bow, the hair is always slackened after playing.

Strings may be of gut or wire, and either plain or wire-wound. Plain gut is not used in modern orchestral instruments; plain wire is only used for the E string of the violin. The cost of a string is related to the length and quality of the wire used: violin strings cost proportionately less than the heavily bound and longer-lasting lower strings of the double bass. The vibrating length of the string is from the metal nut, at the end of the fingerboard, to the bridge. The pitch varies between strings, due to the weight of their material and the tension applied. Thus smaller instruments (threequarter-size, half-size, etc.) designed for use by children can still be tuned to the same pitch. Tension is applied by turning the pegs in the peg box; on some instruments, fine adjustment can be made by a screw adjuster on the tail piece. The strings are numbered from the highest to the lowest in pitch, the fourth string being the heaviest and lowest pitched and placed furthest away from the bowing hand.

Sound is produced by drawing the hair of the bow across the string at right angles. The fine fibres of the hair catch the string and friction is increased by rubbing a dry, slightly sticky, resin (or rosin) on the bow before use. Notes produced from the full length of the string are said to be open notes and correspond to the fundamental note of the unstopped string's harmonic series. Each string can be temporarily shortened by compressing it on the fingerboard with the finger of the left hand, the vibrating length being from the finger to the bridge. Such a string is said to be 'stopped'. By moving the finger up the finger board (i.e. towards the bridge) successively higher pitched notes can be obtained from any string and, if this progression is carefully graded, a chromatic scale can be produced. There comes a point when the stopped note produced by a lower pitched string is the same pitch as the open note on the adjacent higher pitched string: thus the higher positions on the instrument provide alternative fingerings for notes, which allows greater flexibility in difficult passages.

The length of string between each semitone becomes shorter as the finger progresses up the fingerboard and the distance between each position also becomes shortened. A skilled performer can be expected to play in any of nine positions up the fingerboard on each string. In the eighteenth century, orchestral string players utilized the first four finger positions only. The development of technique and of the instrument itself has placed greater demends upon the player.

The quality of a stopped note is smoother than that of an open string and can be further enhanced by the use of vibrato, a controlled vibration of the arm and wrist, which causes the fingertip to roll as it presses on the string. In effect, it slightly shortens and lengthens the sounding part of the string with a steady pulse. Different speeds and amplitudes of vibrato can be used to colour the sound; often, a player will add the vibrato only after commencing a note. Because of the different quality of the stopped string, players tend to use only stopped notes as far as possible, so as to avoid the coarse, uncontrolled sound of the open strings from standing out in a melodic phrase. For a richer sound, or to make a particular effect possible (e.g. a passage of harmonics), a composer may request certain notes, or a whole passage, to be played on a single string. This is signified in the score either by the number of the string (the lowest is IV, the highest I), by *sol–fa* (C = *do*, D = *re*, etc.), or by the terms *sul G* It; *auf der G Saite* Ger; or *sur le sol* Fr.

More than one string may be played at any one time. The simultaneous playing of two notes is known as double stopping. Three- and four-note chords are also possible, but because of the arch of the bridge, only two upper notes on adjacent strings can be sustained. It is usual, therefore, to spread the chord from the bottom upwards and to sustain either or both of the two upper notes.

A much softer and mellower sound can be achieved by slotting a mute over the bridge. Marked *con sordini* (It., *mit Dämpfer* Ger; *avec soudines* Fr.), such passages have a colour of their own, both at piano and forte. The end of a muted section is indicated by the term *senza sordini* (It., *ohne Dämpfer* Ger; *sans sourdines* Fr.)

Bowing effects

Bowing effects are many and varied: several basic concepts should be understood. A downbow (*giù* It; *Abstrich* Ger; *tiré* Fr., or marked ⊓), from heel to point, is usually adopted for emphasized notes, e.g. the first beat of a bar. Upbows (*su* It; *Aufstrich* Ger; *poussé* Fr., or marked ∨), from point to heel, usually alternate with downbows and tend to be employed on weaker beats. Several terms denote the use of the bow on the string: *arco* It; *Bogen, Bog.* Ger; *archet* Fr. They are most usually employed to mark the return to normal bowing after a section of pizzicato or col legno (*see below*). For normal bowing, as opposed to some of the special techniques described below, composers have occasionally used the terms *in modo ordinario* It; *gewöhnlich* Ger; *jeu ordinaire* Fr.

To play with more strength the player may use just the bottom of the bow alone. Composers often specify this by inserting the terms 'heel', 'nut', or 'at the frog' (*Frosch* Ger; *talon* Fr.). Conversely, a lighter, softer and more delicate style is usually associated with playing at the point (*punto* It; *Spitze* Ger; *au bout de l'archet, pointe* Fr.). Bowing needs to be carefully worked out in rehearsal, and not only should the style of bowing at each point be agreed upon but also its unanimity, which is important for good ensemble. Most important, the player should arrive at the right part of the bow, and also use just the right amount of bow. (Many of the techniques outlined below are only effective in precise areas of the bow.)

A crescendo usually is at its most effective when on an upbow, as the strongest sounds can be obtained at the heel. Conversely, a long and gradual diminuendo suits a slow downbow. At times a 'retake' of the bow is necessary, in which the bow is taken off the string and a fresh downbow played from the heel (or occasionally an upbow from the point). This can help the phrasing by introducing a break in the music and emphasizing a particular note. The music may demand several downbows in succession, as where several notes in a row have to be played with some force. (Examples can be found at the opening of Borodin's Second Symphony, and in the 'Tanz' from Carl Orff's *Carmina Burana*.)

A different quality of sound can be achieved by altering the point of contact with the string. *Sul ponticello* (It., *am Steg* Ger; *au chevalet* Fr.), literally, 'on the bridge', this is the term for playing as near to the bridge as possible. The technique produces a slightly scratchy sound most often prescribed for the eerie, sometimes magical atmosphere it evokes when played *pianissimo*. The 'frost scene' from Purcell's opera *King Arthur* is a good example of the effect. It may also be used for the soft opening of *Winter* from Vivaldi's *The Four Seasons*. The opposite style of bowing, i.e. bowing near the fingerboard, is called *sul tasto* (It., *am Griffbrett* Ger; *sur la touche* Fr.). Both sul ponticello and sul tasto can be used in places other than those indicated by the composer to allow the sound of the wind section to penetrate the dense string sound of some scores.

Col legno (*coll'arco al rovescio* It; *avec le dos de l'archet* Fr.) indicates the use of the wood, rather than the hair of the bow on the strings. If executed to the letter, a rather small sound is produced, so judicious 'faking' is sometimes employed by string players, where the bow is turned sideways so that a little of the hair also comes into contact with the string. Mahler inserted a footnote the first time he introduced it into a composition: 'Kein Irrtum! Mit dem Holz zu streichen' (No mistake! Stroke with the wood).

The bow can be turned back to its normal position but still used percussively, striking the string with the hair: a different device called *batutto*. It can produce quite loud effects at times. Mahler indicated this with the phrase 'mit dem Bogen geschlagen' (strike with the bow).

In more recent scores (e.g. Penderecki's *Threnody for the Victims of Hiroshima*), special effects such as bowing between the bridge and the tail-piece are requested. This particular sound is quite uncontrollable in pitch but produces notes of a high pitch. Such techniques require special signs or instructions in the music, which are usually clearly explained in a prefatory note at the beginning of the score.

The bowing effects discussed below are broadly divided into bowing 'on the string', where the bow never breaks contact with the string, and 'off the string', where it is lifted off the string between each stroke. In legato passages, each note may be separately bowed (fig. 8.1a) and anything up to the entire length of the bow can be employed. This is often used in slow passages where a breadth or richness of tone is required, and may be referred to as *Strich für Strich* (*'stroke for stroke'*), *mit liegendem Bogen*, ('with lying bow') or 'lang gestrichen' ('with long line/bow'). If a still smoother legato style is required, several notes can be slurred together (fig. 8.1b). Here the bow moves slowly in one direction whilst the fingers alter the length of the string and, consequently, the pitch of the notes.

Other effects are possible without lifting the bow off the string. A tremolo effect, or a trill, can be achieved by alternating rapidly any two fingers on the string or one finger on an open string (fig. 8.2a). A similar effect can be achieved using rapid short alternating movements of the bow (fig. 8.2b); here, the added advantage is that it can be performed on one note only or on two by double stopping. Care must be taken as confusion can arise between a finger tremolo and a bow tremolo.

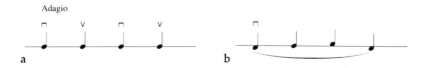

Fig 8.1

Fig. 8.3a is a finger tremolo: each group of notes is distinctly bowed according to the slur; fig. 8.3b is a two-note tremolo with the bow, as there is no slur. This is uncommon: most players will, in fact, play both notes sounding together as a true double stop. It could have been rewritten without changing the manner of performance but reducing the chance misreading, as in fig. 8.3c. A similar effect can be achieved by dividing the section as in fig. 8.3d, which is easier to read.

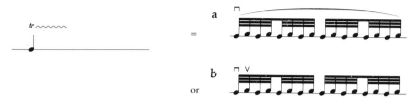

Fig. 8.2

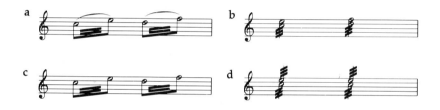

Fig. 8.3

On-the-string legato styles

Détaché

This is played with the middle or upper half of the bow, using short, separate bows played smoothly, neither slurred nor staccato. It is reserved for passages where all the notes are of equal length and not marked with staccato. In fast, *forte* passages that require a full tone (such as the opening of the third movement of J.S. Bach's Concerto for two violins BWV 1043), détaché bowing provides a rich and exciting sound. Détaché is sometimes referred to as *grand détaché, petit détaché* or *détaché moyen* (medium), depending on the degree of separation.

Louré

Also known as *portato* It., this can be performed in any part of the bow. Here the bow continues its motion as for conventional legato but releases pressure slightly between notes so that they become somewhat detached.

On-the-string staccato effects

Marcato

(It., *betont* Ger; *détaché, sec, marqué* Fr; marked). If there is a clear break and attack on each note, whether on the up- or downbow, a short middle to upper bow stroke is usually employed.

Martélé

(Fr., hammered). An extreme form of marcato, this can be executed with the whole bow or with just an inch or two. The bow must be pressed into the string prior to any lateral movement; it therefore grips the string at the start of a note and then is released enough to produce a good quality of tone. At the end of the stroke the bow stops on the string and pressure is again exerted ready for the next stroke. This style cannot be used in fast passage work since the tempo has to be slow enough to provide time to prepare the bow. The style is not restricted to *fortissimo* writing, it can be used just as effectively in *pianissimo* writing where a firm start is required for each note.

Off-the-string staccato effects

Spiccato

The middle to lower bow is dropped on the string and allowed to rebound. The bow is therefore held lightly and used for fast passage-work. It is difficult to achieve very loud playing using this technique. A very light spiccato is sometimes referred to as *saltato* or *saltando* (It., *Springbogen* Ger.). A harder and more brittle effect is usually marked *spiccato assai*. At the other extreme, a 'chopped' effect can be achieved with the heel of the bow. It requires much less dexterity and is usually employed when a spiccato effect is required at a moderate tempo but where the dynamic is greater than *mf*.

Staccato volante

(It., 'flying' staccato). This refers to a series of spiccatos played on one upbow, each one played on the rebound of the previous one. It is often used for lightness in fast passage-work or for repeated notes.

Ricochet (jeté Fr.)

Like the above, this is a series of *spiccato* notes on one bow, generally employed where a repeated motif of two to five notes occurs. The technique becomes unmanageable in longer groups. The right hand controls the number of bounces.

Pizzicato

Some effects may be achieved without the bow. The fleshy part of the finger can be used to pluck the string (*pizzicato* It., 'pinched'). For lengthy passages of pizzicato the players usually put the bow down and pick it up again when the bow (marked *arco*) is resumed. Very occasionally, the fingers of the left hand may pluck open strings whilst the right hand bows. It is not unknown for one finger of the left hand to stop the string whilst another plucks it. Normally a cross sign (+) above the note indicates left-hand pizzicato, but this is by no means universal. The more usual right-hand pizzicato may be performed with one or more fingers. Not only can single notes be plucked but also chords of up to four notes. Chords of two notes can be plucked together but larger chords need to be spread in arpeggio fashion. Composers occasionally specify this by the term *alla chittara* It. In such cases the chord can be spread upwards or downwards. This would be notated using either up- and downbow signs or directional arrows

For lengthy guitar-like passages the violin may be held banjo-fashion in the lap or under the arm. As there is a degree of decay in the sound produced by *pizzicato*, some composers (Bartók, for example) have exploited a glissando effect by moving the left-hand finger to move up or down the string immediately after the string has been plucked. Mahler asked for an aggressive form of pizzicato, where the player pulls the string away from the instrument so that it strikes the fingerboard on its return. Bartók used this 'snap' technique to such an extent that he even invented a new symbol to indicate it. (Cf. Bartók's *Music for Strings, Percussion and Celesta*, bar 116.)

Harmonics

If a finger of the left hand touches the string lightly, rather than presses it against the fingerboard, a bowed note can be produced of a much purer quality. When this technique is used on an otherwise open string, it is called a 'natural harmonic', since the note which sounds is one of those which form the harmonic series of the open string. This can only be effected at those points on the string which divide its length by a simple proportion (e.g. 1:2, 1:3, 1:4, etc.). If it is specifically required by the composer, the sign ° is placed above the note.

'Artificial harmonics' can also be produced on any note in the following manner: the first finger is pressed on the string in the normal way, while the fourth is placed lightly at the interval of a fourth higher. The note produced is two octaves higher than that which corresponds to the position of the first finger.

The Double Bass

The double bass differs from the other members of the modern string section in several ways. The shape is probably the most recognizably different feature of the instrument. Akin to the viol family, the instrument's shape is characterized by sloping shoulders and a longer neck in proportion to body size. The distances between notes on the strings has resulted in a different tuning scheme. Rather than tuning to fifths, as in the violin family, the strings of the double bass are usually tuned in fourths. In addition, the lower range of the instrument is often extended either by having a fifth string, or by the use of a device fixed to the lowest string. Double bass parts are generally notated an octave higher than the sounding pitch, but this is not universal practice. Four-string instruments are tuned to $E'-A'-D-G$. When a fifth string is added, it is most usually tuned to B' or, occasionally, C'.

Other String Instruments

Viola da gamba

This generally refers to the bass member of the viol family, and was primarily used from the sixteenth to the eighteenth centuries as a consort instrument, but today's conductor occasionally comes across it, notably in the music of J. S. Bach. Viols differ from the violin family in that they have flat backs, sloping shoulders, thinner wood and deeper ribs, C-shaped rather than S-shaped sound holes, six strings across a wider and often fretted fingerboard and a flatter bridge (enabling chords to be played). The strings are thinner and less tense and the instrument is held upright like a cello, using a bow held with the palm outwards.

Viola d'amore

This is occasionally found in works by J.S.Bach, Vivaldi, Handel, and more recently Meyerbeer, Richard Strauss, and Prokofiev. It has characteristics common to both the viol and the violin family, with 14 strings, of which seven are tuned strictly in the key of D major and seven, placed below the fingerboard, are free to vibrate in sympathy. There are no frets, and the instrument is held like a violin.

Harp

(*Arpa* It; *Harfe* Ger; *harpe* Fr.). The full-size orchestral model is called the 'gothic' or 'concert' harp. It has ancient origins and finds a place in the orchestra for its beautiful tone, glissando effects and arpeggios. The harp has 47 strings with a range of six and a half octaves; its music is notated in the treble and bass clef, rather in the manner of a piano score.

There are seven strings to each octave, linked to seven corresponding pedals (each with three positions) arranged around the base of the instrument near the player's feet. The positions of the pedals determine whether a particular note (and all its octave transpositions) is flat, natural, or sharp. The pedals are set at the beginning of the piece according to the key signature; accidentals or changes of key require the pedal positions to be altered.

There is no mechanical damping of the strings, which are damped by the hands of the player. If the strings are to continue to vibrate, the terms *laisser vibrer* Fr., and *klingen lassen* Ger. are generally used. The opposite, a rapid damping of the note is indicated by the terms *secco* It; *kurz* Ger; *etouffé le son* Fr. An immediate damping of several strings is indicated by *sons etouffés* Fr. Strings are plucked near to their middle for a full ringing sound. A rather more brittle quality, produced when the strings are plucked nearer to the sound board, is signified by the term *près de la table* Fr. In general, the fleshy part of the finger is employed to pluck the strings; however, Mahler specifies the use of a plectrum (*médiator* Fr.) to give a hard, 'twangy' sound, although players tend to use finger nails for this effect.

Harmonics can also be produced on the harp. For very clear, bell-like sounds the strings are stopped with the base of the hand while plucking with the thumb of the same hand. These are indicated by ° above the note affected, *son harmonique* Fr., or simply, 'harm.'

Transposing Instruments

The human ear is stimulated by vibrations of the air between it and the sound source; the pitch of this sound depends on the frequency of the vibration. The pitch of sound produced by a wind instrument is related to the length of the column of air within it. The sound is initiated by the vibration of a player's lips, as in brass instruments, the vibration of a single or double reed, as in the oboe, clarinet and bassoon families, or by blowing across one end of the air column.

For any given length of tubing a characteristic series of notes can be produced, the lowest of these is known as the fundamental. More forceful blowing (overblowing) produces more rapid vibration of the air column. Usually the next note obtained is an octave above the fundamental, as if the extra force divides the length of the vibration in half, doubling its frequency. Yet more forceful blowing produces faster vibrations and further subdivisions: the series of notes produced is shown in fig. 8.4. The series is known as the *harmonic series*; these are the notes possible from a fixed length of tubing or a string. A different length of tube will give the same pattern of notes but its harmonic series will be based on a different fundmental: the longer the tube, the lower will be the fundamental and the set of pitches of its harmonic series, and vice versa.

Fig. 8.4

The harmonic series has certain other characteristics which are of importance to the conductor. Notes number 7, 11, 13 and 14 of the series (fig. 8.4) are out of tune. The trumpet and horn are not able to obtain the fundamental note in the series, nor, for practical purposes, numbers, 17, 18, 19 and 20 or 21. If the air column is closed at the non-blowing end, as in a stopped organ pipe, the first note obtained on overblowing is the twelfth and not the octave. The clarinet, although not a closed pipe, is unique in that it overblows to the twelfth and, because of this, requires a different type of fingering system to other instruments of the woodwind family.

A single instrument of fixed length limits the player to the notes of one harmonic series and some of these are out of tune or unobtainable. One way of overcoming this problem and increasing the available notes is to have more than one instrument, each providing a separate harmonic series. However, this would prove inconvenient and limiting, since time is required to prepare and change instruments and this may only be possible, between, rather than during movements. It is also impractical and uneconomical to have to carry and maintain a series of instruments each built in a different pitch. Other approaches have been devised to increase the ways of changing the length of tubing of a single instrument and, therefore, increase the number of harmonic series available to both the composer and the player. An early method used in brass instruments was to have a site somewhere along the tube where a segment could be removed and be replaced by another of different length. These detachable segments were called 'crooks' (if a coiled length) or 'shanks' (if a straight tube). The technique was used to change the fundamental pitch of the trumpet and the (French) horn.

Another problem when changing instruments, or when using crooks is that of notation. When the fundamental note of the instrument is C the player can read a part notated in C, and the written and sounding notes correspond. When the harmonic series is based on another note, two alternative forms of notation are available. The composer would indicate the pitch of the required instrument (e.g. horn in D) and, for convenience, notate the part using the notes of the harmonic series; the player used the appropriate instrument or crook. This was the standard method of notation for crooked instruments, since regardless of the crook being used, the player would associate the visualized note at a set point on the stave with the technique necessary to produce the correct intervals, although the sounding note varied. Today, the player has to 'transpose', since it is usual for players of transposing instruments to use one or two instrumets pitched in a specific key to cover the parts that were originally written in the key appropriate to the key of the work. Transposing at sight is today limited to a few instruments, notably the horn and trumpet, since their music prior to the mid-nineteenth century was notated in the fashion outlined above.

Modern woodwind and brass instruments alter the length of tubing not with crooks but with slides, valves or keys. A length of sliding tube was first used in the sackbut and even the trumpet for a time, but with modern instruments the slide is only to be found in the trombone. Valves are designed to divert the airstream into a separate section of tubing. By various combinations of three valves and their corresponding tubes (or 'slides'), the trumpet and horn now posses a fully chromatic range. Valve number two lowers the pitch of the harmonic series by a semitone, the first valve by a tone, and the third valve by a minor third. This mechanism is used to alter the length in most brass instruments. Keys predominate in the woodwind families, where they are used to cover or uncover holes along the body of the instrument altering the length of the resonating air column and in so doing altering the available harmonic series.

The perfection of methods of lengthening and shortening the vibrating length of modern wind instruments has made them very reliable and consistent in tone production over the chromatic range. A set of instruments of different lengths, and with varying fundamentals, is no longer needed. The pitching of every instrument in C would have economic advantages; also, composers could write all orchestral parts in the same key and instrumentalists would not have to transpose. However, a number of wind instruments are built in keys other than C, as indicated in subsequent sections. This is partly traditional, but more importantly the tone quality and range of these instruments has proved to be well suited to orchestral requirements. Instruments of the same family produced in different keys (e.g. clarinets in Bb and A) use the same fingering systems. This means that a note at a set place on the stave is produced by the same fingering although the two instruments sound at a different pitch. Such instruments are named according to their transposition so that a Bb trumpet or clarinet sounds a tone lower than written, i.e. they sound a *b'* flat when written *c'* is played.

The Woodwind Family

The woodwind section of the orchestra can be referred to collectively in scores as *i legni* It; *Holz, Holzbläser* Ger; *les bois* Fr. Mahler refers to the woodwind in his First Symphony as the Holzinstrumente instructing them to 'Schalltrichter in die höhe', i.e. to raise the bells of the instruments as high as the players can manage. (This bells-up special effect is most commonly asked of the horn section.) In France and Germany a mixed wind group, for example in Stravinsky's *Symphonies of Winds*, is often termed *Harmonie*, hence published editions often describe the wind parts of even a full orchestral work as the *Harmoniestimmen*. Other collective terms are *i fiati, stromenti a fiato* It; *Bläsinstrumente, Bläser* Ger; *instruments à vent, les vents* Fr.

Flute family

(*Flauto traverso* It; *Querflöte* Ger; *flûte, flûte d'Allemagne, flûte travèrsiere* Fr; transverse flute, German flute). The **flute** is a non-transposing instrument usually with a range of three octaves ($c'-d''''$). The most natural scale of the concert flute is D major. Military models at the turn of the twentieth century lacked the extension from d' to c' , and were known as 'flute in D', although they were always written for as non-transposing instruments. The flute is held horizontally, and an air stream (sometimes called the 'air-reed') is directed across a hole in the head joint, focused by the player's embouchure. It was common in the late nineteenth century for flutes to be required to play b and even b flat, e.g in Mahler's Fifth Symphony. A foot joint extension is added to the modern flute to obtain b but it does tend to upset the intonation of the instrument: b flat can only be covered if played on an alto flute.

Flute in G (*flautone, flauto in sol* [Stravinsky] It; *flûte en sol* Fr.). This was called the bass flute until comparatively recently in Britain; today it is more generally referred to by its european name, the alto flute. This is a more accurate description, since a true bass flute and a contrabass flute now exist. Where the alto and concert flute are both used, the latter is clearly distinguished by one of its names e.g. flauto traverso or Querflöte. In size and shape the alto flute is usually a longer and wider-bored version of the concert flute but a second variety curves back on itself in the shape of a long narrow letter U. The alto flute is pitched a fourth lower than the concert flute, it is a transposing instrument with the same written compass: its sounding range is from $g-a''''$. The tone quality of the alto flute is extremely rich, soft and velvety.

The **bass flute** and **contrabass flute** are recent inventions and can be seen in flute choirs. Their use in the orchestral repertoire is extremely limited, and in the standard twentieth century repertoire, references to the bass flute can be assumed to be to the alto flute. If in doubt, look at the key signature. Both the bass and contrabass flutes are pitched in C, one and two octaves below the concert flute respectively.

Eb flute. This is a rarity in England, however, it is increasingly written for in the American symphonic band literature, where it often doubles the first Eb clarinet part. One example of its use can be found in the symphonic band arrangements of Bernstein's Overture to *Candide*. Like the Eb clarinet it is a transposing instrument sounding a minor third higher than written.

The **piccolo** (*ottavino, flauto piccolo* It; *kleine Flöte* Ger; *petite flûte* Fr.) is a small-sized flute, which plays an octave higher than the concert flute. Its range differs, however, since it does not possess the foot joint with the additonal two holes. Its range is from $d''-b''''$. Composers from the nineteenth century and the turn of the twentieth century, including Mahler and Verdi, have asked for *c'*. This problem can be resolved by the surreptitious use of a doubling flute player.

Recorder family

The Recorder has had many different names in different languages which have often been derived from various features of the instrument: its 'beak', the fipple or block, or the fact it is held straight in front of the player. The most common names are: *flauto dolce, flauto diritto* It; *Blockflöte, Schnabelflöte, Langsflöte* Ger; *flûte à bec, flûte à neuf trous, flûte d'Angleterre, flûte douce* Fr; fipple flute, consort flute, English flute. The quiet, restricted dynamic range of this instrument found a place in the orchestras of the baroque period, where it could balance the small number of violins and other woodwind, e.g. J.S. Bach's Second *Brandenburg Concerto*, where the recorder takes its part alongside high trumpet, oboe, strings and continuo.

The recorder player is the best authority to consult before choosing the appropriate instrument for baroque music, especially as composers almost never specified the type of instrument to be played. In eighteenth-century scores, the *flauto piccolo* is usually taken to mean the sopranino recorder. The most commonly used instruments are the treble (sounding at written pitch), the descant and the sopranino recorders (the last two instruments sound an octave higher than written). The range of a descant recorder is from *c''–d''''*.

Oboe family

The **oboe** (*Hoboe* Ger; *hautbois* Fr.) is a conically-bored pipe, terminating at its lower end in a flared bell. At the upper end is a short length of metal tubing called the staple into which the double reed is fitted. It is a non-transposing instrument with a fully chromatic range of *b* flat–*g'''*, although *b* and *b* flat are only obtainable by means of key extensions. These are not standard, and many european instruments go no lower than *b*. However, *b* flat extensions are to be increasingly found on modern instruments.

The oboe is keyed upon the Böhm system, but there are several different systems, requiring different fingerings for some notes. Rapid trills are possible but double-tonguing effects are difficult. However, flutter-tonguing has been asked for by Stravinsky in the *Rite of Spring* (four bars after rehearsal figure 10).

The **oboe d'amore** (*Liebesoboe* Ger; *hautbois d'amour* Fr.) is rarely used in modern scores. When an oboe d'amore is not available the cor anglais can be used to cover the same register, although the tone colour is rather darker. It is in effect a mezzo-soprano oboe pitched in A, a minor third below the oboe and ranging from *b–e''* (written pitch), sounding a fifth lower (*e–a''*). It is played by an oboist, as the fingerings of the two instruments are virtually the same.

The oboe d'amore is mainly encountered in baroque scores, for example in Bach's *Christmas Oratorio* and *Magnificat* in D. More recent examples of its use are to be found in Richard Strauss's *Symphonia Domestica* and Debussy's *Gigues* (where it is required to descend to *b* flat).

The **cor anglais** (*corno inglese* It; *Althoboe* [Wagner], *Englisches Horn* Ger; English horn) is the contralto instrument in the oboe family, pitched in F, and, like the oboe d'amore, is a transposing instrument. Its written pitch and range is identical to the oboe d'amore, sounding *e–a''*. It is wider and longer than the oboe, with a thistle-shaped bell. At the upper end the metal crook, or staple, into which the double reed is attached, is generally bent back to facilitate the holding of the instrument. Older instruments have a gently curved shape over the whole length of the instrument, to shorten effectively the overall length and to make fingering easier.

Notation has varied, but today composers use the treble clef, writing for a transposing instrument with the same fingerings as the oboe. The Italians before Verdi's time wrote for the instrument in the bass clef an octave below sounding pitch.

The **oboe da caccia** (*Jagd-Hautbois* Ger.) is a predecessor of the cor anglais and its tone is more strident than that of its younger cousin. Like the cor anglais, it is an alto instrument pitched in F. The instrument is built in the shape of a curved hunting horn and has either an expanded bell or, more frequently, a pear-shaped bell that renders the sound rather less strident. Bach used it frequently, writing for it at sounding pitch in the alto clef.

The **Heckelphone**, invented by Wilhelm Heckel and produced in 1904, is to all intents and purposes a baritone oboe in C, written for in the treble clef and sounding an octave lower than notated. Its range is from *A–g″*.

The Heckelphone has a pronounced conical bore that is twice the dimensions of an oboe and has a bassoon-like sound. It terminates in a closed, spherical bell which rests on the floor. The sound emanates in the lower registers from holes bored in the bell. The Heckelphone was popular in Germany for a time and its first appearance in the orchestra was in Richard Strauss's *Salome*. Strauss asks for an unplayable *F* in the *Alpine Symphony*.

Clarinet family

The **clarinet** is a single-reed transposing instrument. It is a cylindrical pipe and has the properties of a stopped-pipe, that is to say its fundamental note is an octave lower than the corresponding note either of an open-pipe or of a conical reed-pipe of the same length. In addition, it overblows at the twelfth, rather than at the octave. The fingering of the clarinet thus differs fundamentally from that of the flute and oboe.

With the exception of the basset clarinet, basset horn and the bass clarinet (to be discussed below) the written *e* is the standard bottom note of all clarinets and the upward range generally extends to *g‴*.

The sound produced varies markedly through this range and there are four distinct registers. Below *g′* is called the chalumeau register, as it corresponds to the tone and range of an early instrument of this name. The register is soft and beautiful and the easiest to control. Between *b′* and *c‴* is the usual clarinet register obtained by overblowing. It has also been termed the clarino register, due to its likeness to a trumpet (it is possible that the instrument derives its name from that of the clarino trumpet). The notes between these two registers are known as the break, or throat register. They have the least satisfactory timbre and require a great deal of finger changing making it difficult to achieve a true legato. Notes above *c‴* are known as the extreme register; notes higher than *g‴* are rarely asked for and their production depends greatly on the skill of the player and the quality of the instrument; *c⁗* appears in Elgar's symphonic study, *Falstaff*.

The clarinet has the greatest command of dynamic variation in the woodwind section: from the almost inaudible start to a note in the low registers, to the very large fluctuations of volume possible on most parts of the range. The instrument was developed in the late seventeenth century but did not become a regular member of the orchestra for another hundred years. During the classical period, and well into the middle of the nineteenth century, orchestral clarinets were made in three keys:

clarinet in C, a non-transposing instrument written and sounding in the key of the piece; clarinet in Bb, a transposing instrument sounding a major second lower; and clarinet in A, a transposing instrument sounding a minor third lower. Of these three, the clarinet in C is now obsolete. This still leaves a choice for the composer. The clarinet in A is most commonly used for sharp keys and the Bb instrument for music in flat keys. It is not uncommon for composers to ask the clarinettist to change instruments between movements of an extended work or even in the body of a lengthy movement to suit the music's key structure. To change clarinets requires time, since the player normally transfers the warmed mouthpiece and the barrel being used to the second instrument; the conductor must be aware of any such changes, and should allow sufficient time where these happen between movements.

Eb and D clarinets (*clarinetto piccolo* It; *petite clarinette* Fr.) transpose up a minor third and major second respectively. They are virtually interchangeable as far as tone colour is concerned, but the Eb instrument is more readily available. The instrument is required in Berlioz's *Symphonie fantastique* and also in works by Strauss, Mahler and Wagner.

The **basset clarinet** was the instrument for which Mozart's finest works for clarinet (the Concerto K 622 and the Quintet K 581) were composed. It is pitched in A and extends down to written *c* (a minor third lower than the Bb instrument). The versions of these two works generally played have been altered to fit the range of modern instruments. However, the current interest in authentic performance practice has led to the reproduction of the original instrument.

The **basset horn** (*corno di bassetto* It; *Bassetthorn* Ger; *cor de basset* Fr.) is a tenor instrument in F, transposing a fifth lower than written and extending with extra keys down to written *c*. Its written range is from *c–c'''*. Modern instruments resemble a bass clarinet, with an upturned metal bell and a curved upper metal extension upon which the mouthpiece is attached. The instruments of Mozart's day were constructed from boxwood, bent in the middle (or crescent-shaped) and with a large box-like structure into which the lowest keys vented.

Mozart wrote for the basset horn in several of his operas, the *Requiem* and in the Serenade K 361 for 13 wind instruments. These parts, however, are usually transcribed for the Bb clarinet, which can replace the basset instrument if necessary. Richard Strauss also writes for the basset horn in several operas, using both treble and bass clef. (The bass clef notes are written lower than sounding pitch and therefore transpose a fourth up.)

The **alto clarinet in Eb** transposes and sounds a major sixth lower than written. It was replaced by the alto saxophone in the military band, but is now found as an integral member of the wind band and clarinet choir. **Bass clarinets** (*clarinetto basso, clarone* It; *Bassklarinette* Ger; *clarinette basse* Fr.) existed in two forms (Bb and A), both pitched initially an octave below the standard instrument: the Bb instrument has survived today. The early form resembled the standard clarinet, but the bell was near the floor, resulting in lost sound, and the instrument was cumbersome to hold. The modern instrument resembles the saxophone in shape, the curved head joint and upturned bell being made of metal.

Although the instrument has as great a range as the standard clarinet, most compositions are for the distinctive low register. The usual lowest note is Eb. An instrument extending down to written C has been called for by some twentieth-century Russian composers, including Shostakovich, but this instrument has not found favour in Britain. The German method of notation for the bass clarinet is in the bass clef, sounding a major second below the written notes. The more popular method is a French notation in treble clef, as for all the other instruments in the family (so that fingering associations are maintained), sounding a major ninth below written pitch.

Pedal clarinet (contrabass clarinet, double bass clarinet). This is a large instrument used in symphonic bands and clarinet choirs. It is pitched an octave below the bass clarinet in Bb. It is written for in bass clef and sounds a major ninth below written pitch.

Bassoon family

The bassoon is a conically-bored pipe doubled back on itself. The overall length is about eight feet. The instrument can either be held diagonally across the body, supported by a sling, or more vertically held at the appropriate height by a spike. It is notated at concert pitch and has a range from B' flat–e'. However, any note above b is only infrequently asked for. To avoid great numbers of ledger lines, bass, tenor and occasionally treble clefs are used. Composers have called for A flat: when there is sufficient time, an extension can be added to the instrument (such as a paper tube), rather than employ a contrabassoon.

Double bassoon (*contrafagotto* It; *Kontrafagott* Ger; *contrebasson* Fr.). The double or contrabasson is normally notated in the bass clef but sounding an octave lower. It ranges from B " flat–e. The instrument most often seen is of modern German design. Over 16 feet in length, its tube is doubled back on itself four times.

Unusual woodwind instruments

A number of instruments have been employed to play the offstage shepherd's pipe music in Wagner's *Tristan und Isolde*, one of these was developed by the German maker, Heckel: the **Heckel-clarina**. It is in Bb and possesses a written chromatic range of b flat–e'''. The instrument has a single reed and so belongs to the clarinet family, but its conical bore makes it a woodwind saxophone. A cor anglais is often substituted to play this particular part.

The **saxophones** (*sassofone* It; *Saxophon* Ger.) are a family of hybrid instruments, invented by Aldolph Sax, in about 1840. They share the characteristics of several family groups and this has led to many differing views as to their rightful place in the orchestra. The metal body of the instruments likens them to the brass instrument family, while the single-reed mouth piece is similar to that of the clarinet. The bore is conical however, and it has an arrangement of keys resembling that of the oboe.

The original seven members of the military band and orchestral groups were: sopranino in Eb or F; soprano in Bb or C; alto (mezzo soprano) in Eb or F; tenor (melody) in Bb or C; baritone in Eb or F; bass in Bb or C; and contrabass in Eb or F. All are notated in the treble clef with a written range of b –f '''.

Modern notation has followed the French tradition using the treble clef. At the turn of the century, however, Richard Strauss wrote for instruments tuned to C and F in his *Symphonia Domestica* using bass and treble clefs. The saxophone has a great range of tone colour and dynamics. At its purest in the soprano saxophone, the smooth and silky tone can be most alluring, but the middle and lower pitched instruments can produce a very thick, brassy quality liked by jazz players. As there is a strong association of the saxophone with dance bands and jazz, composers have often employed them in orchestral groups to create a jazz 'feel' (cf. Kurt Weill's *Dreigroschenoper* and *Mahagonny*).

Brass Instruments

Horn

The horn originally was a hunting instrument and its simple shape (a tube coiled twice) was suitable for carrying over the shoulder. This form of the horn has been called *corno da caccia* It; *Jagdhorn* Ger; *cor de chasse, trompe de chasse* Fr. The early orchestral instrument was very similar to the hunting variety but was smaller, had a narrower diameter of coil and had a deeper mouthpiece, the latter producing a less brassy tone. This was the form to which crooks of varying lengths could be added to vary the pitch of the harmonic series. This horn is referred to in varying languages by the terms: *corno naturale, corno a mano* It; *Naturhorn, Waldhorn* Ger; *cor simple* Fr.

In its more developed eighteenth-century form, crooks were used to transpose the basic harmonic series of an instrument into a variety of other keys (*see* p.157). Even in natural horns a further method of altering the pitch of the note is possible. The right hand is inserted into the bell and by altering the shape with the cupped hand, the note can be either lowered or raised. This raising or lowering can be to the extent of a semitone, so out-of-tune notes can be tuned and the smaller gaps of the series filled in – hence the name 'corno a mano'. These stopped notes have a very different tone colour, and were sparingly used on the natural horn. Nowadays, hand-stopped notes are used for special effects (*see below*).

The invention of valves around 1814 or 1815 by the horn player, Heinrich Stölzel, paved the way for a horn with an even tone and a fully chromatic register. This obviated the necessity for the player to carry a set of crooks. Composers quite quickly came to recognize the improvement, but there were notable exceptions (such as Brahms, who wrote for the natural horn as late as the 1860's). Wagner contrasted the new valved horn with the natural horn in *Tannhäuser*, where he asks for both 'Waldhorner' and 'Ventilhorner'.

The valved horn had to be distinguished from its ancestor and several labels have been employed: *corno a pistoni, corno a macchina, corno cromatico* It; *Ventilhorn* Ger; *cor ventile, cor à pistons, cor chromatique, cor d'harmonie* Fr. The overall term, French horn, is generally used today. The most confusing nomenclature is the Spanish name *trompa* which is very similar to the Italian term for trumpet (*tromba*). Care should be taken when deciphering the notation. Although the written part appears to be in C (i.e. written with no key signature), players normally use an F horn or a combination or double horn, such as that in F/Bb, where an additional length of tubing (brought into operation by a fourth valve) raises the pitch of the horn by a fourth, and offers the player a complete series of alternative fingerings for notes that are out of tune or involove 'tricky' fingerings on the F instrument. The written range of the instrument is from $F'-c''$. The normal sounding range consequently is from B flat–f'' on the Bb side of the double horn. Bass clef is also used for low or 'pedal' notes. Here confusion can ocur if the player or conductor is unclear of the composer's normal practice, as two systems of notation exist. By tradition, the notes in the bass clef are transcribed an octave down so that the transposition (for a horn in F) to concert pitch becomes a fourth upwards. In orchestration manuals, however, the transposition in bass clef is the same as the treble (down a fifth). In most cases it is possible to work out what the composer intends as some notes in the old notation are impossible if played down a fifth.

In orchestral music, horns are usually grouped in pairs. Early symphonies (from *c.*1750) generally had two horns; Beethoven and his contemporaries asked for four. The first and third horns play the higher lines and are designated as principal and sub-principal in the modern orchestra. A chord played by four horns may be laid out as: 1, 3, 2, 4 with the top of the chord taken by the first player. Bruckner, Mahler and Richard Strauss increased the horn section to eight, deployed as 1, 3, 2, 4, 5, 7, 6, 8. In addition, off-stage horns are scored in some works; in the *Alpine Symphony*, Strauss requires 12 off-stage horns in addition to the eight on-stage players.

Wagner tubas. Some confusion has been created by the description of these instruments as tubas. In fact, they have more in common with French horns. Features which support this are the instrument's narrow bore and the fact that it is played using a French horn mouthpiece. Indeed, it is the horn player who usually plays this instrument when it is found in a score. They are in two sizes: tenor in Bb and bass in F, and correspond with the Bb alto (defunct) and F horns. They have four valves, three for obtaining the notes of the chromatic scale and the fourth for compensating the intonation of the lower octave. The range of the Bb instrument is E flat–*f″* and the instrument in F, B flat–*a′*. Wagner tubas are usually treated as a quartet, two tenors and two basses and are played by the fifth, sixth, seventh and eighth horn players. In the *Ring*, Wagner writes for a quartet of Wagner tubas, adding a contrabass tuba.

Horn special effects. Placing a hand tight into the bell will lower the pitch of the played note; also, if the hand is pressed into the instrument as far as possible, together with tongued accent and a good deal of pressure of the lips, a rather buzzy sound, a semitone higher is produced. This 'closed' note (*chiuso* It; *gestopft* Ger; *sons bouchés, bouche* Fr.) needs to be carefully approached. Lowering the pitch is less often requested, since it results in a soft, almost woolly sound, whereas raising it can add a great deal of excitement to a symphonic texture. The composer usually notates at sounding pitch, marking + for hand-stopped notes and º for open ones, unless he is rather more specific (*see* the introduction of Dukas', *Sorcerer's Apprentice*, where the composer specifies that the instrument is only half stopped). Mutes, such as those used for trumpet and trombone (referred to as *sordini* It; *Dämpfer* Ger; *sourdines Fr.*), can be used, but here the note need not be transposed for the effect (*see* p.164).

A brassy and very loud effect can be achieved by almost overblowing the instrument while hand stopping. It is marked *cuivré* ('brassy') or *gestopft*, with the expression *schmetternd* ('clanging', 'shrill' or 'blazing') or *stark anbläsen* ('blow hard').

The instrument can be played 'bells up' for extra-loud effects, the bell of the instrument being held up in the air (*schalltrichter hoch, schalltrichter in der höhe*, Ger.). Players have also been asked to stand up (see Mahler's First Symphony, fourth movement, rehearsal figure 56). Glissandos are normally executed by altering the tension of the lips, so that only the natural harmonics are employed. However, some juggling of the valves and movement of the hand inside the bell can give the impression of a fuller slide. The 'out-of-tune' harmonics have been requested for special effects: the best-known example is the prologue and epilogue from Britten's *Serenade for Tenor, Horn and Strings*.

Trumpet (*tromba* It; *Trompete* Ger; *trompette* Fr.). Like the horn, early trumpets were without valves. Most were pitched in D or C, so this became the most usual key for orchestral movements using trumpets. Crooks were introduced during the seventeenth century. A notable exception to the C and D instruments is found in J.S. Bach's Second *Brandenburg Concerto,* which requires a trumpet in F. A high piccolo Bb trumpet is now normally used to play the high range with confidence.

The modern valved trumpet is of cylindrical construction, flaring out conically over the last third of its length. The instrument which has found favour in this country during the twentieth century is the Bb trumpet, and many composers now write parts ready transposed for it . The compass of the Bb instrument rises chromatically from written *f* sharp–*d'''* (sounding *e–c'''*.) Most orchestral compositions restrict the range below written *c'''*. However, Strauss writes *e'''* in the *Alpine Symphony* and Mahler calls for the same note in his Seventh Symphony. Very high notes are achieved by jazz trumpeters (the upper limits of this so-called 'super' range may exceed that given above by as much as a fifth), and Bach writes *g'''* (concert pitch) in the Second *Brandenburg.*

Eb and D trumpets are generally used to cover the high *clarino* trumpet parts of the eighteenth century. The **piccolo trumpet in Bb** (usually with a shank attachment to transpose it into A) sounds an octave higher than the standard Bb instrument, notated an octave lower than sounding, and is also used to cover these notoriously difficult high and florid parts. It has an extra fourth valve to extend its range downwards additionally by an augmented fourth

The bass trumpet is used notably in Wagner's *Ring* and Schoenberg's *Gurrelieder.* It is available in three keys, C, D and Eb, and its range (*G* flat–*g'* flat) corresponds roughly with the bottom notes of the tenor trombone and to the top notes of the French horn. It is notated in treble clef and sounds an octave lower than written, and is usually played by a trombonist.

Cornet (*cornetta, pistoni* It; *Kornett* Ger; *cornet à pistons* Fr.). The cornet is shorter in appearance (but not in length) than the trumpet; it has a relatively longer conical portion and uses a more cupped mouthpiece. The two most common orchestral cornets have been pitched in Bb and A; the Bb cornet, like the Bb trumpet, is now the most commonly found instrument, and parts in A usually have to be transposed down a semitone by the player. The range is the same as that of the Bb trumpet. A high **Eb soprano cornet** is also used in the brass band, sounding a fourth higher than the Bb model .

The cornet appears quite often in orchestral music, particularly in nineteenth-century French music. It augments the brass section in the scores of Berlioz and a number of his contemporaries. Cornet parts are often played on the trumpet in amateur orchestras when a cornet or cornets are not available.

Trombone (Fr., *trombone* It; *Posaune* Ger.). The modern orchestral trombone is a brass instrument with a cylindrical bore over much of its length, expanding at one end into a bell. The cup-shaped mouthpiece is somewhat larger than that of the trumpet. The slide, a U-shaped length of tube which forms the middle section of the instrument, affords the player a method of filling the chromatic steps between the basic notes of the harmonic series. So gradual can the movement of the slide be, that a glissando effect of an augmented form can be achieved from the most extended to the closed position.

Trombones are unusual as a family as, despite being essentially transposing instruments (none have the harmonic series pitched in C), they are notated at concert pitch. The range is from *E'–f''*. The standard orchestral ensemble is of two **tenor trombones** (in Bb, but always written for as a non-transposing instrument) and a bass trombone (in Bb/F, extending down to C). The alto trombone, found regularly in classical and romantic scores, is pitched in Eb. Beethoven calls for a high *f''* in the last movement of his Fifth Symphony: do not expect the amateur player to hit this note every time in rehearsal with complete accuracy.

The **contrabass trombone in Bb** is not usually asked for in orchestral scores. The strain on the players lips and lungs limits the effectiveness of this instrument. Wagner made use of the instrument in the *Ring* as does Schoenberg in *Gurrelieder*. The instrument is notated at sounding pitch and can extend down to *B''* flat.

The trombone appears in Monteverdi's *L'Orfeo* linked to the composer's depiction of the Underworld. The trombone remained a source of special effects (cf. Mozart's use of the instrument in *Don Giovanni*) until the turn of the nineteenth century when it found a regular place in the symphony orchestra. The slide glissando first occurs in an orchestral score with Schoenberg's *Pelleas und Melisande*, an effect used subsequently to add both humour (Bartók's Concerto for Orchestra) and shock (the same composer's *The Miraculous Mandarin*).

Tuba Family. There are five members of the tuba family, all of which are to be found in use today. As developments have largely been specific to a particular country, any one may be scored for in an orchestral work. (The tuba family does not include the so-called Wagner tubas, *see* p.165.) The **tenor tuba** in Bb (*bombarda* It; *Baryton* Ger; *basse à pistons* Fr.) is most commonly known in Britain as the euphonium.

Bass tubas (F and EEb). The tuba in F was once the most usual orchestral instrument, but has been dropped in favour of a lower-pitched instrument in C (*see below*). It was not normally used in brass band work in Britain. The tuba in EEb is a regular member of the military and brass band. **Contrabass tubas** (C and BBb). The tuba in C is the instrument most favoured by today's orchestral players. The tuba in BBb, the great double Bb tuba (*cimbasso, bombardone* It; *Kontrabasstuba* Ger.), is the lowest instrument to be found in military or brass bands. However, the *Kontrabasstuba*, which is used by Wagner as the bass instrument to his pairs of tenor and bass tubas, and the *cimbasso*, to be found in Italian scores, are both pitched in C.

Brass band instruments (tuba in Eb and tuba in BBb) have been made in a circular shape so that the instrument can rest around the body of a marching bandsman: these are called *helicons*. The American variety of the helicon, which has a specially designed and forward-facing bell, is called a *sousaphone*, after the bandmaster, J.P. Sousa, whose band first used it. The early tuba was called the *bombardon* which, until recently, was the generic name used to refer to either or both of the band instruments, the tuba in Eb and the tuba in BBb.

Flugelhorn (*flicorno soprano* It; *Flügelhorn* Ger; *grand bugle, bugle* Fr.). The modern instrument used in the contemporary brass band looks and plays very much like a large cornet. However, like the bugle, it has a conical bore; in effect, it is a large bugle with piston valves. It is pitched in Bb (or C if it is used in the German brass band) and is a solo instrument in British brass bands, where it is treated as the upper part of the tenor (sax) horn section. On the continent, it sometimes replaces the cornet as the standard melody instrument as it has the same range as the cornet but a rather mellower tone. Mahler calls for a long and demanding flugel solo in his Third Symphony and Vaughan Williams uses it in his Ninth Symphony.

Saxhorns. The saxhorn family (patented 1843) was developed by Adolph Sax as a means of replacing the disparate group of instruments that were being used in bands in Europe by a set of instruments of uniform quality and pitch. He developed a set of seven instruments built to a standard model based upon the bugle. They were originally designed with a bell-front format but after a year or two he adopted an upright style for all. Subsequent litigation against Sax on the originality of his invention brought him to ruin. However, the term saxhorn continued to be used, and has come to describe any upright band instrument.

The **military bugle** is called *Signalhorn* in Germany and *clairon* in France and *cornetta segnale* in Italy. It is a natural instrument, pitched in Bb with a range of only 6 clear notes (sounding a tone lower than written), the highest is out of tune. They are: (written pitch) *c'*, *g'*, *c''*, *e''*, *g''*, (*b''* flat).

There is also a **bugle in Eb** (D'Indy's opera *Fervaal*), intended to be played, in all probability, on an Eb saxhorn, a smaller instrument than the flugelhorn. This corresponds to the Eb soprano cornet that is played in British brass bands (*see* p.170).

Any references to bugles in scores generally should be taken to be to saxhorns or flugelhorns; the contralto bugle part (in Stravinsky's *Threni*) should, in fact, be played on the flugelhorn. The six soprano, tenor and bass *flicorni* that Respighi asks for in *The Pines of Rome*, where he wishes to represent the *buccine* of the ancient Roman army, refer to the flugelhorns and saxhorns described above. In performance, therefore, use Bb flugelhorns for the *flicorni soprani in Sib*; Eb tenor horns transposed for the *flicorni tenore in Sib* and Bb euphoniums for the *flicorni bassi in Sib*. The **tenor saxhorn** (*flicorno tenore* It; *bugle ténor* Fr.), or tenor horn, is pitched in Eb. It is mainly used as a substitute for the French horn in the brass band. The **baritone saxhorn** or, as it is known in British brass bands, the baritone, is a close relative of the euphonium (*eufonio* It; *Baryton, Tenorbass, Tenorbasshorn* Ger; *basse* Fr.), the instrument that Mahler writes for in his Seventh Symphony.

Mutes

Mutes (*sordino* It; *Dämpfer* Ger; *sourdine* Fr.) have evolved over the years and some that have been stipulated by composers have either become vastly changed or are now obsolete. Decisions about the type of mute appropriate to the required sound should be made after consultation with the players; if necessary, different types of mutes can be tried, although it is best to avoid mixing mutes of metal with mutes of plastic or fibre.

Varieties that have been called for include: wood, metal, plastic and fibre 'straight' mutes (the most common type); 'Wa-Wa', 'Harmon' or extending-tube mutes; bucket, bowler hat, felt crown and cup mutes. Composers often specify muted brass (denoted by the term *con sordino*), and some are quite specific about the type of mute and, therefore, the type of sound they require.

Brass Bands, Military Bands, Symphonic Wind and Concert Bands

Bands of wind instruments have always been associated with outdoor music, whether for military use or for entertainment. Bands and band music have a long history, and developments have followed different lines. The result is that there are many different types of ensemble of wind instruments and a confusing list of names to describe them. The following summary discusses the characteristics of the bands most commonly encountered. The term military band has been in circulation since the late nineteenth century and is probably the most commonly used term to describe the small wind band. In Britain and the British Empire, military bands were very popular. All the major services had military bands and there were also many civilian town bands.

Since the composer/arrangers tended to be a small group of specialists servicing several publishers, the instrumentation remained stable. The conductor works from a condensed score with its own nomenclature. Full scores are very rare but some have been published to meet demands of the American education market.

Opinions differ about how many clarinets should be used, fig 8.5 indicates a common seating plan for symphonic wind band. There should be at least two tubas or one tuba and a double bass; the euphoniums (marked with an *) can be placed in either position. If the brass section is enlarged, corresponding enlargement of the woodwind is necessary also, to ensure that the relative balance of the group is maintained. In some printed editions, parts have been provided for Bb soprano saxophone, Eb baritone saxophone and even harp.

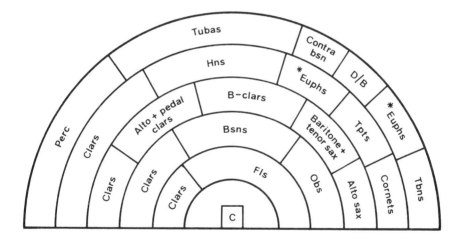

Fig. 8.5

Symphonic wind and concert bands

Both names have become widely used in the USA and refer to much larger bands than the British military band. Whereas the military band can function with between twenty and thirty musicians, the symphonic band normally uses a minimum of forty to sixty musicians. Symphonic and concert bands are a mainstay of musical education in the USA, high school and university bands can have ninety to 120 players. Doubling of parts is necessary in all departments of the band. Sometimes parts for keyboard instruments are included and light music from stage or screen will often have rhythm and bass guitar.

Marching bands

Wind bands have always had a dual role, to provide concert music and to provide martial music for military and street parades. The term marching band is linked to the sheet size of the music. This is about 18 x 13 cms, so that it can fit on a detachable stand (or 'lyre') affixed to the instrument, but it has the disadvantage of being small and cramped. There is no special instrumentation for the marching band. British editions follow military orchestration and American editions of symphonic orchestration.

Wind ensembles and wind orchestras

The wind ensemble provides an opportunity for the principle players of the larger symphonic bands to combine in smaller forces. The term wind orchestra was probably introduced in the 1960s as a more appropriate title that would appeal to players with an orchestral background. One important feature that distinguishes the wind ensemble/wind orchestra from other bands is that it uses only one player per part, in a truly chamber style. The conductor generally has a full score.

Brass bands

In Britain and the Commonwealth, the brass band has established itself as a true alternative to the wind band. Its music is both for concert use and marching and it has a large body of music used for contesting; this has become a popular activity for these highly skilled musicians.

The brass band is a collection of saxhorns with the addition of sections of cornets, trombones and percussion. Its format is rigid and has remained so for over a century. It is one of the most widely encountered amateur instrumental ensemble in Britain and overseas and has proved to be an ideal teaching and instrumental resource in schools. Its popularity is part musical and part social. Despite the demands of a rigid instrumentation and music of set length (about 12 minutes for contest pieces) many notable composers, including Elgar, John Ireland, Holst, Vaughan Williams, and Wilfred Josephs have responded with major works for the medium.

A typical modern band comprises 1 Eb soprano cornet; 4 Bb solo cornets; 1 first tenor trombone; 1 second tenor trombone; bass trombone; 1 'ripieno' Bb cornet; 1–2 Bb second cornets; 1–2 Bb third cornets; 2 Bb flat euphoniums; 2 EEb bass tubas; 1 Bb flugelhorn; 2 BBb contrabass tubas; 1 Eb solo tenor horn; 1 Eb first tenor horn; 1 Eb second tenor horn; timpani and tuned percussion (three players); 1 Bb first baritone horn; 1 Bb second baritone horn; and other percussion. Except for the bass trombone and percussion parts, all parts are written in treble clef. Today, the occurence of brass bands at school level means that most trombonists, euphonium and tuba players read in both treble and bass clefs and adapt well to wind bands and orchestras.

Some confusion with terminology is possible when older American publications refer to the brass band. This is an unfortunate misuse of the term and really refers to a full symphonic band. Traditions of wind and brass band playing exist in the Soviet Union, Germany, France, Netherlands, France, Spain and Italy.

The Percussion

The percussion section has been greatly expanded in the twentieth century as composers have drawn upon more and more tonal colours of non-western cultures. As the use of such instruments is still relatively new, confusion arises when composers ask for a particular instrument employing one of the variety of names by which it is known, and when other names are used which have become out of date or are ambiguous (as in the case of the gong and tam-tam). To do the subject justice requires a volume in its own right. This outline of percussion instruments, therefore, although quite broad, is by no means exhaustive, and reference to specialist books on the subject is recommended (*see* **bibliography**).

In the following section, classification is based on the method by which the sound is produced, rather than by the shape of the instruments or by the materials used in their construction. Four main categories cover this immense variety of instruments:

Idiophone: *vibration of the entire body of the instrument.*
Membraphone: *vibration of a membrane or skin.*
Chordophone: *vibration of a string or strings.*
Aerophone: *vibration of an enclosed air column.*

Each category may be further subdivided into those tuned percussion instruments of definite pitch and those instruments usually considered to be of indefinite pitch but which can be tuned. In printed scores and parts the percussion section may be referred to using the collective term: *battaria* It; *Schlagzeig, Schlagwerk* Ger; *batterie* Fr.

Idiophones

The sound of these is produced by the vibration of the entire body of the instrument. Some, such as those with a keyboard-like arrangement of bars, may have amplification in the form of tubular resonators placed underneath the instrument. Most are made to sound by being struck, but some untuned idiophones are sounded by shaking, scratching or scraping.

Tuned idiophones with wooden or metal bars in the form of a keyboard

Xylophone. Composers have used some unusual descriptions for the orchestral xylophone: *de bois et paille* (Saint-Saëns: *Danse macabre*), *Holz-und Strohinstrument* (Richard Strauss: *Salome*), *Holzharmonika* (Schoenberg: *Gurrelieder*), 'hammerwood' (Percy Grainger). Other names adopted have been *silofono, zilofono, xilofono* It., and *Xylophon* Ger. The modern xylophone and marimba have a set of hard-wood bars laid out in the style of a piano keyboard. The chromatic notes are usually raised, but may be level with the diatonic keys on some instruments. Whereas early xylophones were made without resonators, giving a very dry and brittle sound, modern examples have tuned tubular-metal resonators underneath the keys, developed from those of the modern marimba. This gives the instrument a much richer and more sustained tone. The range is between two and a half and four octaves upwards from c'. It is becoming customary to notate at concert pitch; however, many parts have been written an octave lower than the sounding pitch, so beware! The most common orchestral instrument is the three-and-a-half-octave model.

The **marimba** has a mellow, more 'booming' tone than the xylophone, caused in part by larger metal resonators and the use of soft beaters, rather than the hard beaters of the xylophone. It has developed from native African and Latin American models that have keys of variable size and thickness, and gourds, tuned to the pitch of each key, to act as resonators. The modern instrument is much larger than the xylophone with very long U-shaped resonators. Often these are so long that, in order to ensure the keyboard is at a playable height, the resonators have to be turned upwards at the bottom. The marimba has a standard range of four octaves (c–c'''), although the modern American instrument occasionally reaches down to A and some continental instruments range up an additional fourth to f'''. The lower range of the instrument contains its most characteristic tone and, because of this, some modern instruments do not have the top octave. Some bass instruments have been produced and are notated at sounding pitch (C–c'). Milhaud composed a Concerto for marimba and xylophone; Orff uses it in *Carmina Burana* and other scores.

A hybrid model, the **xylorimba** (or *marimba-xylophone*) is a somewhat larger xylophone covering the ranges of both instruments. It is not usually part of the normal equipment of the modern symphony orchestra though it is becoming much more common in contemporary scores. However, Stravinsky calls for the instrument in *The Flood*, and Berg used it as early as 1914-15 in the *Three Orchestral Pieces*.

The **vibraphone** has a keyboard made of aluminium alloy bars, with both chromatic and diatonic notes on one level, which facilitates the playing of chords by the simultaneous use of four or more mallets. It was developed in America during the 1920s and was most probably developed from the glockenspiel or the marimba. However, it has a much more mellow sound, which is quite resonant in nature. This resonance can be enhanced by raising the bars off the felt damper by the use of a damper pedal which acts, in effect, like the sustaining pedal of a piano. The instrument's characteristic vibrato is produced by an electric motor, turning discs at the top of the resonating tubes, which alternately open and close the pipes. Both pitch and volume is slightly altered by the fluctuations in air pressure caused by the movement of the discs. They also have the added effect of sustaining the sound for a fraction longer.

The beaters have yarn- or cord-wound heads and are produced with a variety of cores with different degrees of hardness. This provides different tonal effects, attack characteristics and degrees of volume. Consequently, a melody line can be brought out and contrasted with the accompanying chords. The standard vibraphone has a range of three octaves (f–f'''). There is controversy as to whether the instrument is notated at concert pitch or an octave lower than sounding. Its symphonic use is rare: Berg used it in *Lulu*, and Tippett scores for the instrument in his Third Symphony.

The **glockenspiel** (Ger., also *Stahlspiel* Ger; *campanelli* It; *carillon* Fr.), like the xylophone, has a keyboard-like arrangement of steel bars with the raised chromatic notes. It has neither tubular resonators or damping. The sound rings for some time, so much so that in rapid passages a characteristic blurring of the notes is apparent. The standard instrument has a compass of $g''-c''''$ or $c''-c''''$. The instrument sounds two octaves higher than its written pitch. It can be played with a variety of mallets or beaters, ranging from those with soft rubber heads to those with brass balls mounted on flexiglass. The hardest beaters can only be used on an instrument with steel bars, since alloy bars are easily damaged. Sibelius avoided any confusion between *Glocken* (bells) and the glockenspiel by specifying *Stahlstaben* (steel bars) in the symphonic poem, *The Oceanides* (*see* steel plates p.176). Orff wrote for a lower-pitched and larger instrument than the standard, giving it the name *metallofono*. The simple metallophone is often found in the classroom; it became part of the group of tuned percussion instruments developed and written for by Orff in *Das Schulwerk*.

Bell-lyra (lyra glockenspiel). This is a form of glockenspiel designed specifically for use in marching bands. The keys are held vertically on a lyre- shaped frame, which itself is carried on a staff supported by a belt round the player's waist. The bars are arranged as a ladder with the chromatic notes on the left and the diatonic on the right, struck in the same manner as the orchestral glockenspiel. A hard beater is the most effective for outdoor use. The range is usually no more than two octaves. The instrument has been referred to ocasionally as the lyra or military glockenspiel. Britten scores for it in *The Burning Fiery Furnace*.

Keyboard glockenspiel (*jeu de timbres* Fr.). This is very much like a celesta (*see below*), with hammers operated inside a box by a mechanism linked to a keyboard. It has a very bright, thin sound, and usually is best substituted by a hammer glockenspiel. Where chords are specified or fast and highly chromatic music is written, impossible on an ordinary hammer glockenspiel, the celesta provides an adequate alternative. The keyboard glockenspiel has a range of up to two and a half octaves. Handel called for a keyboard glockenspiel or 'carillon' in a number of his works, including *Saul* and *L'allegro, il pensieroso ed il moderato*.

Other names for the keyboard glockenspiel include *Glockenspiel mit Claviatur*, and *carillon avec* or *à clavier*. The term, *jeu de timbres*, is applied usually to the version of the instrument with keyboard, although instances can be found where the term is associated with the mallet instrument. The Italians use the term *campanelli tasteria*: Puccini called it the *campanelli giappa*. The keyboard glockenspiel is the most likely instrument called for by Mozart in *The Magic Flute*, to produce the sound of Papageno's on-stage bell playing. Here, it is referred to as a *strumento d'acciaio* ('steel instrument').

Celesta (It., *céleste* Fr.). The celesta differs from the keyboard glockenspiel primarily in that its steel bars are attached to a tuned wooden resonating box. This gives the instrument's timbre a far more rounded and sweet quality than the keyboard glockenspiel. It is also a much quieter instrument, with only a slight gradation of dynamic range possible. The range of the standard instrument is five octaves from c, although Mahler writes for an instrument which extends downwards for an extra octave. Sounding pitch is an octave higher than written. The celesta is played in the orchestra by a pianist.

Tuned idiophones (without keyboard)

Tubular bells (*campane, campanelle* It; *Glocken* Ger; *cloches* Fr.). These are brass or steel tubes, chromium-plated, and hung in a frame by cords from their upper end. They are made in sets of up to 18, chromatically rising from $c''-f'''$ and notated at concert pitch. Tubular bells are arranged in two rows, with the chromatic notes placed behind the diatonic notes. A mallet, usually with a rawhide head, is used to strike the top rim of the tube, the sound being damped by a foot pedal. Tubular bells should be employed where a score specifies 'campani', 'cloches' or 'glocken'. The terms *jeu de cloches* and *Röhrenglocken* are also to be found.

Gongs. Gongs and tam-tams (*see* p.176) are terms often confused by non-percussionists. The term gong, in English-speaking countries, has been used until recently to describe all gongs and tam-tams, whereas, on the continent, tam-tam is considered to be synonymous with gong. The two instruments, however, have separate and distinct features and characteristics, and significantly different sounds.

The gong came to western music from the Orient, notably Burma, China, and Java; it began to appear in the western orchestra with an increasing degree of regularity from the end of the nineteenth century, though it had been used by Gosssec as early as 1791. Gongs are made in sets from bronze or an alloy of copper and tin. They have a much deeper and more focused sound than the tam-tam. The main feature of the gong with definite pitch is its central dome, beaten out originally to tune the plate. Gongs of indefinite pitch are flat faced with a shallow-lipped rim. The sounds produced can vary from pure to harsh, depending upon how the instrument was cast and beaten. Sets of tuned gongs have been referred to by many names, but are often known as Thai gongs.

Crotales. In ancient times, these were two small pieces of metal, wood, bone or ivory fastened to the thumb and fingers and played like castanets. Today, the term refers to the small metal cymbals, of definite pitch, which can vary in shape from that of a Turkish cymbal (akin to the modern orchestral instrument) to small, thick cups of inverted brass. Ravel and Debussy score for *cymbales antiques* ('antique cymbals'). The clear ring produced by crotales is achieved by striking, edge against edge, two matching discs held together by one cord. Modern crotales are produced in fixed rows of pitches, rather than in pairs held together by a single cord. They may be struck either with other crotales or with beaters.

Flexatone. This is a modern invention and resembles the 'musical saw' in concept. The sound is produced by a rapid oscillation of a wooden knob at the end of a flexible strip. The knob strikes a long curving metal plate. The extent of the curvature of the plate and thus the pitch of the note is controlled by the thumb. Schoenberg writes for the instrument in his Variations for Orchestra (1928).

Untuned idiophones

The following instruments are predominantly idiophones, the only exception being the cuica. They can be divided into those instruments that are struck and those that are shaken, stroked or scraped, each group being further divided into instruments of metal or wood construction.

Struck untuned idiophones

Metals

The **triangle** is a triangular steel bar left open at one corner. The instrument can be hand held, or suspended from a stand held by a loop of gut cord. They are made mainly in three sizes, 6 in (15 cm), 8 inches (20 cm) and 10 inches (25 cm), the player chosing the instrument most suitable for the music to be played. The instrument's pitch is indefinite. Different beaters may be employed to produce varying effects: the usual beater is a metal rod of medium weight; however, a wooden drum stick may be used to obtain a soft, delicate sound. A thin metal beater will produce a light, silvery sound.

Cymbals (*cinelli, piatti* It; *Becken, Schellbecken, Tellern* Ger; *cymbales* Fr.). For the greater part of the orchestral repetoire cymbals are used in pairs clashed together. Since the turn of the twentieth century other methods of playing have been adopted. For these a single plate of the cymbal may be suspended, leaving the hands free as discussed below.

Clashed cymbals come in pairs, matched together so that one produces a higher pitch than the other. They come in a variety of sizes and gauges but a large plate size of 17 to 22 inches (43–53cms) of a medium–heavy gauge metal (usually an alloy of copper and tin) is best for general orchestral use. The lighter-gauge models produce a brighter sound than those of heavier metal. Pairs of cymbals are held by leather · straps, which run through the holes in the instruments' central domes. For *forte* attacks, they are clashed together with an oblique motion ending with the plates held apart. To increase reverberation time, they can be held high above the head, with the face of the plate towards the audience. For *piano* effects, the plates need only be touched lightly and for extremely delicate effects only a small part of the rim of one cymbal may come into contact with the other.

The terms used to denote a return to the usual clashed method of execution following the use of another technique are *gewöhnlich* (i.e. in the 'usual' manner) Ger; *naturale* It; and 'clashed'. Damping is achieved by touching the plates on the chest. A tie above a single note indicates that the plates should not be damped. Other terms used to show this effect include *lasciar vibrare* It (L.V.); *verklingen lassen, nicht dämpfen* Ger; *laisser vibrer* Fr.

The plates need not be clashed at all. A very effective metallic noise (indicated by the term *strisciato* It., 'trailed' or 'grazed') can be achieved by rapidly scraping one of the plates across the other: *roulee* (Roussel), *cymbales frottées* (Ravel), *à main* (D'Indy), 'rubbed together' (Vaughan Williams). The pressure of contact controls the volume and quality of the sound.

Suspended cymbals (*Zymbal* Ger.). A stand may be attached to the centre of the sound plate with rubber or felt rests, which prevents undue damping of the sound or the introduction of extra metallic vibrations. There is a greater range of gauges than with clashed cymbals, extending from paper thin (giving a piercing high-pitched ring) to extra heavy. Variety of tone can be achieved by the use of a stick or sticks and other beaters (denoted by the terms *colla bacchetta* It; *mit Schlagel* Ger; *avec la baguette* Fr; struck) and from striking different parts of the plate. Harder sticks encourage a brighter and harsher sound from the plate, and striking nearer the edge of the plate can produce a splash of sound not unlike that of the tam-tam: an extreme is the use of a triangle beater (marked *Stab* Ger.). A brush is sometimes asked for, although there is no standard term (one such is *verghe* [Prokofiev]). More sonorous effects can be achieved nearer the central dome, since here the higher harmonics are at their weakest. For full-toned effects, two sticks – one hard and one soft – may be employed. Damping may be achieved with the fingers of the free hand.

Sizzle cymbal. Loose rivets are inserted into the plate to increase the duration of the sound and to heighten the high pitched components. The **hi-hat** comprises two cymbals on a stand, clashed together by the use of a foot pedal. They can be choked by allowing them to touch; alternatively, they can ring freely. They can be used in combination with sticks, the most effective being side-drum sticks.

Tam-Tam. In Europe, the term tam-tam is used often by musicians to describe all gongs and gong-like instruments. Strictly, the tam-tam is a form of gong, of Malayan origin, although the term has now come to describe all gongs that emit sounds of indefinite pitch. However, clear and distinct effects are possible: for example, a soft heavy beater, when lightly striking the instrument's centre, produces quiet, clear sounds made up of rich and low harmonics. Higher harmonics are produced at the edge of the plate and so the instrument is struck just off centre to produce the fullest range of sounds. The shape is somewhat different from the gong in that it does not have a pronounced dome at the centre, the rim is not as large, and the whole plate has a slightly curved shape. The orchestral tam-tam should be provided with a stand from which it is hung, and a large, heavy wooden mallet (covered in lamb's wool) with which to strike the instrument. Hard-wood and metal beaters may be used to produce more brilliant effects.

Cowbells. Authentic cowbells (or *Herdenglocken*, as Mahler refers to them in his Sixth and Seventh Symphonies) do not usually have clappers and are hung from leather thongs so they are free to knock together. Other references to these have been made by Richard Strauss (*Herdengeläute*) and Henze (*Almglocken*). The modern equivalent (*cencerros* Sp.) are wedge-shaped and are of bronze or chromium-plated metal. They are mounted rigidly on a frame in sets of up to five or six and are played with side-drum sticks. They are not considered tuned percussion but are notated as in relative pitch (i.e. high, medium or low). Unlike the Herdenglocken, which evoke an Alpine atmosphere by their tone colour and characteristic 'randomness' (they are simply shaken together at the appropriate moments), the cencerros can take part in complicated rhythmic patterns when required, and are very much associated with the Latin-American percussion section. Messiaen uses the latter instrument in his *Coleurs de la cité céleste*.

Anvil and metal blocks (*l'incudini* It; *Ambose* Ger; *enclume, blocs de métal* Fr; metal blocks). The anvil either can be a block of steel or a large and heavy round bar which is suspended and hit with a hammer (alternatively, it can be placed on a pad). Although some tuned anvils were used in the nineteenth century found in scores by Verdi and Wagner – 18 are called for in *Das Rheingold* – these are no longer readily available. The **lujon** is an instrument with six large squares of metal suspended by a frame above box resonators. The resonators either can be fixed below, as in the marimba, or the plates themselves can be placed inside a resonating box. Berio employs this instrument in *Circles*.

Bronze sheets. These are long sheets which may be buckled and flexed, or struck with mallets or hammers. They are often used for thunder effects.

Steel plates. These need to be quite thin in order to produce much sound when hit with a hammer. Mahler calls for *Stahlstäben* (steel bars) in his Seventh Symphony. In this piece it is understood that he is describing deep, untuned bell-plates. However, Sibelius uses the term differently (*see* glockenspiel, p.172). A single sheet or plate is often referred to as *Stab*.

Woods

Claves are two similar-sized cylindrical blocks of wood beaten against each other. They are normally made of a very hard wood to give the deep, 'woody', penetrating sound typical of the instrument.

Wood blocks (*cassa di legno* It; *Holzblock, Holzblocktrommel* Ger; *bloc de blois, tambour de blois* Fr.) can be of solid construction, but most usually are hollow boxes of wood cut longitudinally near the top and bottom to provide greater resonance, struck with side-drum sticks on the upper surface. They have quite a high-pitched sound compared to temple block, which have a deeper, more hollow sound. Double blocks of different pitches can be used in combination.

Temple blocks are sometimes called **Chinese** or **Korean blocks**. Some confusion has arisen in certain scores, where the term Chinese blocks has been used to describe both temple and wood blocks. Temple blocks are usually made in sets of five supported by a stand. They are rounded or oval in shape, and at one end have a wide aperture, rather in the fashion of a smiling dragon. Like wood blocks, they vary in size and, although they are occasionally tuned to the pentatonic scale, they are most often used as unpitched instruments notated with only an approximate gradation of pitch. The sound is deeper and more hollow than that of wood blocks, because of the instrument's large resonating chamber.

Whip (*frusta* It; *Holzklapper* Ger; *fouet* Fr; slapstick). The modern orchestral instrument is, in its simplest form, two evenly matched lengths of resonant wood, hinged at one end, which are slapped together. Ravel uses the whip to open his Piano Concerto in G.

Wood drums (*Holzschlitztrommel* [slit drum], *Holzplattentrommel* [woodplate drum] Ger – the latter is most likely the *tamburo di legno* required in Puccini's *Turandot*.) The log drum is usually a cylindrical hollow of wood, sealed off at each end with wooden stoppers or plates. Along the top is one large slit – this is the point at which the instrument is struck with the beater. The slit drum is shaped like a deck boat with cut-off stem and stern. The top is flat with two wide slots in line communicating with the internal cavity. The edges of the slots vary in thickness, so that different timbres may be produced by striking different parts of the instrument. Woodplate drums are usually made by glueing thin wooden heads into the tops of tom-tom shells to form single-headed drums, but without tensioning screws.

Shaken, stroked or scraped untuned idiophones

Metals

Sistrum (*sistro* It., Sp.). This instrument dates back to ancient Egypt. Examples can be found in many cultures, both ancient and modern, around the world. It is a rattle, and originally consisted of a handle and a horseshoe-metal frame, with loose cross bars that rattled when the instrument was shaken. The sound is enhanced in more modern examples by the addition of loose metal discs strung along the cross bars (cf. *bell-tree* below).

Sleigh bells (*sonagliera, capello Chinese* It; *Schellen* Ger; *grelots, pavillon chinois* Fr; bell tree, jingling Johnny, Turkish crescent, jingles.) Jingles are a set of small spherical bells attached to a leather strap. They are often to be seen tied around the ankles and wrists of Morris dancers. In this form, they are identical to sleigh bells. They can be found in other forms, with perhaps the most common of these being those where

the jingles are arranged on a wooden frame or 'tree'. A *bell-tree* may have jingles resembling miniature bells, rather than the spherical jingles of the sleigh bells.
Chains (*Ketten* Ger.). In orchestral works, these are normally lengths of large iron links rattled or shaken. Placing them on a metal plate or gong increases the sound. In *Gurrelieder*, Schoenberg describes them as 'einige grosse eiserne Kettern' (some big iron chains), where they help to conjure the image of dead souls rising from the grave.

Woods

Castanets (*castagnette, nacchere* It; *Kastagnetten* Ger; *castagnettes* Fr.). These are made of wood. Unlike the Spanish hand-held variety, the orchestral version is fixed on a board or has a handle. This makes it possible for more intricate rhythms to be executed on the orchestral model than on the traditional instrument. **Maracas** are of Latin-American origin and normally come in pairs. Each is a gourd or calabash-shell shaker filled with dry seeds. Prokofiev scores for them in *Romeo and Juliet*.
Güiro (rape). This is a dried and empty gourd with serations cut into one side evenly along the length of the instrument. A scraper is then pulled across the serations, the body of the instrument acting as a resonator. It can execute quite precise rhythms as well as continuing a straightforward ostinato. Stravinsky asks for both 'rape guero' and 'guero (rape)' in *The Rite of Spring*.
Sandpaper blocks. These are two blocks of wood covered in sandpaper and rubbed together. One may be fixed on a stand so that only one hand is required to play the blocks. A similar sound is provided by a metal cannister filled with sand called a *sanbuchse* or *Sandrasseln*. Hindemith writes for the latter in his *Kammermusik* No. 1.
Wind machine (*eoliphone* Fr.). This instrument consists of a cylindrical wooden frame which can be made to revolve by turning a handle. The framework is covered by a silk cloth, which is fixed so that a wind-like sound is produced when the wooden slats stroke the silk. Notable examples of its use occur in Strauss's *Alpine Symphony* and in Ravel's *Daphnis et Chloé*.

Membraphones

These instruments produce sound by vibration of a membrane.

Tuned membraphones

Timpani (It., *Pauken* Ger; *timbales* Fr; kettle drums.). The resonating shells or bowls of the timpani are usually made of copper. Fibreglass bowls, although inferior in sound quality to copper, are far more durable, lighter, and are more easily transported. Drumheads may be of prepared calfskin or a plastic substitute. Heads made of the latter are less prone to the effects of extreme atmospheric and temperature changes.

Two types of timpani may be distinguished: 'hand-tuned' (occasionally 'tap') drums and 'machine drums' (*timbales chromatiques* Fr.). For the latter, three types of mechanism exist to enable the player to change rapidly the pitch of the instrument: pedal-operated, hand-tuned by one master screw, and rotating bowl instruments. All three cause the tension on the drumhead to be raised or lowered (with a corresponding change in the pitch of the drum) by raising or lowering the counter-hoop that keeps the drumhead in place. Pitch is primarily determined by drumhead tension and bowl diameter. The diameters of modern machine drums vary from 81 to 27cm, with a corresponding pitch range of *D* (flat)–*b* flat. This range is covered conventionally by three drums, each with a range of a fifth.

The bowl of the kettledrum magnifies certain of the overtones in the harmonic series. The shallower bowl tends to clarify the principal notes whereas the deep shell tends to increase its resonance. If a bowl is too deep, however, the pitch has a tendency to flatten on impact. Slight tonal differences can be compensated by the player striking different positions of the head. It is generally true that the nearer its edge the drumhead is struck the drier and less resonant the tone becomes. This characteristic can help heighten a passage employing wooden sticks. A further peculiarity is to be found when the response is different for *forte* and *piano* passages. In a sudden change from *forte* to *piano* the tone of the *piano* notes will seem flat.

Untuned Membraphones

Snare drum, side-drum (*tamburo piccolo* It; *kleine Trommel* Ger; *caisse claire, tambour* Fr; *tambor, caja* Sp.). Beware of the confusion that may arise because of the similarity of the term tambour to that of tambourine (*see* p.180).

The shell of the drum is normally made of metal (originally brass) over which at each end is stretched a skin. When the top face, the batter head, is struck, taut gut, silk or metal strings vibrate against the lower or snare head to give the drum its characteristic sound. The sound can be muffled by placing a hand or a cloth on the batter head, indicated by the terms *coperto, gedampft,* or *voile*. The snares can also be switched off to give a more normal drum sound (*senza cordes, ohne Saiten*). Wooden sticks, called side-drum sticks because of their characteristic shape, are the standard implements. However, modern composers may stipulate other beaters such as various timpani sticks or that different parts of the drum head and body are to be struck for various tonal effects.

The *rim-shot* is a loud crack produced by placing the left-hand stick so that the tip touches the middle of the head and the shaft is laid on the rim. The stick is then struck hard by the right-hand stick. The *hoop-crack* is an alternative when there is no time to prepare for the normal rim-shot. Here either stick can strike the vellum and rim together as part of a series of strokes. The sound is less forceful.

Although the snare drum, tenor drum and military drum are different instruments, they have been greatly confused by composers. It is worth consulting an authority on the subject when in doubt as to the sound most apt for a specific work.

Military drum (*tamburo militaire*, field drum). This is lower in pitch than the snare drum as the shell is deeper. **Tenor drum** (*cassa rullante, tamburo rullante* It; *Ruhrtrommel, Wirbeltrommel, Rolltrommel* Ger; *caisse roulante* Fr.). The shell is deeper than the military drum in relation to the diameter and there are no snares: the sound therefore is deeper and hollower. It is in fact half way between a snare drum and a bass drum.

Tabor, tambourin. The tabor is a rarity in scores, but its nearest is the tambourin (Provençal long drum). The tabor has no snares but the tambourin has one. The true tambourin is very long in proportion to its diameter and has a head made of soft calfskin. A single hard beater (sometimes of bone) is employed.

The English tabor on the other hand, has a very shallow rim (a wooden hoop) and only one head. It is traditionally held in the left hand and beaten with a hard stick with the right. Modern versions are very similar to the tambourine (*see below*) except without the jingles. The parchment head may be tightened or loosened by means of rods and nuts placed around the head.

Bass drum (*gran cassa, cassa gran, tamburo grande, gran tamburo* It; *grosse Trommel* Ger; *grosse caisse* Fr.). This is a large drum, the wooden shell is narrow in relation to the diameter. The heads may be tightened or slackened to alter the sound, either by altering the tension of the cord holding the braces around the body of the instrument or, on more modern instruments, adjusting the rod screws. There is no standard size and interestingly, the larger the drum size does not mean the greater the ensuing volume or quality of sound. Some large drums are placed on their backs so that two players may strike the same face (Berlioz's *Symphonie fantastique*). Sometimes the composer requires the drum upright so that both faces may be struck.

The single-headed gong drum is often employed in professional symphony orchestras because of its superior tone quality. Very few scores, however, indicate the form, size or shape of drum required.

The stick normally used is heavy with a large, soft-padded head. On occassion, however, late romantic composers, such as Mahler and Richard Strauss, revived the practice of specifying a twig or split-rod switch (*Ruthe, Rute* Ger.); it seems to have been a fairly commonplace method in Haydn and Mozart's time. Mahler employs it in traditional fashion, on the head of the instrument, but also less conventionally on the rim ('auf dem holz'). The swishing sound of the sticks before they hit the drum is a part of the effect.

For a different tone colour timpani sticks can be employed. These give a rather more focused sound as they are smaller and normally harder. A roll may be achieved by using two heavy sticks (sometimes called *mailloche* or *mazza*). A double-headed stick has also been designed for the purpose, but this is not commonly found.

As the drum vibrates sympathetically with other orchestral instruments, it is worth ensuring that the player places a cloth over the instrument when it is not in use so that unwanted sounds are damped.

Tambourine (*tamburo piccolo, tamburo basco, tamborino,* It; *Baskische Trommel, Schellen Trommel* Ger; *tambourin, tambour de Basque* Fr.). Beware of the confusion that may arise because of the similarity of the tambourin to that of the Provençal long drum, (*see* p.179) and the tamburo piccolo to the snare drum (*see* p.179).

The instrument consists of a small wooden hoop with a single head of parchment. The hoop is cut away at intervals to allow for the insertion of jingles (small pairs of metal plates). The instrument may be shaken, in which case only the jingles make any sound, or struck, most usually with the knuckle, though the flat of the hand works just as well, especially at the end of a shaken roll (sometimes referred to as *batutto cola mano*). More measured trills (or *tremulos*) can be executed by wetting the thumb and rubbing it round the edge of the head (*mit dem Daumen* Ger; *avec la pouce* Fr.). The degree of control for this technique is not great: for more complicated rhythmic passages the player may rest the instrument on his knees and strike it with both hands.

Two other forms of the tambourine are known. The first, a hoop with no parchment but with jingles, is used only very rarely in the orchestra The other is equally rare, the hoop with parchment but no jingles. It has been specifically called for by de Falla using the description, 'pandero sia sonajas'. This, therefore, is very similar to the tabor.

Tom-toms. These are small, high-pitched drums with a single or double head and a tapering body. They often come in pairs tuned, if not to a definite pitch to high, medium or low. They can be played with either hard sticks (side-drum sticks) or soft sticks for a mellow timbre and less vital attack. As they can be accurately tuned they can be used as substitutes for high timpani or to extend the timpani range upwards.

Timbales (*creoles, timbales creoles* Fr.). Timbales are of Latin-American origin. They are single-headed instruments usually played in pairs and are normally intended to be struck with wooden sticks. Their tone is metallic with a pronounced ring (presumably because the heads are highly tensioned).

Chordophones

These instruments produce sound by the vibration of struck strings.

Piano (*pianino* [upright piano] It; *Klavier, Flugel* ['baby' grand], *Konzertflugel* [concert grand] Ger.) Scores in which the piano is employed as a member of the percussion section in a conventional manner need no further comment. Of more interest to the conductor are those in which the player is asked to produce sounds other than by depressing the keys. Although some of these effects are produced with the body of the piano, the majority are produced inside the piano on the strings themselves. These effects can be divided into those that require no preparation of the piano and those that require some addition of extra materials to the piano to alter the tone colour.

a. Prepared pianos. Here, materials acting as mutes or sound modifiers are placed between the strings with the intent of changing the instrument's tone colour and texture. Mutes include screws, bolts and rubber wedges. Generally, only a selected number of strings are treated, and the composer either dwells solely on these notes or contrasts the textural differences between treated and untreated notes.

b. Non-prepared pianos. Fingers can be used to pluck the strings of the instrument. Paul Patterson, in his *Kyrie* for choir and piano, writes out separate parts for two pianists, one for the player of the keyboard, and one for the player who plays the inside of the instrument. Effects can range from shouting into the instrument, tapping the frame or sound board, to plucking or scraping the strings. The sustaining pedal can be depressed to give a large, broad effect. A ruler is sometimes required for bold effects, the finger nails being used for more intimate sounds. Single strings can be scraped longitudinally to give a sustained sound on a chosen note, or several adjacent strings can be scraped in a lateral motion akin to a harp glissando. Some degree of control of dynamics is possible with these effects.

Zither. This is a folk instrument used chiefly in Bavaria and Austria. It is occasionally encountered in the orchestra, an example being found in Johann Strauss's waltz, *Tales from the Vienna Woods*. It consists of a flat wooden sound box, over which are stretched four or five melody strings and as many as 37 accompaniment strings. The melody strings are stopped on a fretted finger board by the left hand and are plucked with a plectrum worn on the thumb of the right hand.

Aerophones

These instruments produce sound by vibration of an enclosed air column. Though strictly not percussion instruments, i.e. not made to sound by being struck, they are usually entrusted in the orchestra to percussionists.

Whistles. These are quite varied and include 'bird calls' and police, train, steam, slide and tin whistles. The slide whistle has a plunger which alters the length and pitch of the instrument.

Sirens. These are employed only ocasionally in western art music. The most effective sirens are those operated by the turning of a handle, slowly for low-pitched sounds and faster for high-pitched and louder sounds: they have a button for stopping the sound instantaneously.

Bull roarer (thunderstick). This consists of a long, thin piece of wood fastened to a length of string which, when whirled rapidly around the head, produces a menacing roaring sound.

Motor horns. The old-fashioned rubber-bulb horns are the most obvious examples and will suffice for most scores. Several firms now produce sets of horns specifically for performances of Gershwin's *An American in Paris*.

Pitch

The pitch of vocal and instrumental music has varied over the centuries. Whereas a specific, but non-standard, pitch was integral to the development of the vocal and instrumental characteristics of the music of a country, region or musical institution, the lack of a 'fixed' standard of pitch often inhibited the free exchange of musical thought and ideas from one centre or one genre to another: e.g. sacred and secular music was usualy performed at two distinct and separate levels of pitch. Although much of what has been written about early vocal pitch is speculative, research on the pitch of early instruments gives an indication of the preferences of different nations and generations.

More accurate comparison of relative pitch became possible with the invention of the tuning fork in 1711 and of the pitch pipe $c.1750$: Handel's London tuning fork ($c.1740$) showed a' to be 422.5 Herz. The music of Mozart and Beethoven was of a lower pitch than that of their predecessors and during the eighteenth century a' varied from 415 to 430 Herz, Mozart's piano of 1780 being at $a' = 421.6$. Pitch was not universally constant however. Touring virtuosos (Mozart included) had several violins to accommodate deviations in local standard pitch, and to avoid loss of tone or damage to instruments or strings by excessive retuning. During the nineteenth century there was a general tendency towards a higher level of pitch, especially in Britain. The Philharmonic Society in London established its 'Philharmonic' pitch of $a' = 423.5$ in 1813. In 1880 Steinway pianos of New York tuned their instruments to $a' = 457$. An early attempt to standardize a' at 440 cycles per second (by a congress of physicists in Stuttgart in 1834) was unsuccessful. In 1858 the French Government nominated six physicists and six musicians to investigate the problem. The group, including Berlioz and Meyerbeer, recommended that $a' = 435$ Herz; this was enforced by statute in France. New Philharmonic pitch of $a' = 439$ Herz was introduced by International agreement, although British military bands did not follow this recommendation until 1928. The current standard of $a' = 440$ Herz followed an International Conference in 1939, and this has now gained universal acceptance.

Appendix II

Preparation of Manuscript Copy

The conductor of an amateur orchestra, band, or choir often has to arrange and copy out parts. Though he will probably not be able to match the hand of an experienced copyist, he should produce an accurate, easily read and unambiguous manuscript. Outlined below are a number of points worth remembering when making hand-written copies.

Type of paper. The paper used should be non-porous, mat-finished, white, with clearly lined staves and adequate space between them. Various sizes of manuscript paper are available: for most purposes a 10- or 12-stave layout with 2cms between staves is desirable. Choose a format to suit the task in hand; most needs can be served by paper 210mm x 297mm. Pages of 24 staves may be required for copying a full score, although copyright laws must be checked if this is necessary.

Tools required: *Soft pencils* – 2B or 3B may be used to map out the page. Marks made with such pencils are easily erased; *Ink pens* – A fine nib should be used for bar lines and words (either of a vocal line or for instructions such as tempo or dynamic markings). Always use black ink for the notes themselves. Coloured inks are useful for marking rehearsal figures clearly. Use a broad-nibbed pen to produce fine vertical and wide horizontal lines; *Rulers* – Two types are required: a short one with a raised edge for notating note tails and beams, and a longer one for ruling bar lines on full scores; *Extra tools* – A razor blade and liquid paper will be needed to make corrections. If a mistake is made, the ink should be allowed to dry and the error carefully removed with the edge of a razor blade (or sharp penknife). The paper can be restored by removing any residual marks with a typewriter eraser. Add any corrections before removing mistakes. For more substantial errors, a patch-on manuscript paper can be pasted over the offending section.

Notation

Solid notes should be oval and slightly oblique, with open or white notes more rounded. Note stems usually occupy the length of three spaces, unless a tail or beam is to be added, and should pass downwards on the left or upwards on the right side of the note head. Generally, stems from the third line or below pass downwards and the remainder upwards. Exceptions to this occur where more than one line of music appears on one stave, as in short scores, piano scores and divided parts, when upper parts always take upward-facing stems and lower parts take downward-facing stems. Tail bars on single notes should be angled or curved and pass towards the note head, always to the right of the stem.

It is best to form head and stem in one movement, with the head produced before the tail. Try to avoid a style of writing that attempts to reproduce the shapes of printed notation, but aim to be consistent over the size of note heads and stems. The guiding principle should be to keep note shapes as simple as possible, so that with practice a fast and accurate writing style can be developed. The hand should move freely without unneccessary pressure being used. A useful and detailed discussion of the manual strokes required to form good copy can be found in Archibald Jacob's *Musical Handwriting*.

Key signatures should be repeated at the head of each successive stave. Accidentals in the course of a phrase take up the same space as a note, are placed immediately to the left of the note they alter, and cancel previous key inflections up to the next bar line (or beyond, if the note is held). If there is any confusion over where an accidental should be cancelled, 'cautionary accidentals' may be added for the sake of clarity.

Planning the page

Bar lines should only be inked in after the correct proportions for each bar have been decided upon. Avoid dividing a bar between the end of one line and the beginning of the next; if this cannot be avoided, it is essential that the bar to be broken is divided exactly in half. Bar lines are carried across for groups of related instruments. This requires a good deal of advanced planning, and it is best to write the 'busiest' part first to ensure adequate horizontal space. In heavily scored material it may be necessary to write out a bar at a time, working vertically down through the score. Ensure that enough room is left for tempo and expression markings, and the words of a vocal part or parts.

When writing out parts for individual instruments specific attention must be given to the appropriate clef or clefs to be used. If a part is to be transposed to help a player, ensure that the key signature is correct and that the transposition is accurate. Rest bars must be carefully numbered, and rehearsal figures and appropriate cues are added (usually a prominent theme just before the re-entry of the resting instrument). Also include any cues which the player may have to 'cover' if a particular instrument is unavailable either for a rehearsal or a performance. Each page of manuscript should be planned to end (or the following page to begin) with enough rest bars for the player to turn his part without undue haste. This is particularly important to players of large or cumbersome instruments, who may be separated by some distance from their music stands. Where playing has to begin almost immediately after a page turn add 'v.s.' or *volti subito* to the foot of the page to be turned.

Bibliography

General

Arnold, Denis (ed.): *The New Oxford Companion to Music*, 2 vols (Oxford: OUP, 1983)
Barlow, Harold and Sam Morgenstern: *A Dictionary of Musical Themes* (London: Williams and Norgate, 1949; revd edn London: Faber & Faber, 1985)
Barlow, Harold and Sam Morgenstern: *A Dictionary of Vocal Themes* (New York: Crown Publishers Inc; 1950; London: Ernest Benn Ltd, 1956)
Barton, Marianne (ed.): *British Music Yearbook* (London: 1972-3, annual publication; Rhinegold Publishing, 1985–)
Boustead, Alan: *Writing Down Music* (London: OUP, 1973)
Jacob, Archibald: *Musical Handwriting* (London: OUP, 1937; 2nd revd edn, 1947)
Jarvis, Pam: 'A Practical Guide to Arts Event Promotion' in *Arts Festivals in Great Britain and Ireland*, Sheena Barbour (ed.) (London: Rhinegold Publishing, 1989)
Sadie, Stanley (ed.): *The New Grove Dictionary of Music and Musicians*, 20 vols (London: Macmillan, 1980)
Thorn, Eric Arnold: *Understanding Copyright: A Practical Guide* (Tunbridge Wells: Jay Books, 1989)

Technique

Boult, Adrian: *A Handbook on the Technique of Conducting* (Oxford and London: OUP, 1920; repr., London: Paterson's Publications, 1968)
Carse, Adam: *Orchestral Conducting* (London: Augener Edition, 1929)
Green, Elizabeth A: *The Modern Conductor* (Englewood Cliffs NJ: Prentice-Hall, 1987)
McElheran, Brock: *Conducting Technique for Beginners and Professionals* (Oxford and London: OUP, 1966)
Malko, Nicolai: *The Conductor and his Baton* (Copenhagen: Edition Wilhelm Hansen, 1950)
Miles, Maurice: *Are You Beating Two or Four?* (London: Novello & Co., 1977)
Rudolf, Max: *The Grammar of Conducting* (New York: Schirmer, 1949)
Scherchen, Hermann: *Lehrbuch des Dirigierens* Eng. trans as *Handbook of Conducting* (Leipzig: 1929; Eng. trans., London: OUP, 1933)
Wood, Henry J: *About Conducting* (London: Sylvan Press, 1945; repr., 1972)

Choral Conducting

Corp, Ronald: *The Choral Singer's Companion* (London: B.T. Batsford, 1987)
Decker, H. A. and J. Herfords (eds): *Choral Conducting: a Syposium* (Englewood Cliffs NJ: Prentice-Hall, 1973)
Holst, Imogen: *Conducting a Choir: A Guide for Amateurs* (Oxford and London: OUP, 1973)

Interpretation

Brown, Howard Mayer: 'Editing' *The New Grove*
Caldwell, John: *Editing Early Music, Early Music Series* 5 (Oxford: OUP, 1985)

Dart, R[obert] Thurston: *The Interpretation of Music* (London: Hutchinson, 1954; 4th edn, 1967)

Del Mar, Norman: *Orchestral Variations* (London: Eulenberg, 1981)

Donington, Robert: *The Interpretation of Early Music* (London: Faber & Faber, 1963; 4th revd edn, 1989)

——: *A Performer's Guide to Baroque Music* (London: Faber & Faber, 1973)

Fuller, David: 'Dotting, the "French Style" and Frederick Neumann's Counter-Reformation', *Early Music*, 5/4 (October 1977), 517-43

King, Alec Hyatt: *Four Hundred Years of Music Printing* (London: The British Museum, 1964)

Neumann, Frederick: *Ornamentation in Baroque and Post-Baroque Music with Special Emphasis on J.S. Bach* (Princeton: Princeton University Press, 1978)

——: 'The Overdotting Syndrome: Anatomy of a Delusion', *Musical Quarterly*, 67 (July 1981), 305-47

Instruments

Adkins, H. E: *Treatise on the Military Band* (London: Boosey & Hawkes, 1931; revd edn, 1958)

Baines, Anthony (ed.): *Musical Instruments Through the Ages* (Harmondsworth: Penguin Books, 1961; revd edn London: Faber & Faber, 1966)

Baines, Anthony: *Brass Instruments* (London: Faber & Faber, 1976)

——: *Woodwind Instruments and their History* (London: Faber & Faber, 1957; 3rd revd edn, 1967)

Bate, Philip: *The Flute: An Outline of its History, Development and Construction* (London and New York: Ernest Benn, 1969)

——: *The Oboe: An Outline of Its History, Development and Construction* (London and New York: Ernest Benn, 1956)

——: *The Trumpet and Trombone: An Outline of Its History, Development and Construction* (London and New York: Ernest Benn, 1966)

Bevan, Clifford: *The Tuba Family* (London: Faber & Faber, 1978)

Blades, James: *Orchestral Percussion Technique* (Oxford: OUP, 1973)

——: *Percussion Instruments and Their History* (London: Faber & Faber, 1970; 3rd revd edn, 1984)

Brindle, Reginald Smith: *Contemporary Percussion* (Oxford: OUP, 1970)

Carse, Adam: *The Orchestra from Beethoven to Berlioz* (Cambridge: Heffer-Broude, 1948)

——: *The Orchestra in the XVIIIth Century* (Cambridge: Heffer-Broude, 1940)

Del Mar, Norman: *Anatomy of the Orchestra* (London: Faber & Faber, 1981)

——: *Companion to the Orchestra* (London: Faber & Faber, 1987)

Donington, Robert: *The Instruments of Music* (London: OUP, 1949; 4th edn, 1970)

Janetzky, Kurt and Bernhard Brüchle: *The Horn* (Eng. trans, London: B. T. Batsford, 1988)

Joppig, Gunther: *The Oboe and the Bassoon* (Eng. trans, London: B.T. Batsford, 1988)

Meylan, Raymond: *The Flute* (Eng. trans, London: B.T. Batsford, 1988)

Sadie, Stanley (ed.): *The New Grove Dictionary of Musical Instruments*, 3 vols (London: Macmillan, 1984)

Tarr, Edward: *The Trumpet* (Eng. trans, London: B.T. Batsford, 1988)